HOW TO BE BRAVE

SELF-HEALING TOOLS FOR LOVE WARRIORS

LAURA DI FRANCO

FEATURING: COLLEEN AVIS, JULIE BLAMPHIN, LESLIE ENGLE, JANE ANN GUYETTE,
BARBARA E. HANLEY, R. SCOTT HOLMES, MICHOL MAE, VAL MEOLA, LAURIE MORIN,
DR. ARLENE NOCK, DONNA O'TOOLE, DR. PAMELA J. PINE, ANGEL ROHRER, GLENN SCHUSTER,
DR. RUTH A. SOUTHER, LAURA RENEE SPINNER, JANETTE STUART, MICHELE TATOS,
TIFFANY THOMAS, SUSAN THOMPSON, BRADFORD W. TILDEN, ATLANTIS WOLF, T.L. WOODLIFF

HOW TO BE
BRAVE

SELF-HEALING TOOLS
FOR LOVE WARRIORS

With Warrior Love,
Laura

LAURA DI FRANCO

FEATURING: COLLEEN AVIS, JULIE BLAMPHIN, LESLIE ENGLE, JANE ANN GUYETTE,
BARBARA E. HANLEY, R. SCOTT HOLMES, MICHOL MAE, VAL MEOLA, LAURIE MORIN,
DR. ARLENE NOCK, DONNA O'TOOLE, DR. PAMELA J. PINE, ANGEL ROHRER, GLENN SCHUSTER,
DR. RUTH A. SOUTHER, LAURA RENEE SPINNER, JANETTE STUART, MICHELE TATOS,
TIFFANY THOMAS, SUSAN THOMPSON, BRADFORD W. TILDEN, ATLANTIS WOLF, T.L. WOODLIFF

"What a beautiful path I just traveled through the chapters of *How to Be Brave*. It was as if each author were set up alongside the way, awaiting my arrival, offering me a chair, encouraging me to open my mind to the story and tool in store. 'Come, sit down, make yourself comfortable. It's time I share.'

I was touched by the common vision of bringing bravery to life through carefully selected words, painted scenes, and important characters, and the love poured into meditations, prompts, activities, and medicine to close each chapter. The authors are wonderfully diverse, and I found a unique connection with every human Laura Di Franco has gathered in this collection.

As I finished the last page and my journey through *How to Be Brave* ended, I closed the book and smiled, knowing I can call up any one of these authors, they'll answer, and I can let them know, 'I have seen your brave heart, I love you, please tell me more.'"

~ Natalie Petersen,
Author, Speaker, Mentor, Bloomstruck

A Phenomenal Journey of Bravery

"Laura Di Franco's *How to Be Brave: Self-Healing Tools for Love Warriors* is a remarkable collection of stories from experts sharing their experiences of bravery in various forms. The book explores how bravery can manifest in unexpected ways and underscores its essential role in our lives. Through its pages, the authors guide readers through profound lows and exhilarating highs, offering deep insights into the true meaning of bravery—what it feels like, looks like, and sounds like. This book has profoundly enhanced my understanding of bravery and inspired me to elevate my own courage.

Moreover, it provides practical tools that can be used with clients or for personal growth. If you want to boost your bravery, *How to Be Brave* is the book for you. You won't regret it."

~ Joey Natale,
Mindset Relationship Coach, Founder of Grow Our Light LLC

"In a world that often equates strength with invulnerability, *How to Be Brave* stands as a beacon of truth, illuminating the profound strength found in embracing our vulnerabilities. This transformative work delves deep into the human spirit, showcasing the incredible power that lies within each of us when we choose to walk our own path and claim our inherent power.

The authors masterfully weave personal experiences with universal truths, illustrating that true bravery is not the absence of fear but the courage to face it head-on. Through poignant storytelling, we are reminded that our vulnerabilities are not weaknesses but rather the very source of our strength. It is in these moments of openness and authenticity that we discover the resilience of the human spirit.

One of the most compelling aspects of *How to Be Brave* is its emphasis on the power of acceptance of the *now* and making our own choices to define value and meaning of our lives. The authors encourage readers to break free from outside expectations and carve out their own unique paths. This journey of self-discovery and empowerment is beautifully depicted, showing that when we claim our power, we not only transform our own lives but also unlock the potential to offer our unique gifts to the world.

The book is a call to action, urging us to embrace our true selves and recognize the gifts we have to offer. It is a reminder that our personal journeys, filled with both triumphs and challenges, can inspire and uplift others. By sharing our stories and standing in our truth, we create a ripple effect of empowerment and healing.

In conclusion *How to Be Brave* is a profound exploration of bravery, vulnerability, and the indomitable human spirit. It is a testament to the power of choosing our own paths and claiming our power. This book is not just a read, but an experience that will leave you inspired, uplifted, and ready to embrace your own journey with newfound courage and conviction.

Well done, this book will be a resource I offer to clients I serve."

~ **Laurie B Teal**,
Integrative Wellness NP in Psychiatry, PLLC

"*How to Be Brave*—the latest book collaboration and *Brave Story Medicine* by Laura Di Franco—is a profound resource for healing and empowerment.

As a reader, therapist, healer, and author, I am deeply impressed by this remarkable compilation of wisdom, transformative codes, and practical tools.

Each contribution is a testament to the expertise and heartfelt vulnerability of the authors, creating a treasure chest filled with a kaleidoscope of approaches, strategies, and guidance on dealing with trauma and fears, as well as on our courageous path of healing and expansion. This amazing book is a must-read for anyone on a journey of personal and professional growth."

~ Nydia Laysa Stone,
Somatic Therapist, Life Transition Coach,
and Master Teacher of the Healing Arts

Get access to **The Brave Healer Resources Vault** with thousands in training/master classes and workshops for author-entrepreneurs:

https://lauradifranco.com/resources-vault/

DISCLAIMER

This book is designed to provide competent, reliable, and educational information regarding holistic health and wellness and other subject matter covered. However, it is sold with the understanding the authors and publisher specifically disclaim all responsibility for any liability, loss, or risk, personal or otherwise, incurred as a consequence, directly or indirectly, of the use and application of any of the contents of this publication.

In order to maintain the anonymity of others, names and identifying characteristics of some people, places, and organizations described in this book have been changed.

This publication contains content that may be potentially triggering or disturbing. Individuals who are sensitive to certain themes are advised to exercise caution while reading.

The opinions, ideas, and recommendations contained in this publication do not necessarily represent those of the Publisher. The use of any information provided in this book is solely at your own risk.

Our authors represent cultures worldwide and as such, there may be differences in language and expressions. As a global publisher, we have made the conscious choice to not edit these nuances so each chapter is authentic and in its author's own words and language.

Know that the experts here have shared their tools, practices, and knowledge with you with a sincere and generous intent to assist you on your leadership journey. Please contact them with any questions you may have about the techniques or information they provided. They will be happy to assist you further and be an ongoing resource for your success!

DEDICATION

To Danielle, who chose to walk on my path in this lifetime and teach me the true definition of being brave. I love you so much.

To Jonathan: I watched you step into your courage and change your life this year without looking back. You're a badass. I love you so much.

I'm so proud of you both. I'm such a lucky mom. Thanks for picking me.

To Chris, who taught me that being brave is sometimes simply about saying, "I love you," and risking your heart.

To the Brave Healer community, my gratitude is so huge. Every morning I wake with fear-busting purpose, raise my hand to my heart, and wonder: *How am I so lucky?* I dedicate this collaboration (and its energy and spirit) to you. May you find the courage you need to do the impossible things and thrive. And may you never feel alone on the journey.

The Lightbearer by Jenny Hawkyard

Jennifer Hawkyard is a multidisciplinary artist and designer living and working in remote West Wales. She specializes in creating intuitively led channeled artworks and messages for her clientele all over the world. Her work is multi-dimensional, colorful, and imbued with layers of insight, love, and significance. She has worked with best-selling author Kyle Gray to create *The Angel Guide Oracle*, *The Gateway of Light Activation Oracle*, *The Divine Masters Oracle*, and *The 22 Archangels Oracle*. She has also self-published her own creativity journal filled with inspiring artwork and channeled messages to encourage the reader to explore their creativity and intuition. Find Jenny on the internet under the pseudonym Jezhawk on most platforms, and a wide variety of prints and products on her website https://www.jezhawk.com.

The Lightbearer

I come to you now as a bearer of the light, a symbol of the light that resides in all of you, the energy and pure vibration that resides in all of you that can be dampened, can be shrunk, and can be ignored but can never go out. It is yours, dear ones; it is yours and only yours, and nothing will ever extinguish it. Some of you guard your flames closely, keeping them cupped within your hands, protected by the winds and the wilds of the world, but trust me when I say that your light can become a roaring inferno when you allow it. When you stoke it and when you treasure it. It is not a light that can ever be extinguished, and if you nourish it every day and come more closely to its warmth, you will feel it start to react, to radiate, and to emerge from you vibrant and glorious and much needed in this world.

Many of you have been taught to dampen your flame, your spirit; many have been told to keep quiet and to keep unheard, but now is the time to shine brightly—let your flames ring out, your light shine out like the great tolling of a wondrous and magnificent bell. For much like that bell, that frequency you emit as a result resonates and reverberates through the fiber of the Earth and the realm you reside in, and it can shake things up; it can activate more than you realize—not to mention the very cells in your body.

So feel the shimmering core of your light within you, visualize it daily, and nurture it. Sometimes, you may need to retreat to gather fuel for your fire; other times, it may be roaring merrily. Allow it to do so. Visualize it emitting from all around you, from the very center of your being like a supernova, like a star wave, a magnificent crest of light shooting out in all directions through all dimensions, clearing and clarifying and activating all that is around you. Do this daily, return to your light daily, bask in it, nurture it, grow it, and it will become ever more your guide and your temperature gauge on how you are doing, how connected to your soul you are. Ever will it then guide you if you will reside within the light of your own being. And so it is.

TABLE OF CONTENTS

INTRODUCTION

"I have this huge cry inside. A four-year-long cry. It won't come out. I've tried everything. I can't touch it. I can't access it. I live with this baseline level of anxiety, a constant breath-hold, bracing against something that isn't coming. I'm tired of trying to analyze it. I'm tired of feeling this way. I give up. I surrender."

I confided in one of my healer friends, and for the first time, I felt a crack in the titanium-plated, terminator-like armor around my heart. I felt a slight possibility things could shift. Hope settled in my chest, and warmth spread through me. The next breath was so much deeper than usual. Man, it felt so good.

I survived trauma by bracing. I will thrive by opening my heart and feeling the pain. *That* is brave.

Being brave in terms of living the life you know you were born to live—one of immense joy and abundance—requires awareness and the willingness to dive into a healing crisis with curiosity and courage.

If you're reading the words 'healing crisis' for the first time, cool. Feeling this in your body is the first step toward everything good. Understanding how to deal with those feelings will change your life.

A healing crisis comes when any sort of mind-body restriction, pain, or trauma that needs to be released surfaces. It feels like you're going to die, hence the word *crisis*. When you jump through to the other side (face and feel the pain), you realize that the wall of fire you're facing is a millimeter thick. You'll look back at it and smile and wish you jumped through sooner. Recognizing a healing crisis—that awareness—can change your life. It can be the opportunity you have to process, resolve, and heal trauma (in mind, body, spirit, or soul).

This book is called *How to Be Brave* because I want to help people understand what's possible for healing and all the ways we can move through life with courage. I asked my Brave Healer colleagues to help me with it because there are more than a few ways to be brave. I've already written a whole book about this topic. *How to Have Fun with Your Fear* was my teaching memoir about how to show up in the world in a bigger way. For *this* book, I wanted to bring together all the unique voices and experts on the topic to give you all the ways (and new hope) to address the parts of you in pain or pieces of your life that aren't working as you planned. There are so many ways to be brave and to heal.

Why do you need to be brave? Leaping into fear and being vulnerable takes a ginormous amount of courage. Your vulnerability is your strength. Your surrender to vulnerability is how you show up with world-changing strength. It's how you live the juicy, amazing life you're craving with integrity and without regrets. Brené Brown has researched this vulnerability superpower. We love her for that. And there are thousands of us healers who haven't just researched it; we've used ourselves as the experiment, done the work, and then boldly gone out to teach it by example. You can talk about being brave, or you can show up and model it. Watch as the authors here do just that.

Love warriors—my brave healers—commit to this path. When we come up against something that limits us, we don't run in the other direction. We stand tall inside our worthiness, trust something bigger is supporting the journey, and face pain with an open heart, knowing we'll be guided. This is our lifelong practice and mastery. Turning pain into purpose is a superpower, and it's available to anyone.

This book is your guide for that kind of life, and we're so glad you picked it up. That means you're tired of the old, unhelpful ways you've tried to survive, and you're ready to take a step that leads toward health, wellness, joy, freedom, abundance, and connection—the life you know you're here to experience. *You* are our love warriors.

We're going to help you fully feel everything so that, along with the pain, you can feel the ecstasy.

We're going to help you connect to your inner wisdom, the place that has all the intuition, answers, and clarity you're looking for.

We're going to offer our own vulnerable stories so you know you're not alone.

We're going to pay forward the tools we use that helped us master our own lives and live with purpose, passion, and bigger warrior love.

We'll help you alchemize your fear into fuel and lean into that love.

We'll be there for you when you reach out. This isn't just a book; it's a community of people who care.

Choosing love over fear is what takes courage. It's easier to be confused. And it's okay to be angry. It takes much more courage to practice awareness and do this life from the seat of love.

Authentic healers know they can't fix you because there's nothing broken. They empower you to find the answers yourself. They provide tools, strategies, and practices that get you closer to that connection and finally mastering your Self—yes, big-S Self. They sometimes serve as channels for higher energies to help activate that energy in you. They are master facilitators of the process.

This excites me so much! I feel like everything in my life points to this collaboration. This book is so much of why I was born. Gathering with the master healers here is a dream. To create this book, knowing we're meant to do this together, gives it so much power and magic.

My intent was to gather all our voices and perspectives on courage and bravery because we need every single one of them. We know each individual voice, story, and life experience will be the one that resonates with the right person. We know one tool doesn't always work for everyone and that each tool doesn't work every time you use it, so we wanted you to have many at your fingertips—a master toolkit.

Lastly, we know that being in the right, aligned, and safe community heals. So we're giving you that, too. Belonging to a community of like-minded, heart-centered, purpose-driven healers is badass and part of how you do this healing journey well, with more awareness and more courage. You might do the internal work alone, but you're not meant to do the journey alone.

It's both the solo path and the community connection that bring you to a place of health, wealth, and joy. I'll talk more about that at the end. For now, cannonball into this mastery (or maybe dip a toe in with one chapter).

We're so glad you're here. It's time to grab hands.

It's time to be brave.

Awakening

~ Laura Di Franco

This fear isn't mine.

I looked seven generations behind.
The lightbulb blinded me.
Confusion disappeared.
The very straight line
pointed to me.

Fear was stuck
thick-crusted and glued to my heart.
I pried away pieces for years
pulling off huge chunks of flesh
to save myself from the pain.

I discovered octopus powers.
Something brand new grew
whenever the sharks dismembered me.

All I needed was time to heal
awareness to feel
wisdom to recognize the deal
I made with God.
And I knew. . .

. . .I'll be the one to alchemize the fear into fuel.

I'll be the one to clear the line.

I'll be the one who alters time.

I floated and breathed.

I noticed the crow's wings

illuminated gold by sunrise beams.

I stared into a circle of rainbow spears

shimmering in the sky.

I touched my third eye

and remembered to listen—closely.

It's time to be brave.

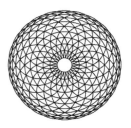

Your fear of not-good-enough is boring.
This isn't about you anymore. What if the thing you're still
a little afraid to share is exactly what someone needs
to hear to save their life? It's time to be brave.

~ Laura Di Franco

CHAPTER 1

BRAVE STORY MEDICINE™
WRITING TO HEAL TRAUMA

Laura Di Franco, MPT, Publisher

MY STORY

It's been one and a half years since my daughter's abuser was sentenced to ten years in prison, and I still can't seem to release the clench in my gut that started the day I took the witness stand.

The mahogany box the sheriff ushered me into felt like a coffin. And "buried alive" was pretty close to how the hours felt during that three-day trial.

My daughter is way more brave than me. But "brave" is relative, isn't it? I've reframed how I think of myself after surviving these past few years. *Brave* isn't how I feel. However, I'm very proud of being able to stay present in every excruciating moment that week–something my thirty years as a healer prepared me well for.

Awareness is everything. It's what helped me survive the worst events of my life, and what makes me feel fearless. Fear is just a feeling. Being brave just means you got good at taking action with that feeling in your body.

There's some pressure in being known for being the Brave Healer. I also call myself an alien. This road is lonely sometimes.

"Laura's intense, isn't she?"

"Laura, people have to have some stamina to hang with you."

Over the eight years since Brave Healer Productions was born, I've heard many similar versions of what people think of me. While most are positive (including the two above), a tender heart sometimes takes what it hears and turns it into something bad.

They must not like me.

It's okay if they don't like you. You're not here to please everyone.

Being yourself (even when it's not accepted or liked by others) is brave.

When I realized everything I made life mean (my thoughts) was exactly how I manifested my life, I paused. **How exciting is it to realize that when you take responsibility for every single thing in your life, you can have any life you dream of?** It's a fricking amazing moment of freedom.

Except it's not that easy, is it? Awareness is everything, but once you have it, you can't go back.

I hear what people say and notice my teeth coming together in a familiar holding pattern that, after a while, starts to ache into the back of my skull. Sometimes, I wake up with it throbbing. I catch myself in the car sometimes, waiting at a red light with my left hand balled into a fist so tight my forearm starts to cramp.

What is wrong with me? Breathe!

Taking responsibility for every word, action, behavior, reaction, response, and move in your life feels like a huge job. Not to mention when something bad happens.

What did I do to attract that?

Oh, wait, isn't everything that happens happening for me?

Fuck all of this! This is impossible.

Even if I try, I'll never get it perfectly right. I don't have what it takes to do this like how they say is possible.

And. . .

What else is possible?

Answering that last question—defaulting to curiosity, wonder, awe, and possibility—is my practice. I do it by writing my way there as an awareness practice. And that has saved me so many times. Last year, it felt impossible. I had to find new ways to be aware. Writing became a life line.

♥ This chapter is me doing the awareness process I'll teach you.

♥ This chapter is me healing.

♥ This chapter is a way to call out the demons, pain, hurt, disappointment, frustration, anger, guilt, shame, doubt, worry, anxiety, and fear and create something magnificent with it.

♥ This is me manifesting my life. Right here. Right now!

I'm really good at it—that manifesting thing. In fact, it's become such a powerful force I've had to be careful what I wish for. It's not lost on me that one of the biggest traumas of my life created an other-level awareness and practice that forced me to shift my thinking in a way that granted me this superpower.

Lay the feeling of certainty over your desires and then bask.
Inspired by Esther Hicks, Philadelphia, June 1, 2024

You can try it, too! Grab your notebook and pen and spend five minutes with this:

What I want right now is _____. Write as fast as you can without censoring yourself!

When I founded Brave Healer Productions (my second successful business), I realized that I never asked myself what I wanted. I was 48 and lived life on autopilot. I checked all the boxes and made great achievements based on what I thought (what I was taught) would make me happy—two degrees, a great job, marriage, kids, a house, a retirement plan, vacations, cars, a second home.

Holy cannoli, Laura, you've never spent any dedicated time asking yourself what you really want or writing any of it down! You have no idea what you really want, girl!

That aha moment was huge. It changed everything. That awareness stirred the pot. It created huge shifts (asking for a divorce), transformations (finally feeling worthy), and monumental challenges (letting go of my first business).

I sat down and, for the first time in my life, journaled about what I wanted. Do you know what happened? I stared at that blank page for a really long time. I ran my hand over the thick cardstock paper, tracing the edges repeatedly, spinning my Pilot Fine Point pen on the table between my right thumb and index finger over and over. My dog looked up from his spot on the floor in front of the sunny sliding glass door when I sighed.

I have no idea what I want.

What makes you happy, Laura?

I don't know, puppies?

Thinking about puppies always brought a smile. And that would be a key because what brought smiles, laughter, and joy became my compass. Dog videos on Instagram always did the trick if I had a bad day. Cuddling with *my* dog was super therapeutic. I mark my decades with the dogs.

I love dogs. I always have. Loving dogs is easy and the hardest thing I've ever done.

Having dogs (or any pet you love) is brave. It takes something to willingly sign up for that journey, knowing your heart will eventually be torn out of your chest.

Every single dog I've ever owned sat at my feet while I journaled about life. Leo's here right now, sleeping. An occasional puffing dream-sigh escapes his snout. *Love you, Leo.*

I appreciate everything that has happened for me to bring me to the place I am now.

Inspired by Esther Hicks, Philadelphia, June 1, 2024

What else do I love?

Like the 'What do you want' question, this one was worthy of pondering, too.

I looked back at the woman going through the motions of life for decades, pursuing happiness (she looked a little zombie-ish, and don't get me started on the polo-shirt-khaki-pants uniform—holy crap) and saw someone following every should, supposed-to, and obligatory duty she was taught made her a good girl. This included loving people she was supposed to love, even if they were toxic.

Maybe you, like me, spent a lifetime finding your voice and your Self, reclaiming your worthiness and power. I salute you, you badass. It's our time.

As of the writing of this chapter, I claim the end of the worthiness pursuit and banish paralyzing shame for what it is—self-sabotaging and destructive.

I'm worthy. I'm a badass.
It's okay if people don't like me.
I'm here to spread good vibes and brave words and help the world understand what's possible for healing. I was born for this, and I will die leaving a legacy of love and courage.

Phew, that last paragraph was awesome. Wanna try writing a power mantra, too?

Grab your notebook and pen. Write as fast as you can without censoring yourself:

What will you let go of today? What sentence would you pick to bold and center on the page?

What are you claiming for your life moving forward?

When it's out loud, it's real.

Go for it!

"Shame is ridiculous."
Abraham-Hicks

Journaling has been an awareness practice and healing modality for me since I was 15. It morphed into even more of a therapeutic process when I started blogging for my physical therapy clients, and then it up-leveled again (in terms of needing to be brave) when I decided it was time to write and publish my first book.

Living, Healing, and Taekwondo (published in 2012 by Balboa Press and re-published by Brave Healer Productions in 2015) wasn't very well-written. The cover sucked, and I misspelled a word in the title. There was no editing to speak of, and "show don't tell" was barely noticeable in that first 2012 version.

But isn't that what the next book (and step in life) is for? This is a practice. If being perfect is paralyzing you, then wake up to the fact that **imperfect action is the perfect solution to your paralyzing fear.**

I use writing to conquer fear and un-stick myself (when I feel down about something not working like it was supposed to), to be aware of limiting thoughts and beliefs (like, *you'll never be able to do this*), and to realize my dreams, vision, purpose, and legacy (journal new ideas, to-do lists for programs, or outlines for books or new empires!). I write my way to the next step, idea, inspiration, motivation, program, or plan. I write to process (every time a dog died, someone was hurt, through my divorce, and when I was inspired by the midnight sky). Writing is my therapeutic movement, energy shifter, and magic wand. Most of all, writing is my self-discovery tool.

Your intention and energy are more important than your opinion.
Inspired by Esther Hicks, Philadelphia, June 1, 2024

Writing is also my meditation practice (picture me right now, outside on the back patio, sharing the chair with Leo (and his super-bad dog breath), listening to the breeze ruffle the leaves and the circling hawk crying above). Writing is how I curate my energy and set my intention.

Laura, you got it. This is it. This is what you're born for. Keep it up, goddess! I see you down there!

That was the hawk message, y'all.

Feathers are a sign (and another love) for me. If it's a huge live bird, even better. There's a hawk couple that hangs in our neighborhood. I love them. They're up there crying down at me a lot.

You're on the right track! Don't quit now! Everything is working out in the best way!

Things haven't always been fun, easy, or happy. However, my life overall has been an amazing, fabulous miracle. The biggest challenge of my life delivered some pretty humongous gifts—patience and the capacity for bigger love. Another gift was the decision not to wait around for life to happen but to take action and go on awesome adventures.

My daughter was sexually abused by her cheerleading coach when she was 14. She was under my watch during the abuse. It was the same year I separated, divorced, and had to move out of the house for a year. It took her three years to tell me. It took the justice system four years to convict him (due to the COVID backlog and fuckery). We sent him to prison for ten years. He's served one and a half at the time of this book's publishing.

Laura, why didn't you see it?

This is your fault.

You're an idiot to have allowed this person into your home. What were you thinking? Now look at what you've done.

Rather than take you, dear reader, into the pit with me, here's what my survival story looked like. I wrote the pieces I was allowed to write throughout the ordeal. I published a few. I talked about it a lot to safe people who knew how to listen. I talked to professionals who were familiar with the court system. I asked for support. I asked for thoughts and prayers during the trial. I asked a lot of questions of all the professionals. I said yes to chats when offered (when my norm was to say, "Thank you so much, but I'll be okay."). I moved through feelings of guilt, shame, and pain and tried to speak and write about it.

**What makes us want to express hardship
is the need to justify our path
and receive approval for it.
Don't seek harmony with others' opinions.
Seek harmony with your inner being.**
Inspired by Esther Hicks, Philadelphia, June 1, 2024

I listened when my friends offered these retorts to my self-sabotaging, traumatized mind-body:

"Laura, he was a master manipulator; nobody would've seen it. He fooled many, not just you."

"This is by no means your fault. He is the perpetrator. He is to blame."

"You thought he was a friend and that he cared about you and your family. You haven't done anything wrong. He is seriously ill."

I listened. And I journaled—a lot.

Remember the opening message of this story?

How exciting is it to realize that when you take responsibility for every single thing in your life, you can have any life you dream of?

Here's what I know. It's our *response* to life that matters. It's our awareness process. It's how we live, breathe, speak, act, and behave during and after something happens. It's how we take what happened (past trauma) and practice being in our now moment (the only one you can do anything about).

Nothing and no one can be your point of attraction. You control what you feel. With awareness, you have a choice.
Inspired by Esther Hicks, Philadelphia, June 1, 2024

This awareness practice saved my life so many times. Writing is part of that. Writing helped me heal trauma and then turn it into something that saves others' lives. I create energy on the page. I claim my life out loud, right here. Words don't create; energy does. But I found the purposeful use of brave words helps me shift my energy and choose something healthier and more aligned any time I feel like it.

This is me (here on this page) writing, healing, and changing the world.

Now, it's your turn!

THE TOOL

Brave Story Medicine™: Three Steps to Healing Trauma (and Thriving) with Writing

What you need: A quiet, sacred writing space where you won't be distracted and your notebook and pen.

The idea in Step 1 is to move words, ideas, thoughts, and beliefs onto the page. If you're worried about someone else reading them, then you can burn the pages later. What's more important is the process because it shifts energy, increases awareness, and heals. If you're worried about hashing up old trauma, think about this for a moment: If the trauma (that is still sitting in your myofascial tissue) is ready to be healed, it will surface. If it's not ready, it won't. You have total control here. Be brave. Please read about how John F. Barnes Myofascial Release can help to heal mind-body trauma at MyofascialRelease.com.

Step 1: Be in your body

Find any comfortable position and practice any form of body awareness you enjoy. Breathwork and sound healing are my two go-to's. Try noticing what you feel. It's really that simple. This practice can be more detailed or complex; however, it's really about spending time noticing what you feel and sense. Do that for five minutes or more. If you need more ideas about how to get in your body, please check out *The Ultimate Guide to Self-Healing* book series.

Step 2: Write

After you've cleared your mind and grounded and centered yourself in your body, set a timer for five minutes, grab your notebook and pen, and write as fast as you can without censoring yourself. Fill in the blank:

I feel _____.

Nowadays, I don't need any prompts, but when I want to use writing as a healing tool, and I don't have any ideas to write about, I just use the "I feel" prompt to get me going. There are no rules here. Just write. When I get stuck (I'm thinking too much and out of my body), I try to pause for a deep breath and start again. There's no writer's block.

The "block" happens when you move out of your body and into your overthinking mind.

Step 3: Share

This is about putting the vibration of your voice to your words. It can involve just you or a safe friend. You can read what you wrote out loud to yourself. You can read it out loud to your friend. Or you can ask that your friend read it to you. Try any version and see what you notice. You may even write some more about how that made you feel.

As someone who shares "out loud" through writing, speaking, and publishing, here are a couple more advanced steps for my love warriors. Step 4 is about writing for others to read: blogs, social posts, email newsletters, and books. And Step 5 is about grabbing a microphone. Eeek!

I don't do these things without fear, y'all. I just learned how to do them with that feeling inside—how to take action with the feeling. Fear is just a feeling. And it's stealing your show!

At the beginning of my journey, the fight-flight-or-freeze feeling was real and visceral. I shook through being on stage so many times before I got it under control enough to allow me to do it more often. I lost feeling in my legs. I sweated through my shirts.

I've wavered over the last several years with thoughts like: *Why are you doing this to yourself? Why don't you just live a quiet life and go sell coconuts on a beach somewhere?*

It always comes back to my purpose: to wake the world up to what's possible for healing we need to be out loud about it. Writing and speaking are the path. Maybe it's yours, too!

To continue to be brave and share those words with the world, your purpose has to be burning inside you and not based on what everyone else has taught you you should want. If nothing else, go back and do that first prompt: What I really want right now is_____.

Follow the joy. Be relentless about that!

Writing (and speaking) to manifest your awesome life.

The last message is one of conscious creation and the opportunity that lies before you.

Talking smack about anything, especially your own goals, desires, and dreams, will create resistance to achieving them.
With awareness, you have a choice.
Inspired by Esther Hicks, Philadelphia, June 1, 2024

Every thought, spoken word, and feeling matter. And rather than shrinking back from that huge responsibility, realize its freedom. This is the freedom to create a life of your dreams. It's the magic, the secret, the way, the how, the thing maybe you wonder if you can do. You're either pointing forward or backward. Take notice. Practice the awareness. Be a ninja for your own life.

Excuses aren't a part of the love warrior's code.

Big Warrior Love,

Laura

Laura Di Franco is the CEO of Brave Healer Productions, an award-winning publisher for holistic health and wellness professionals and those who serve them. Read more about her in the About the Author section at the end of the book.

https://BraveHealer.com

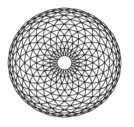

Fire, walk with me.

~ David Lynch

CHAPTER 2

BURNING TO BE FREE

CLEAR THE PATH TO YOUR HIGHEST DESIRE

Atlantis Wolf

MY STORY

"The embers are 1200 degrees or hotter," said Jeremy, pacing inside the circle of students assembled for the final shamanic initiation. He was barefoot in blue jeans and a t-shirt with his hair pulled back and his open hands coming together and apart, fingertips tapping as he walked. His Italian heritage showed in his dark skin and hair. But his eyes were blaze-green and looked like he once stared into an inferno without blinking as a child. The fire left its mark.

I remember that moment as I see him and his wife, Stephanie, in the circle of my fire ceremony at the Brave Healer Writers Retreat in the Catskills. Tonight I'm pacing. I'm teaching how to remove mental bindings that limit our potential and to become the storytellers of our reality.

Often, before a shamanic ceremony, there's an initiation. Mine arrived at lunch today, sitting at one of the round tables assigned to our group in the Honor's Haven Resort cafeteria. The room reminded me of high school, but with a better view—a former golf course and miles of mountainside. Also, less yelling and BO. We ate on ceramic plates with a rainbow of food offerings instead of paper plates and institutional pizza. But with the same level of social calculations and predatory practices.

The meal was finished. Few of us remained. I saw a woman at the next table and considered my move. I saw her the first night of the retreat.

Skinny jeans and Brazilian blowout, I thought to myself. *She's probably been married 20 years and does whatever she wants. Not my people.*

I've been a single mom since my kids were four and six. My ex-husband left six months before my mom died of cancer. Grief-stricken, I quit my job as a project manager at Charles Schwab and became a licensed medical massage therapist. No one would hire me without experience, so I worked for myself out of my house. Five years later, I started taking care of twins and brought them in as family. Their mom is still an alcoholic. All the kids are in college. Still in business 14 years later with an office and a second therapist, I wear my life experiences like war medals.

But something about her pulled me.

She probably plays golf, I thought.

My dad raised us to examine everyone in the same way: judge, criticize, and dismiss. If we drove past a golf course, a sport he disliked because it wasn't basketball, it might go like this: "Look at those jerks wasting time on that chemical grass, too rich to sweat at a real sport. What a bunch of a-holes."

That was the pattern imprinted from birth. I watched it spin around my mind like a familiar song on a record. But I'm not under my dad's roof anymore. Not for 30 years. Or in his car. The pattern still exists, but it's as uncomfortable as old shoes.

I can stay here, observing myself, I thought. *Or not.*

"Hey, Ellen!" I said across my table. "Can I talk to you?"

She walked over and sat next to me, only an empty chair between us. "What's up?"

"I, uh, want to say that you remind me of people in high school," I said. "Not a specific person, more of an archetype of the kids who used to make fun of me."

Her smile sank. "But I..." she said before I cut her off.

"No, no, not that you are them. It's a reminder. An old feeling. I used to weigh 85 pounds more than I do now. And dressed in Goodwill clothes and just basically didn't fit into rural Ohio."

I leaned in closer, talking with my hands.

"So, here I'm seeing you as one of the popular rich kids, but then I listened to how you spoke to Greg when he sat between us yesterday at breakfast. The way you speak to people, how you turn your body to face them and ask such open-ended questions, bringing out their quiet thoughts. It's a marvel to witness. It's like watching angel wings wrap around a person. I'm in awe of you."

I watch her face change from what she shows the world to what she feels inside, like looking down a path into the forest and seeing deeper into the darkening wood.

"When I was 16," she said, "My life circumstances changed, and I became homeless."

I'm such an a-hole, I thought.

We looked into each other's tear-filled eyes, seeing each other. Instead of trading wounds as women are conditioned to do, we traded stories of battles won. Two warriors meeting on the mountain; two sisters who found each other. A master ayurveda teacher and a master shaman finding the common lineage in their background.

Sitting with her was an awakening. Raised by a rageaholic who erupted over me in no predictable way, I wasn't prepared for the presence of colossal kindness. It startled me to be with someone so vulnerable and emotionally mature. I felt seen and accepted.

The last to leave, we hugged, and she noticed our bodies were both warm below the waist.

"Whoa!" she said, putting her hand on her belly. "Our bodies are so warm right here."

"Womb sisters," I said, smiling.

That night, I saw her striding up to the fire circle with her black Lululemon shoulder bag.

"Hey, no purses or phones at the ceremony!" someone said.

"Oh, this goes everywhere I go," she said, sitting down. "My phone's off."

I smiled and thought: *My sister is so cool.*

I walked around the circle with a basket, greeting each person and giving them a pinecone with a piece of papyrus paper wrapped with twine and a separate square of paper. Javier, who worked for the resort, lit the fire. He also found fuel for the tiki torches and lit them.

The tree frogs were talking to us as the wind spoke through the leaves in the tall maples and oaks as we gathered together.

The clang and ripple of my Himalayan tingsha bells quieted the conversation.

"Fire is the element of transformation," I said. "It does not destroy. It changes what it consumes into heat and light, smoke and spirit, so it can be reassembled and returned to you as a gift."

Pointing to the cement ring surrounding the lit wood, I said, "Here at the east-facing point is a blue alabaster egg from Egypt representing water, birth, and beginnings. Here is a bronze copalera from Italy holding gold copal from Mexico representing earth, labor, and midday. Here is carnelian to the west, representing fire, endings, and wisdom. And here is a metal Katrina skull from Oaxaca representing air, ancestors, and the spirit world."

"The stones are from Bradford, sitting right here," I said, smiling. "He has more for sale."

"The skull came from a trip I took with Stephanie and Jeremy to Oaxaca to celebrate where the Day of the Dead tradition began. And the copal came from the pyramids at Teotihuacan, Mexico on a book project trip with Stephanie and Jeremy. Are you seeing a pattern here?" I said, smiling at them.

"I'm also adding incense, palo santo, and tobacco to Grandfather Fire to honor him."

I began drumming on my 27-inch cow-skin drum, looking into the flames. I guided the group through a meditation and asked them to imagine they were collecting details of a story into the pinecone held in their hands.

"What keeps you separate?

What makes you small?

What is your prison?

What shackles you to a dark wall?"

I guided them to draw a symbol, a glyph, or a letter on the pinecone paper to represent the story. Then draw it on the square paper and put it in their pocket. They were instructed to put the pinecone into the fire when they were ready to let it go, agreeing to never tell the story again.

I drummed as they reflected in private silence. Stephanie and I sang the fire song. Some people joined in. One person got up in seconds and hurled their pinecone into the heart of the fire like a baseball. Some lobbed it. Some cried, cradling the pinecone before setting it gently on its voyage to ash. Some cones fell off the fire and needed a second try.

I kept drumming and said, "I have extra pinecones if you want them."

Jeremy came around with the basket and many people took another and another. The flames were high and bright as the crowd delighted in releasing themselves from old patterns and limiting beliefs.

I release myself from anger that wasn't mine.

I burn away this small prison.

I remove these chains and hand them back.

I purge the poison.

My face full of flame and eyes blazing, I stopped drumming.

"Stay as long as you need. Use the fire as a scrying tool, meditate by gazing into the embers, and see what message arrives for you. You might see something, sense a presence, or hear the voice of an ancestor. Be still and silent. Wait for what comes."

The stars sparkled like tiny fires, and the wind whispered over our heads.

"When you are ready, return to your room and journal with the symbol in your pocket. Retell your story in a new way. See the lesson, where it led you, and how it shaped you. See it as medicine."

I sat and drummed, pausing to say, "And anyone who wants to meditate with fire dragons, stick around for another guided meditation."

I sat close to the fire, fed it more incense and tobacco, watching the sparks and snapping wood form shapes in my glowing eyes—dragons, fire sprites, and green-purple spirits hovering over the licks of flame.

I reached back to the memory of the night of the last initiation of shamanic training in the Smoky Mountains of North Carolina. Jeremy built a multi-level star out of wood. We wrote our intentions on paper and pushed them between the logs. The flames were so high and hot I felt like I was looking into the sun.

I remember his words before it was lit. "Don't walk unless you are called. You don't have to walk. No one will know," he said. "If the fire doesn't pull you, don't walk. You'll get fire kisses. We don't say burned."

The wood seared to embers as we sat nearby and meditated.

What if I can't walk? What's pushing me forward?

I spent so much money and effort to get here.

Three people are taking shifts feeding my kids.

I'd disappoint everyone.

We reassembled in a circle, barefoot, with a drum or rattle in our hand. In the blackness, a glowing carpet of embers with a long, mounded line on either side was laid in front of us. At the front of the path was an arch in the shape of two flames, like hands, forming a portal made of iron and steel. Liquid propane filled each side with fire.

"Stand at the doorway and wait to see if you are called to walk," Jeremy said.

We all drummed and rattled, watching the glow as Stephanie sang the fire song.

"Fire, Sacred Fire,

Come to me in the night."

One person stepped forward and walked, banging their drum and howling to the stars as they walked the five steps to the far side. We cheered and howled with them.

I'm not walking.

It's fine.

My body feels like cement.

I'm rooted underground.

"Come to me in the Dream-Time.

Bring me visions of light."

Stephanie sang the song over and over, louder and louder, until we knew the words. We all started singing, mesmerized by the waving vibrations of heat, drumming, and rattling so loud I couldn't hear a thought.

"Spiral down, circle round,

To these arms open wide."

I walked to the flaming arch, drumming and hardly breathing, seeing the sparkling fire eggs in front of me.

1200 degrees.

1200 degrees.

Or hotter.

Why am I here? What called me here?

I'll turn around. No one back home will know.

What's pushing me forward?

I looked across the path through the lines of wavy, radiant heat to the other side.

What would give me the courage to do this?

I exhaled, drumming and relaxing. I had a vision of my kids standing and looking at me. Then the spirits of my grandparents and ancestors I don't know. Future grandchildren. Then my animal guides—wolf, buffalo, sea turtle, and dragon. Above them all, my mom stood in her angelic form, white wings spread wide, and arms outstretched to me.

You're bigger than you can imagine, she said.

It's about what I'm walking towards, I thought. *Not what is pushing me forward. It's all the love waiting for me on the other side, the days yet to come.*

"Healing light, burning bright,

Dry these tears I have cried."

I cried and drummed, walking easily to the other side, dissolving every belief that kept me small and quiet. A crowd of spirits and friends embraced me. Not believing I did it because I didn't feel any heat, I got in line and walked again. And a third time. And fourth. Then, it was time for the mounded lines to be raked to the middle, saving the hottest embers for last.

"If you are called," said Jeremy, "come dance in the fire. Dance with your shadow!"

I jumped onto the coals and danced, drumming and howling in the forest, free to begin my path as a shaman.

THE TOOL

What idea or belief keeps you from achieving the dream you desire? Let's identify it and transform it so you can begin living your dream.

1. Dream

Given unlimited time, physical strength, and financial resources, what would you achieve? What do you want to bring into the world? What change do you want to make in your life? Take time to be still and silent while you journal all the possibilities. Unbridle your imagination and write as many things as you can.

If it feels overwhelming, go for a walk in nature. Get into a forest, on a beach, or in a meadow and be with yourself for an hour or two while you ponder the question: What is my heart's desire?

2. Do

Choose one goal. If you can't pick one, write them all down on scraps of paper and fold them in half twice. Put all the papers in a bowl, close your eyes, and pull one out. Begin there.

Write down all the steps you need to achieve that goal. Even if it takes several days. Ask people for help if you get stuck on some of the steps that may need professional advice, like building a website or getting a visa to go to a foreign country. Make the goal 108 steps at a minimum. Even the smallest step will be a success, a victory worth celebrating. For example, if losing 50 pounds is your goal, make losing a half pound a step. That's 100 steps right there!

3. Die

Create your personal fire ceremony. Gather something in nature that you can tie a piece of paper around. It could be a pinecone, a bundle of sticks, or flowers. Bring them with two pieces of paper, twine or string, a pencil, and your journal to your fire.

Set your intention to release the block or barricade between you and your goal. It's okay if you can't name it. Light the fire and feed it your favorite incense, dried flowers, or herbs. Make it personal. Call in your ancestors who have passed away to come now and sit with you. Ask them to help describe the block and give you the strength to release it to the flames.

Write a symbol, picture, or word to represent your limiting belief. Tie it to your bundle. Send all the details into the fire - How old were you when this first happened? Who told it to you? Where do you feel it in your body? Give it all to the fire.

Wait as the story turns to smoke and ash. Ask your ancestors, friends, or the universe for help retelling your story. Write that new story in your journal, promising yourself never to tell the old story again. It's not about negative to positive; it's about creating your reality.

For example,

Old Story: My dad was a rageaholic who erupted at me with bellowing, unpredictable anger that made me feel scared and small. I stopped talking so nothing I said could upset him.

New Story: I am resilient and composed in the face of even deadly anger. Thanks to my dad, I can feel a person's energy when they walk into the room. I reflect on my words before I speak my mind.

The old story puts my dad at the center. I reacted to his actions. And keeps me in the past. The new story puts me at the center of the present. I initiate and choose my action. See the difference? Standing in your power versus someone else controlling your behavior. Start your new story with "I am…"

4. Fly

As you celebrate each step, be prepared for the grief that can arrive. Living a dream often means letting go of familiar patterns. Giving up smoking can mean not seeing your best friend for a smoke break. Not going out for happy hour can make you feel out of the loop with co-workers. Have faith in the journey. You're bigger than you can imagine.

I'm Atlantis Wolf, and I believe in you.

Emily Atlantis Wolf is a professional healer and teacher. (That means she gets paid to invent ways to heal people.) She climbed corporate ladders in civil engineering and financial investment services until 2009 when her mom died. She pivoted into the healing arts, training to become a Licensed Medical Massage Therapist, Usui Reiki Master, Seneca Wolf Clan Shaman, and Master Breathwork Facilitator, among others.

Since 2010, she has helped over 3,000 clients confront and care for their physical and metaphysical pain in-person and online. From chronic muscle tightness to trauma to unexpressed emotions, Atlantis combines practical and intuitive modalities. Part of her secret is connecting to spiritual realms using breathwork, drumming, and fire ceremonies. She also asks for the guidance of galactic dragons.

Her joy is creating live experiences for group gatherings. Atlantis runs four-week coaching sessions that take clients through the four cycles of change, creating permanent and lasting change for any personal goal. She also offers online calls, writing courses, breathwork events, and retreats.

Sign up for Atlantis's email list to receive part one of her four-part online course called, Take Flight: A Map to Your Heart's Desire.

Connect with Emily Atlantis:

Web: https://www.atlantiswolf.com/

Email: SanoTotum@gmail.com

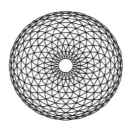

I call this self-inflicted devastation

~ Kala

CHAPTER 3

BUT HOW?

NO ONE EVER TOLD ME
HOW TO STAY SOBER

Dr. Ruth A. Souther, DoD, LRMP, Hypnotherapist

MY STORY

"I'm more than my recovery. Why don't people understand that?"

Kala's wide blue eyes filled with tears. "In AA, they say to work the program, but they never tell me how to stay sober. The same 12 steps over and over.

"But *how?*" Kala shook her head, her long, blonde hair waving in distress. "I know I did some awful stuff and mistreated people. For that, I lost contact with my child, and my family won't speak to me.

"They won't forgive me. They won't even listen. They expect me to get drunk and do more shameful things. I get depressed and lonely, and then I live up to their expectation. How do I change that?"

Kala's pain was evident.

"My family tells me to reach out, or I should have contacted them when I thought I would backslide. But they don't want to hear it. They shut me out, and I feel worse. So I drink more.

"AA people talk about sobriety. Nothing else is ever on their minds. I know I'm being judgmental, but if that's all I think about, I want to drink. It's like being on a diet, and I can't focus on anything except what I want to eat. It doesn't help."

Kala paced around my office, touching things as if to ground herself in the physical moment.

"Give yourself to your higher power. I don't know what my higher power is. It certainly isn't the God they talk about. How can I 'give myself' to something I can't even describe?

"I don't feel the need to completely define my higher power. I'm confused by conflicting ideas of AA. Some people will say they are *only* able to stay sober because of God.

"But then, we have free will and have to make the decision every day not to drink. So then, which is it?"

Kala's agitation grew as she described her experience with the local AA chapter. Her body language changed as she slouched over, head down. She's much taller than I am, and by the time she finished speaking, she was nearly at my height.

She was broken and would try anything.

A mutual friend recommended Kala to me in the hopes I could help her sort out her feelings and perhaps provide a new path to sobriety. He thought my alternative healing methods would fit Kala's needs. He thought breathwork would help, as he heard it was a natural high.

Based on what she said, breathwork is that, but it didn't fit as an approach for Kala. My specialty is PTSD and anxiety through methods based on intuitive connections to my clients rather than clinical ones.

Addictions are emotionally based, either because of the physical satisfaction or the anxiety that drives someone to continue the search for numbness.

That's a simple description, but it's much more complicated and individual for those who seek my support. I don't like to use the word 'help.' That implies I have all the answers and can 'fix' the issues. I can't.

By the time clients get to me, they've exhausted traditional avenues and feel hopeless.

"What's the point in trying to stay sober?" Kala continued. "Everyone expects me to be a screw-up, so I might as well be one."

"But you're here, so there's hope." I gestured to my inner office, where I practiced hypnosis. "Tell me why you started drinking."

"I didn't start drinking until college. It was fun, and I felt fearless and attractive for the first time in my life. But drinking became a priority very quickly."

Kala fiddled with the hem of her shirt. "I never thought it would end up controlling every bit of me."

"No one ever does. Alcoholism is a sneaky bastard."

Kala laughed and, for the first time, began to relax.

"You're in a safe space; anything you say is confidential. You can lay it out so I can better understand what we need to do." I already had an idea of how to go forward.

Kala had little trust in anyone or anything. She'd seen everything crumble before her eyes because she wanted to have a good time. That's what alcohol was to her, even when it destroyed her self-integrity. Two things were happening.

She could not trust herself.

She could not forgive herself. Or would not. Or didn't know how. The concept of self-forgiveness was foreign. She thought everyone had to forgive her before she could heal.

I deeply respect AA—the solid work done in that community and the lives saved because of the program. Yet something was missing, and that was Kala's most significant issue.

How can she move forward when she is constantly reminded how she failed? How could she possibly find self-forgiveness when her inner demons continued to torture her with the words of others?

"I don't think I can be hypnotized." Kala shifted in her chair.

I darkened the room, allowing just the soft glow of a Himalayan salt-filled bulb in a stained glass lamp. The shade has colorful dragonflies on it—a subtle symbol of transformation. More importantly, it represents the connection between the physical and spiritual worlds.

"Maybe not, but it doesn't matter. Your unconscious will hear everything I say even if you plan your grocery list while I'm talking."

"I didn't realize that about hypnosis. It will help me relax even if I don't get deep? I'm not doing it wrong if I can't go into a trance?"

"There is no wrong way." I smiled.

Kala laughed again, and it was music to my ears. The connection between us was building. She wouldn't remain just a client—she would become my friend and my adopted 'spirit' daughter.

I knew this instinctively but needed to keep my focus.

Kala got comfortable on the massage table I used during hypnosis. Lying down allows the body to relax even if the mind refuses, and everyone I ask prefers it to a chair.

"If you don't want to close your eyes, just look up where the ceiling meets the wall. Let your eyes roll upward as you take a deep breath. Allow yourself to sink into the bed's coziness, feel the blanket's texture, the firmness of the support beneath you."

Meditation music played in the background as we began our first session.

Kala made improvements during the months we worked together. I became her touchstone—someone to text or talk to when she felt like drinking.

I learned a lot about her life growing up, her siblings, her friends, and how she longed to have her daughter back in her life. She achieved that goal and now has shared custody—a huge success.

Kala texted me late one night, sober and deep in thought.

"Wow, I can't sleep. I keep thinking about how my adult life has been such sadness. So often, I'd have a boyfriend, and when that relationship ended, my heart ached, but there was nothing I could do."

I could feel Kala's grief through the words. I wanted to hug her, but she was miles away.

"There'd be a person I could relate to, someone I felt close with, and then, when I got drunk, they would drop me. I felt so abandoned."

My chest constricted, reading her anguish, yet all I could do was 'listen.' It's what she needed. It's what she wanted. No advice. Just listen.

Kala continued her late-night musings. "People just moved away and never contacted me. I'd be alone again."

"Or I was so focused on drinking I lost a lot of family connections and would just be alone again. It wasn't until I got sober that I met new people.

"I discovered I still have a few folks who have been in my life for a long time and still care about me. But they don't live near me.

"It's hard to realize I couldn't be a good friend unless I were sober, and it was hard to stay sober.

"Then, when I started drinking again, I lost all those people again. I don't blame anyone for ending it with me when I was a complete mess and kept doing the same thing repeatedly.

"It's depressing to watch someone do that to themselves. I also lost friends in AA when I got drunk one night. I had a group of girlfriends in recovery/AA.

"They all cast me out. The motto of AA is to be there for struggling fellow alcoholics. Instead, I was treated like I was trying to get attention and like I was toxic.

"People expected me to apologize for hurting them by drinking. 'Sorry that you made my relapse about you.' My drinking had nothing to do with them.

"I have never and never will apologize because I think that was very selfish of them, and although my support system came crashing down, it made me realize I didn't really want to be associated with them.

"They weren't following the principles their program teaches. I understand keeping your distance from someone who is constantly relapsing and affecting your life negatively, but just one night when I almost had a year sober is wild.

"Man. Such a sad cycle. It wasn't always sad, but I remember that lonely, depressed, and lost feeling too often. But I know I've accomplished a lot of positive things. And my life is so much better now, and I'm actively trying to make new female friends."

There was no need for me to reply. I just sent a heart emoji. I was with her on this journey, and she knew that.

Another random text after many things went wrong on a single day, but Kala did not resort to drinking.

"I'm adulting hard today."

She was, and I told her how proud I was of her ability to go with the flow and not resort to alcohol.

Kala turned her energy toward stand-up comedy.

Kala's recent text to me:

"I love making people laugh. Maybe it's the validation or how easily you can connect with strangers over laughter. I don't know why I decided to do it, though, because I have anxiety and hate speaking in front of large groups of people.

"I was thinking about my life goals in March 2023, and stand-up comedy kept popping into my head. It felt like I needed to do it for whatever reason.

"My talent/ability has nothing to do with anyone else's talent or ability."

There it was: the confidence to be authentic, stand in her power, and take back her life.

She hit a few rough patches and, on occasion, would slide back into drinking. She always returned to her desire to stay sober as her life turned around.

Two months sober, then drunk. Depression playing games with her. Back to square one.

Four months sober and a bottle of wine was the downfall.

Six months sober, another slide back.

As I write this, Kala is at the 11-month sobriety mark, and her year token has been purchased. I'm proud to say she asked if I would present it to her. Her request made me cry.

Her recovery coin says "Change" on one side, and on the other, it says, "The secret of change is to focus all of your energy, not on fighting the old, but on building the new."

THE TOOL

Kala could not get forgiveness from those in her life who perceived her to be unsalvageable. Her salvation was self-forgiveness and letting go of expectations.

Use this meditation to release the emotional baggage that never belonged to you in the first place. Find a small stone to hold as a reminder of your healing promise.

Record it in your voice and allow yourself to sink into the oceanic waters.

Imagine or remember a time when you were pure water, a vast ocean stretching from one distant shore to another. Breathe in the scent of saltwater and sea creatures.

Let yourself be rocked as one with the waves, noticing that it feels natural, and you fall easily into the rhythm. Back and forth. Back and forth. Sleepy, dreamy, and relaxed.

Allow your body to blur around the edges as you begin to dissolve into the water. You become part of the water, feeling the tides ebb and flow as you expand further and further out.

There is nothing except you. You are this great vessel of blue, deep and mysterious, holding all the mysteries of life within its complex existence.

You ask, who am I? Where did I come from? Where am I going?

Then you know. You are life itself, held in trust and tranquility. Sink into this feeling and let it support every cell, every thought, and every emotion.

Connect to this higher form of the nurturing unconscious and let the oceanic power flow through you.

Without water, there would be no life and no energy. You hold the answers to creation. Bask in this knowledge and allow all your doubts to seep out with the tide.

As the waves roll back in, let them bring you the ancient wisdom of the sea.

Commune with the energies and know you are the magic of humanity. Open yourself to this connection. Allow emotional clarity and confidence to fill you with the power to change your life.

Allow yourself to go wherever you need to go. Experience, even for this short moment in time, the emotional truths that allow you to be held in healing waters.

See yourself grow, expanding further into the expression of your sensitive nature.

Hold this energy as long as you can. Let the memory return you to your original state of compassion and kindness toward yourself. Let forgiveness flow through, holding you in its eternal arms.

When ready, return to shore and bring your emotional temperament back into your physical presence. Breathe deeply, inhale and exhale three times, and fully return to your body.

Open your eyes and be fully present in the moment.

Let your stone continue to hold this energy and propel you forward with compassion toward all emotional decisions for the future. Feel the difference. You are no longer holding onto the past. You are strong, centered, and held in the protection of self-forgiveness.

Write about the changes in yourself, your perceptions, and the influence this connection has on your daily life. Observe the rain; where did it flow, and what did you discover? What are you willing to heal?

Ruth Souther has practiced metaphysical and natural arts for 35 years. She is a Master Shamanic Breathwork facilitator, Master Reiki practitioner, hypnotherapist, ritualist, and minister. She co-facilitates with Stephanie Urbina Jones and Terran Woodliff the Alchemy: A New Earth Priestess Mystery School.

She wrote *The Heart of Tarot* (an intuitive guide to the cards), *Vega's Path: The Elemental Priestess*, and three novels: *Death of Innocence, Surrender of Ego*, and *Rise of Rebellion*. The fourth, *Obsession of Love*, is forthcoming. She is the Writing Wrangler for the *Shaman Heart* book series and has written multiple chapters for Brave Healer anthologies.

She is an Initiated Priestess through Diana's Grove and has taught with the Reclaiming Collective of San Francisco at Missouri and Texas Witch Camps. She has studied Tarot and Astrology since 1990, teaches many classes in both subjects, and provides readings in person and online.

Ruth created Vega's Path Priestess Process, which has been ongoing since 2012. She is a facilitating member of The Edge of Perception and The Sanctuary of Formative Spirituality—a NFP spiritual organization. She is a contributing author, and board member/Chief Editor of Crystal Heart Imprints. This independent co-operative press supports and guides authors in their creative projects.

Connect with Ruth:

http://vegaspath.com

http://facebook.com/vegaspath

http://edgeofperception.com

http://facebook.com/edgeofperception

http://crystalheartimprints.com

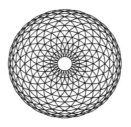

---

*"Congratulations!" we exclaimed in anticipation of having
and seeing a new life among us. With a sigh of exhaustion,
the woman, worn and gaunt, lying on a thin mat in her one-
room, earthen home, looked up with true remorse
on her face and responded:
"Would someone please get me some birth control?"*

~ Dr. Pamela J. Pine

CHAPTER 4

BRAVERY
BEYOND BOUNDARIES

RISING THROUGH CHANGES IN COUNTRY, CULTURE, HEART, AND MIND

Dr. Pamela J. Pine

MY STORY

Before anyone had heard of it and it hadn't yet gained its unfortunate and devastating current international reputation as a harbor for terrorists and a war catastrophe, I journeyed along with a group of other mostly young Americans to Yemen. We were to perform what we internalized as benevolence—in equal part, at least, with adventure. I was freshly out of the university, a middle-class Jewish kid with something to prove and hell-bent on finding and achieving her 1970s women's-movement-inspired independence. What I found there was all that and much more.

On the ground, after 15 hours in the air and a car ride from the airport, we were met by workers from the U.S. who had been there a year or longer. They were browned. I look at my arms. We arrivals are so white due to our wintering, we almost look oddly blue; it feels uncomfortable, perhaps even embarrassing. I squint in the brightness of what seems like a wholly different sun. We were shown to our temporary quarters while in Sana'a, the Capital City. There, I was to attend Arabic lessons for three months taught by three young male Yemeni college students. After walking up the many 16-inch-high, stone block chiseled steps to the upper levels of the dwelling, we then got to pick our spots on the floor to sleep. We had our first Yemeni meal of beans and *khobs* (hand-baked flat bread), chatted a little, and turned in early.

I startled awake at 3 am, sitting straight up with the worst headache I ever had, the kind that had me crying, holding and pressing each side of my head, feeling like I needed to hold it together or it would explode. I was in so much pain. Later, I chalked it up to altitude sickness—Sana'a lies at over 7,000 feet—or travel. Sleep eluded me, and by 5 am on the first morning, I was further beaten down by a sound I had never heard, high-pitched and so close by, it felt unfair at any hour: *"Allahu Akbar. Allahu Akbar. Ash-hadu la ila il Allah. Ash-hadu la ila il Allah."* It was the morning prayer being proclaimed from the next-door mosque's minaret. With no alternative, I arose after a while from the thin mattress on the floor: miserable, sick, jet-lagged, and tired, tired, tired. I dressed, ate, and ventured outside.

Outside, it was dusty and hot, and the later seasons would make it hotter—the kind of heat that makes your brain shut down and numb. I walked around, first aware of the what-I-assumed-to-be rabid packs of snarling yellow mutt dogs I'd very soon feel the need to protect myself from by carrying large rocks. I noticed how close the buildings were to each other and the little alleyways. I ventured down one until I realized that, given few functioning internal toilets, this is where most people went to relieve themselves; the alleyways were lined with human excrement.

I ended up focused on bodily functions a lot over the months (and the two and a half years) in Yemen. I had on-and-off nausea and diarrhea from unclean foods and parasites, and "snail burps"—the massive indigestion that crawled up from the entirety of my stomach to my esophagus, releasing with a horrid taste I could only describe as the taste of unwashed, slimy snail. I peed down holes cut in concrete or dirt floors that ran against the outside stone walls of the stacked, hand-built, layer cake houses that went up and up, decorated on the outside in white, lime lacing. The pee had to run down the outside of the houses; you could not urinate in the same hole through the floor where you defecated because that system needed to stay dry and could thereby be maintained less noxiously. And those bathroom spiders! They were so huge that I could see their eyes watching me.

What have I done?!

But the Arabic classes, taught by the three young male Yemeni students, were a treat even though they were six to seven hours every day, six days a week for three months: a worthy challenge. The teachers had very little English-speaking ability, so there were no "it means this" possibilities, and we were compelled to figure it out. I learned the grammar and new sounds of the Arabic language: the *qa*, the *dhel*, the *Ta*, and the *kha*. Mohammed, one of our teachers, had our entire language class (*"kula wahid al'an"*—"everyone now") practicing sound combinations one day with the repetition of "fuq, fuq, fuq, fuq." There was total falling-off-chair hysteria in the classroom that day.

Being my mother's daughter (she, a former speech therapist), I'm a good linguist and not shy about making a fool of myself in other languages. I can copy any sound and I learn fast. I went down to the taxi stand a month after Arabic lessons began: *"Min futhluk, eshti imshi ila el suq."* *"Ta-yib,"* said the taxi driver. And off we went to the market, down the steep mountain hill.

The marketplace (*suq*) in Yemen is biblical. I was transported by the smells and colors: Frankincense, saffron, myrrh, gold, and silver. Everywhere, the men were in *futahs*—that cotton "skirt" the skinny, little Yemeni men wrap around themselves that goes down to the bottom of their calves, with their *jambiyas*, the curved daggers that sleep in their decorated belted bands to be awoken only in case of a rope or whatnot needing to be cut, or, as the situation demanded (really demanded) in honor-threatening situations. Their sports jackets completed the outfit.

The women—those women allowed by their men to go to the *suq*—were in black *sharshefs* worn over their colorful dresses. Part of the garb is the headscarf with a black red-banded, thin, long scarf that goes on top of the scarf and wraps around the forehead, nose, cheeks, and chin, allowing only the eyes to peek through the small space left after tying that wrap in the back of the head. There are two veils, laid on top of the scarves from the middle of the top of the head forward, running down the front of the face. They hang down, covering the breast, the top one embroidered on each under-lower corner with shiny silver threaded designs so that when that upper veil gets tossed backward over the top of their heads, one can easily see that special touch. These veils are held on with a black, hip-length headpiece and shawl that also ties behind the head but right above the neck. Each "wing" is then brought forward to snap under the chin, covering the arms and down over the hips. The rest of the *sharshef* is a full black, shiny skirt hinged at the waist on the left side that goes down to the floor. Friends dressed me up once with glee; I became their doll. In the picture taken of me, I disappeared in the darkened background. But go to a woman's party, and all that black gets peeled off, revealing beautiful, shiny, colorful, silver-and-gold-embroidered full dresses and pantaloons. And we all whooped it up!

Ultimately, I was assigned to a post I requested in Taiz, the second major city in Yemen, working in a Hansen's Disease (leprosy) sanitarium run by Mother Theresa's Missionaries of Charity. On the day established for me to begin work in Taiz, I went to introduce myself.

I lived just above the base of a mountain and found their house as I walked down by asking various locals for it as I walked: *"Fein el dar el-rahibat ma' el thobe baithe?"* ("Where is the home of the nuns who wear the white robes?")

I rang the bell posted on the wood framing around the corrugated iron door that was mounted in the stone wall surrounding their home and small compound. Tall in Indian terms, Sister Saachi came to the door and opened it with a surprised but welcoming expression.

"Hello," she said, smiling a curious but sweet smile. "Come in," she invited as she opened the door wider to the small garden in the front of their convent home where flowers and vegetables grew. Later attempts to grow roses in that dusty soil failed miserably.

"One moment, please."

Sister Saachi then went in, and then out came Sister Cairistiona, a strong-willed, wise, and spirited sister who spoke to me in the garden that first meeting day. I met the other three of the five Taiz-placed sisters later on the first "real" day of work. Thin Sister Priya, the Sister Superior, was the nervous sister whose eyes darted when considering situations. She was the one who was responsible for decisions made and work performed.

Sister Janani was the round, sweet, quiet, dark sister from Southern India. Little, wiry Sister Gloriana was the one with the black-rimmed glasses.

Sister Cairistiona explained that they could not pay me. "No problem, others will support my way."

"When would you like to begin?" she said with what appeared to be a sly smile.

"Anytime."

With a teasing look in her eye, likely picking up my nervousness about working in a leprosy sanitarium even though that's what I chose to do, she said, "Well, let's go." I stood there blankly.

She smiled and said, "You can begin tomorrow morning."

"Are you Christian?"

"Yes," I lied, it being Yemen, after all, and I being Jewish, "but not religious."

She invited me to come to mass. I thanked her but declined: "I really don't attend church." Well, that was true!

Later, in some twist of the universe's irony, I ended up—given I sang well and told the sisters that before I told them I was Jewish—invited again to Sunday mass to provide a rendition of "I Don't Know How to Love Him" from the show *Jesus Christ Superstar* for their service and small congregation. Standing there, it was nice to have people smiling and my singing appreciated. After the service was over (and not yet knowing it was a mortal sin), the priest assigned to Taiz and the Christian flock there invited me to take (and I took) the holy sacrament. I brought with me one of the world's most prominent religions and surrounded myself with others. Certainly, I must be triple blessed!

On my actual first day of work, we traveled together in their Jeep, me in the back, bumping along, silent, listening to "Hail Mary, full of grace. . .," which, in short order, I could repeat the whole of in my head. After about a half hour, we arrived at *Medinat e'-Noor* (the City of Light).

Most of the patients at the City of Light entered with one or more noticeable signs of the disease: loss of eyebrows, sagging eye and facial muscles, claw hand and/or foot, worn away fingers, large lepromatous boils on their faces or other parts of their body. And, because one of the medications they took was often some form of steroid to reduce inflammation, their faces sometimes came to reflect what the books call a lion or moon face, one that looked bloated and devoid of eyebrows, thereby feline or otherworldly in appearance. There was constant pain.

It's a Wednesday at *Medinat e' Noor*. My jobs were varied. I attended to the fat chickens and horrid, blood-drawing roosters I got from the U.S. government for fresh eggs (and baby chicks) for the patients. I performed sister-trained diagnostic and treatment work and did whatever else was needed, teaching classes to the children of patients and even painting a mural on the dispensary wall of the sisters walking on the mountain.

After chores, Cairistiona and I walked to the home of a woman in the village who grew up around the clinic (patients stayed due to the stigma of leprosy and not welcome home, built simple stone and clay dwellings surrounding the sanitarium). She had just given birth to her fifth child. We headed over when we heard about the birth, bringing with us our excitement and plans to congratulate her. We entered her dim, one-room, earthen home. The new mother was worn and gaunt and lying on her bed, a thin mat on the floor.

We walked in with smiles: *"Mabrook!"* ("Congratulations!") we exclaimed in anticipation of her happiness and of having and seeing a new life among us.

With a sigh of exhaustion, the woman, barely looking up but with true remorse on her face, responded: "Would someone please get me some birth control?" I was struck; there was a thud in my heart.

With a bright smile, Cairistiona said, "God gave me my life, and God gave you yours." My face dropped with the dismay I felt.

We walked out of the birthmother's home, and I turned to Cairistiona: "Cairistiona," I said gently, "I know the sisters run Medinat E'-Noor, but we are in their land, and they are Muslim, and they don't have the same beliefs as you or me." She did not say anything that I recall. We went home that afternoon, as usual, but I was upset and angry: "Hail Mary..."

That afternoon, I walked around Taiz, going to every nearby dispensary, clinic, and hospital, gathering various types of contraceptives available in Yemen: condoms, IUDs, pills, etc., and put them all in a bag.

We drove toward the sanitarium the next morning, as usual: "Hail Mary. . ." All six of us got out of the Jeep, and the Sisters headed toward their work for the day, to the exam/dispensary building or the single-standing long wards (three concrete buildings with long, screened windows in each for fresh air), which the Sisters ensured were kept spotless and germ-free. One man spit on the floor one day, which was not an unusual practice outside. What a tongue-lashing he got!

I, however, went back to the birthmother's home. *"As-salāmu 'alaykum"* (traditional Hello greeting, meaning "Peace upon you.") "I came back to show you what's available for birth control in Taiz and to tell you where you can get it. I cannot give it to you; I'm not a clinician, but you can get a taxi and go to the place that has what you want."

With that, I took everything out of the bag, explained what each was, how it worked, and where to get it, and put it all back in the bag just as Cairistiona came in.

"I prayed on what you said to me last night. I think you are right; we don't have a right to tell them how to conduct their lives."

I was so surprised, grateful, and impressed, all at the same time. Extraordinary.

"Oh, that's good because I went and gathered all the birth control available in Taiz and brought them to show her," I said with a little, perhaps sly, smile, and dumped everything back out of the bag.

"Please just don't give it out."

"I wouldn't. I can't. I'm not a clinician."

I left Yemen in 1980. I incredibly do not remember saying goodbye to these wonderful women. How could I not remember? I don't know. Maybe they had become a part of me, and I took them with me, so remembering the goodbyes is unnecessary.

★★★

I saw Cairistiona two more times in her life, once in Yemen and the last time in Egypt while on short work trips to those countries.

In the din of a Cairo street, she said, "Oh, Pam, the terrible things I've seen since I last saw you. I was so naïve." I sighed. I'd begun to see those things, too. More would come. It's hard to explain the world I know to myself, let alone anyone else who has not seen it or felt it.

A friend called me some years back: Cairistiona passed. I was saddened, as if a close family member had gone. She was—she is—my mentor. I have very few, and she sits at the top of my list.

She taught me so much of what I continue to hold dear today. I love her.

THE TOOL

What we assume about the pictures in front of us is akin to interpreting a modernistic masterpiece. Was it done in oils, watercolor, pastel? What is the color palette? Is it brave and bold in its application? What, in fact, does it mean? As often as not, the answer may be: "I don't know." And that may not matter.

This story is one part bravery in the face of differences, recognizing we may not understand what's in front of us, though it seems plain, at least at first glance. Once there, this story is about:

- Bringing our best core and gut selves to any circumstance.
- Trusting our instincts and truths.
- Practicing integrity.

With these, we can rise to occasions we don't understand or seem beyond our control and make a difference beyond our queued responses.

The second part is about what it means to us individually to be brave, how we go about it, and the effect it has on others. This story is intended as an offering of how large the effect of our growth and healing can be— might I even say, "*should* be," and how our actions can impact our lives and others' lives as we understand them.

How *I* have done that, honestly, is almost too simple to pronounce as a "method," although perhaps it can be called a "tool," but it is true: I check in with my head, body, and spirit and "pull out" the truth—*my* Truth—of the situation. How do my brain, stomach, and muscles feel? I feel a change when something is right, and also when something is wrong. I sit with that, at least for a little while. Then, I decide what the right thing to do is. And then, I do it.

Find *your* Truth. Follow it. Make the world a better place.

Dr. Pamela J. Pine has been an international health, development, and communication professional throughout her adult life. She has worked broadly and worldwide to enhance the lives of the poor and otherwise underserved, focused on leprosy, tropical diseases, HIV, TB, maternal and child health, childhood vaccination, reproductive health/family planning, and economic development. For the past 20 years, her primary focus has been on the prevention, treatment, and mitigation of child sexual abuse (CSA) and other adverse childhood experiences (ACEs). She was the Founder (2002) and former CEO of Stop the Silence®: Stop Child Sexual Abuse, Inc. and, when Stop the Silence® became a Department of the Institute on Violence, Abuse and Trauma (IVAT) in January 2021, she became its Director.

She has also been a multi-media artist and artistic promoter throughout her life, using music, theatre, film, still art, and other venues to raise awareness and open hearts and minds toward action. More recently, she became a best-selling author. She is the Lead Author of *Stop the Silence® - Thriving After Child Sexual Abuse*, a best-selling collaborative book written by 23 international "thriver" authors who tell their stories and provide helpful guidance for healing, published by Brave Healer Productions (March 2023). She is also a contributing author in five other collaborative books of stories and poems, also published by Brave Healer Productions. The chapter in this book (and one other to be published in 2024) will make eight contributions through 2024. She's also working on a novel.

Dr. Pine's degrees are from the University of Maryland School of Public Health (PhD), Johns Hopkins Bloomberg School of Public Health (MPH), Ohio University (MAIA-International Affairs), and Cornell University (BFA). Life taught her the rest. For more on Dr. Pine's life and work, see https://www.drpamelajpine.com and https://www.ivatcenters.org/stop-the-silence.

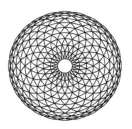

Breathe and move. Breathe and move.
Touch your heart and breathe. Fear and anger will melt.
Your action plan will become clear.
Positive action brings freedom.
Freedom brings joy and life success.

~ Laura Spinner

CHAPTER 5

FROM FEAR
TO COURAGE TO FREEDOM
KEYS FOR LIFE PLAN SUCCESS

Laura Spinner, LCSW, Licensed Brain Gym Instructor®

TRIGGER WARNING: Note to the reader: The following chapter includes a graphic scene of rape, including physical and psychological torture and sex trafficking.

MY STORY

My breathwork saved my life. The sex trafficker and his partners did not win by taking me. I succeeded in surviving by using breathwork to stay conscious and act to escape. That horrible day is seared in my memory.

Rotting stench—the dark abyss, a vegetable storage room off the open-air restaurant, smothered me with life threats from my four captors and the rot of vegetable decay.

Paralyzed. I am paralyzed.

No one anywhere to help.

I'd be better off dead than kidnapped for sex trafficking.

Unbelievable!

I would never have guessed this would happen to me. Sixteen years ago, on the honeymoon trip we never had, I was taken right from beneath my husband's (of thirty years) nose. The most heavenly day of snorkeling, enjoying a waterfall, and lunch beachside turned into a nightmare.

My kidnapper, the sex trafficker, loomed in front of me. The Jeep to take me into the jungle of Yelapa, Jalisco Mexico, stood a mere few feet away, ready to take me to Hell. Murder, or much worse, a lifetime of slavery and torture awaited if I allowed them to put me in that Jeep.

The young man, my restaurant waiter, maybe twenty, touched me. I cringed in terror, but drugged and unable to move, I remained still and available for him. The other three men leered waiting to have their turn.

Satan, get away from me.

My bikini bottoms were yanked down around my ankles. My top was stripped off and tossed on the floor. The kidnapper traced an infinity sign around my nipples. Drawing a figure eight around both breasts, his finger dripping warm water, he enjoyed the intimidation ritual before the rape.

"Hey, look at her. Our buyer will like the blonde hair and trim muscular body. Imagine what she will be able to do for him." He bragged to his three helpers as he explored me in front of the three onlookers.

Move. Scream. Hurt him. Run. The raicilla (a root substance used to impair victims) immobilized me. This waiter drugged me, and now I couldn't move. Fully aware and conscious, my skin became clammy as the water and hand intruded.

Help me. Someone help me! Only I could hear the screams in my head.

No sounds came out.

My mind replayed earlier how the kidnap was orchestrated.

"Would you both like a drink?" our waiter asked.

"Laura, we can cover a drink. I added the cost of the tacos and chips, and we're fine. I'm getting a beer. Get a margarita, hon." Chris smiled, and we enjoyed talking about the beauty of the waterfall at our beachside table in the small restaurant.

After the meal, we were shocked to see we were charged more than we had with us.

"Laura, I need to head to the boat for more money. I'm confused about the bill, but they insist we pay it the way it stands."

"I'll be fine here, Chris." I glanced around and was reassured by being amidst the tables of the tour group. Our tour guide sat at the next table within eight feet of me. "I'll sit and watch you hike the beach. That way, they know we're going to pay."

It was a total setup by the waiter and his partners. They manipulated the check to leave me alone at our table—a trick they had used many times before to take women from the restaurant to sell to online buyers.

I wanted to use the restroom to splash my face with water, but the drink inhibited my motor movement. I struggled to get up, and the waiter came to take me.

"Oh, no problem. The restroom is this way. Let me help you to it."

I couldn't control my body; my mind was clear.

No, someone help. Moving or making a sound was impossible.

No one notices. The tour group and patrons think I am intoxicated and see a helpful waiter escorting me to the restroom. The waiter slipped his hands underneath my shoulders and guided me to the back room.

Someone, anyone, look into my eyes; you will see what's happening.

Authorities later explained this group of sex traffickers had a location in the jungle where the women were hidden. They were taken from the restaurant, secluded, and shipped out the next day. Boats transported them to various destinations.

The partnership included a boat owner, the restaurant owner, the waiter, and several local men. They clocked the walk to the boat and back, and the time to open the safe and get the money to be forty minutes, and could complete a rape and run in that time.

My tormentor's vicious smile widened, revealing a gold plate on one front tooth. His knees grazed mine as he moved in close. I focused on the tooth, trying to disassociate myself from reality. My frightened face stared at me in the gold's shimmer. Alone and afraid, my head pounded, driven by my heartbeats. My heart exploded into racing, heavy beats, so painful tears trickled down my cheeks.

"Ha, mi preciosa." A taunt and sneer as he slipped a water hose between my legs.

Mocked and invaded, my muscles locked as he and his compadres enjoyed the game they played with me. His laughter rang and echoed in the storage room behind the open-air restaurant tables and kitchen.

Nowhere to look. No way to get away. God help me. It will take Chris twenty minutes to get to the boat to get the cash for our lunch. He won't make it in back time.

"Hey boss, how scared do you think she is? Too bad the raicilla masks the fear. I would love to make her scream in agony," a second voice threatened.

Help. I am being raped. My pleas and screams remained internal. My voice wouldn't work. The pressure in my chest mounted.

A third voice piped up, "Is the Jeep gassed up? The buyer is four hours into the jungle." This young man pressed my invader for confirmation they could make the trip to sell me without a problem.

"Yes, no worries, we have time with her and plenty of gas," the golden tooth smile responded.

Mounting hysteria began as he penetrated with God knows what.

Fear is winning.

"How do you like that, Chica?"

Suffocating, can't breathe. Don't give up. You will live out your life in Hell! Silent self-talk rampaged. *Do something. Don't focus on the attack. Focus on how to get out.*

"Are you having fun?" My attacker teased.

Get away. God, he's toying with me. My brain was beginning to shut down into a fear-to-freeze reaction. *Don't give in. Use your breathing. Stay awake. Think.*

"Your stupid husband left you and will have to live with it. Such a weak fool not to question the bill and leave. The tour group will pass him on the beach, returning to the boat, and you will be with us long gone in the Jeep, before he gets here."

The fourth man, silent until now, uttered, "Stupid Americanos!"

In and out. Circular and paced, keep it up. Breathe. In and out. Coherence and strength flooded me as I coached myself into diaphragmatic breathing.

"I need more water pressure—the hose is dribbling." The mistake, his mistake, created the opportunity.

"Hey man, you are taking a long time with her. Get it over with and have your come. There are three more of us before we put her in the Jeep." This guy and the two others challenged their leader. My breathing kept me from becoming undone.

In two, three, four. Out two, three, four. In two, three, four. Out two, three, four.

"Quiet!" My attacker shouted at them and then turned his gaze back to me. "You still have a bikini on." More slime from him. He referenced my white skin and tan lines, chuckling. He stared, mesmerized by my snow-white breasts, and then dropped his eyes to the stark tan line surrounding my bottom and pubic area.

As he compared the stark contrast of my two-toned skin, I took advantage. My breathing provided me with power. No longer would he control me with fear.

I can play a game too. I can control you. I am a woman, and I have what you want. I can turn this around and take over.

On purpose, my smiling eyes beckoned him. *Hi, sugar, come and get me. I want you.* His ego took over. Distracted by my seduction, he became immersed in self-pleasuring and lost caution. *Try to take him off guard by inviting him. He could become careless.* A plan and encouraging thoughts surfaced while breathing.

My body, breath, and mind began functioning together. My spirit started its work to find the opportunity to get out. *Tense. Release. Tense Release.* My muscles responded to my thoughts to take action as I tightened and relaxed.

In two, three, four, five. Out two, three, four, five. My breath and body joined in subtle coordination. *I am strong. I am capable. I am powerful.* My mind joined in with positive self-affirmation. My heartbeat slowed into a regular rhythm. I felt energetic and powerful.

A small guttural groan rumbled in my throat. My voice began to work. In an almost imperceptible movement, I leaned into him, asking for him with my body. He fell for it.

"Boys, where is the water," he snapped. He wanted to penetrate me with both the hose hurting me and then himself.

"Asshole. Asshole. Our turn." Anger took over the three men, and they increased the water flow to the hose a little too quickly and too much. The warm water turned to cold quickly and shocked my system.

The blast of the water surged and opened floodgates of energy to my muscles. My head cleared of fright. My throat opened. My mind was sharp, and with lightning speed like a panther, I pounced on the critical moment, allowing me to gain control. My action plan worked.

"Do you hate me because I'm American or a woman?" Startled and off guard, he stepped back. Seizing the opportunity to flee, I knocked over boxes of onions, creating havoc.

My breathing kept me focused and allowed me to experience a mental vision of him being a little boy being beaten by his mother. He became small in my eyes. *I am more powerful than him.*

We were both shocked as I yelled, pushed, and screamed at the top of my lungs. "Get off of me."

The cooks heard, ran to the door, and I stumbled out naked. The four men were outed. Off they scrambled, jumping into the Jeep.

I fled into the open-air restaurant. A woman helped me to my husband on the beach. "Good for you. You acted despite your terror. My name is Lumiere. It means light. I will help you," her sweet voice soothed me. Chris came to me, and they both covered me in safety. I felt joy in my freedom.

Breathwork transformed my trauma state. My frozen terror, the impact of the sex trafficker, and his inflicted drug, both paralyzing, left me as I did conscious circular breathing. Breathing brought clarity, energy, and powerful action to succeed in my plan to escape.

We flew home the next day. My doctor reinforced I would be fine. I participated in breathwork over the weekend and four days later was solid emotionally and went back to work. The kidnappers were never caught. However, the rhythms of home and my ongoing commitment to and participation in self-care support me in a very productive and wonderful life.

Breathe, move, act, choose freedom, and succeed in every moment of your day. You will achieve powerful outcomes by reducing anxiety and fear with your breath.

Breathe, move, act, create freedom, and create your successful life plan.

I am now committed to asking others, having written my story, "How are you brave?"

"How are you brave, Pri?"

Cypriana Adams, my twenty-four-year-old hairdresser, replied, "Knowing I can change people's lives by using my skills and talents to help them with their appearance. I get up every morning, breathe, and go to work. It's a tremendous responsibility. I'm scared or anxious many times. I know how my clients feel about themselves, and my creations in hair and makeup are so important. How I make them look is critical. My skills come from inner knowing and self-trust. I breathe and do it. Breathing frees me to act and do. I don't let my anxiety take over. Acting and creating for them makes me strong. Knowing your talent is there and using it to help others is brave. Helping other people makes me feel brave. If I help someone feel better, it helps me be brave."

Cypriana says yes to herself every morning and uses her breath to free herself up to move and act. She uses bravery to pursue her career as an artist in hair and makeup creations by breathing and acting.

My fifteen-year-old granddaughter Camden Spinner shares, "It's on the poster I made at age four in my playroom." She faces high school cliques and pressure, which are sometimes very intense. She also faces rejection, as many do at this age.

TO BE BRAVE:

"DO YOUR BEST.	(I AM WORTHY)
SING IT LIKE YOU MEAN IT!	(BREATHE)
DON'T BE NERVES (NERVOUS)	(INTEGRATE)
AWIS (ALWAYS) SING WHEN YOU WANT TO.	(TAKE ACTION)

MAKE THE WHOLE WORLD   (EXPERIENCE LIFE SUCCESS
      YOUR STAGE."   AND JOY IN THAT FREEDOM)

No matter the experience that creates the fear, whether it is driving a car, saying no, loving yourself through learning something difficult, or saving your own life, you have all the resources you need to create your life plan success. Breathwork and movement unlock the resources. Breathing leads to making positive plans and moving into action using positive choices. Action helps you obtain freedom in life and personal success. The result is joy.

Thank you for reading my story.

THE TOOL

Remembering my story, I honor the keys or tools of noticing and my breath. These personal resources are so powerful. They protected my freedom and my life. I use them in daily living, too. Everyone experiences trauma reactions or mind-body reactions that create fear to fight, fear to flight, fear to freeze, and fear to fawn responses. We can become stuck throughout the day.

1. Noticing (Self-Awareness) Noticing provides a way to put intentions into action. It's a tool for monitoring one's needs, well-being, and self-development. Another word that might be used for noticing is self-awareness.

   a. Self-noticing can offer sensory baseline information. In other words, you can self-assess if you're stuck by noticing what's happening in your body. Scan your body from head to toe and toe to head.

   Where are you tight? Where's there muscle tension? Where is there pain—small, medium, or large? How is your breathing? Are you holding your breath? Is it shallow and fast, or slow and labored? How's your heartbeat? Fast, slow, pounding, shallow, or fluttery? Is your skin cold, warm, hot, or flushed? Are you sensitive to noise or touch?

b. Noticing negative critical self-talk or perseveration is essential for setting a positive action and goal statement in the present. By creating and verbalizing your goal in a positive "I am" statement, you can ensure positive experiences and progress toward goals. Examples of positive goal statements: "I'm safe." "I'm peaceful and trust my decision." "I enjoy taking on new learning even though it is difficult." "I'm an expert and enjoy practicing new things." "I'm successful and memorize my script lines."

c. Verbalizing a clear, positive, active "I am" statement grounded in the present time, interrupts perseveration (negative patterns in repetitive thinking), and stimulates commitment to the positive action we require for ourselves. Action can include rest as well as doing.

d. Our mind, body, heart, and soul integrate, and positive action becomes possible as we learn to notice our unintegrated state as we practice our body scans and identify our negative thinking. We develop an ability to understand ourselves, and clarity occurs. This clarity leads to positive choices for personal success.

2. One primary tool guaranteeing positive action is breathing. You can choose from many other tools; however, diaphragmatic breathing is one of the most powerful tools available to coordinate a clear and powerful action plan and create the movement and action you need for success. Breathing creates clarity in goal-making. It stimulates the actions for success in achieving your personal goals.

a. When your breathing is correct, abundant oxygen is taken in which guarantees optimal function in all areas (communication, focus, organized thinking, integrated sensory experience, positive choice-making, and emotional stability).

b. Inhale through your nose, and initially breathe out through your mouth. Blow gentle puffs out from puckered lips. Breathe in and out without forcing your lungs to expand.

As you relax into your breath, your diaphragm will begin to relax. Your lungs will drop further into your body cavity, allowing you to receive more oxygen and enhancing brain and body function.

c. Practice diaphragmatic breathwork daily. Count to three, four, five, or even a little longer, breathing in and out to the same number or sometimes a slightly longer breath out. The next step is to breathe in and out of your nose.

d. Next, rest your hand on your lower abdomen (or place a stuffed toy there), allowing it to rise and fall. Rising on the inhale and falling on the exhale. Breathing helps with centering, grounding, decision-making, improved vocalization, and expression.

e. A few minutes of practice a day will guarantee more life success. Practice moves you from fear and anxiety to decisive, positive action.

Noticing and diaphragmatic breathing create a foundation for positive functioning. All functioning can improve when using correct breathing.

Breathe, set your goal, move, and act to achieve it. Experience joy and freedom in your success.

Laura Spinner, Licensed Clinical Social Worker, has over forty-five years of psychotherapeutic experience in mental health, education, chemical dependency, child welfare, medical, and private practice settings. She created and supervised programs in two mental health centers and one chemical dependency treatment setting. During her thirty-two years in the schools, Laura created successful wraparound programs planning for the needs of children and families in all life domains.

Her specialty license is as a Brain Gym Instructor through Breakthroughs International. Laura maintains certifications as a Reiki Master Level 4, Shamanic Breathwork Facilitator, and Touch for Health Practitioner Level 4. She secured training through Epona Quest in facilitating groundwork in equine therapy. All experiences provide depth to her physical, cognitive, emotional, and spiritual support skills.

Her expertise in helping others work with anxiety, trauma, grief, abandonment, and learning problems to create personal breakthroughs and obtain success in their lives is extensive and invaluable.

Her interest in social work and the healing arts began at age twelve. She realized loving relationship is the true healing property during one of her many major surgeries. She's survived three near-death experiences.

Laura has a husband/partner of forty-nine years (Chris Spinner), two sons (Nick and Sean Spinner), and one grandchild (Camden Spinner). Two of which have extensive medical histories.

Her favorite activities include kayaking, swimming, bicycling, camping, drama, dance, music, reading, writing, and horseback riding. Being with family, pets, and friends, and enjoying nature are important to her. She's had a houseful of children and animals for the past four decades.

Thank you to Paul and Gail Dennison, and Breakthroughs International. Thanks to Helen Cox at Options Center in Peoria, Illinois, Carol Ann Erickson of Movement Exploration, and all my teachers.

Thank you, Star Wolf, Venus Rising, and Aahara, for supporting my spiritual growth.

Connect with Laura: https://www.lauralcsw.com/

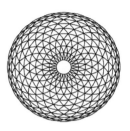

The way you live your life is your legacy in the making.
Writing your legacy letter now serves as a reminder to live
in alignment with your values. It will nudge you back
when you have taken a detour from your true path.
In the end, you will be remembered for the unique way
you expressed your gifts to touch hearts and souls.
Use it as your true north, and you will leave a legacy of love.

~ Laurie Morin

CHAPTER 6

WRITING YOUR LEGACY LETTER
A PATH TO LOVING YOUR MORTALITY

Laurie Morin

MY STORY

"It's intermediate bone marrow cancer, not low risk," the doctor said without looking up from his computer screen. "Two to three years."

My partner and I looked at each other in shock. My last oncologist said it was low risk, with a median life expectancy of eight years. Since I'm on the low end of the age group he usually treated, he assured me my odds were much better.

"Two or three years to what?" I asked when I recovered my breath.

"Until death," he said matter-of-factly. "Of course, I don't put much stock in those numbers."

That was the end of my second opinion with the esteemed doctor. His nurse practitioner came in to pick up the pieces he left gasping on the floor.

"That was a shock," my partner Denise told her to break the ice. "He wasn't very encouraging."

"Don't worry," she responded. "It's his job to give the statistics, but every case is different. I've seen a lot of patients your age do really well. You can stay at this stage for years before you progress to leukemia."

Her words gave us hope. We knew that once you got leukemia, a bone marrow transplant was the only cure. By then, I might be too old to survive one.

"I can't believe he just blurted that out," Denise said, "what terrible bedside manners. We should call him Dr. Doom." Stunned, we spent most of the ride home from Duke Hospital Cancer Center in silence.

During a stop for dinner at our favorite restaurant, we nurtured ourselves with the spicy aromas of our favorite Indian food. When we got home, snuggled up with our four-legged fur babies Blondie and Pete, mindless television comforted us. Distraction from the horrific "elephant in the room" gave me a chance to rest from the reality of the appointment.

When it came time to go to bed, knowing I'd never be able to sleep, I powered up my iPad to do a little research on Dr. Google. If you've ever been down that rabbit hole, you know it's the last thing you should do if you're looking for comfort.

I binged on horror stories of debilitating fatigue, bone pain, and mysterious infections raging out of control. When I couldn't bear it any longer, I popped a couple of Benadryl and crept into bed.

The next morning, I woke up with my usual determination.

I am going to show this doctor. I will beat the odds and go into remission. I'll ignore all the naysayers and focus on positive, inspiring stories to help me on my healing journey.

If only it were that easy. The reality is it has been a bumpy ride. One day, I'm sure I have the power to heal myself. The next day, death seems imminent. One day, making healthy lifestyle choices takes center stage. The next day, I fall into an abyss of self-blame and doubt anything I do will make a difference.

The roller coaster ride is a challenge, but facing mortality helped me figure out how to live a better life. Many philosophers and healers teach these lessons, but they gained significance when a death sentence hung over my head.

1. Self-care isn't a luxury. You can't help others if you don't take responsibility for yourself first.

It all started in a *Write-to-Heal* workshop with Dr. Lissa Rankin, author of *Sacred Medicine,* and Dr. Frank Anderson, a psychiatrist specializing in internal family systems. From them, I learned to trace the roots of my physical and emotional health to childhood trauma. By communicating with each of the "parts" of my wounded psyche, I identified the reasons for some of my unhealthy patterns.

For two years before my diagnosis, I was the primary long-distance caregiver for my 88-year-old mother in Massachusetts. She was legally blind and on the declining side of dementia, which led to scary hallucinations and crippling anxiety. Self-care fell by the wayside while I answered her panicked phone calls at 3 a.m., jumped in the car and drove 750 miles when things got out of control, and became her sounding board when she got angry at the world.

This wasn't new behavior. Since childhood, I had been my mother's loyal protector. My "parts" from early childhood and adolescence still carried the burden of parenting a mother who never hugged or kissed me or read me bedtime stories.

In our last conversation, Mom was sitting on the couch wringing her hands. "I don't know what to do, Laurie," she moaned." I sat next to her and put my arm around her fragile shoulders. "There is nothing you need to do," I whispered. "I am right here. You can relax now." Soon, she fell asleep, and her caregiver helped me carry her into bed. She fell into a deep sleep and never regained consciousness.

My parent's relationship was volatile, and I was the self-appointed peacemaker. I did anything to keep them from fighting and restore things to normal. When the hostilities got out of control, I retreated to my bedroom and cried into my pillow.

These patterns followed me into adulthood. I tried to please everyone and maintain harmony among my colleagues. I took on extra responsibility without reward or recognition to keep my boss happy, negotiated peace between the administration and faculty, and responded to frantic student emails at all hours of the day, even on weekends.

I felt like I carried the weight of the world on my shoulders. To cope with the heavy burdens I placed on myself, I over-indulged in rich food and fine wine and rarely took the time for long walks on the boardwalk. By the time I retired, I had gained 40 pounds and had high blood pressure. Then along came COVID and my mother's slow decline.

It's a natural response to blame oneself when faced with a challenging medical diagnosis, and many spiritual healers reinforce that notion. But I knew that path would lead nowhere. I had to take responsibility for my healing without blaming myself for all that led me there. It helped that the medical literature claimed that the only known cause of my disease was chemical exposure. My doctors assured me nothing I ate or drank would've changed the diagnosis.

On the other hand, that meant changing my diet wouldn't help cure the disease. That didn't make any sense to me. If the doctors didn't know, it was time to trust my intuition and make serious changes to my habits. I finally learned to prioritize my health and stop taking responsibility for others. As a result, I'm feeling better mentally and physically than I have for many years. It may not cure my cancer, but it will improve my quality of life for whatever time I have left.

2. Take responsibility for your path but let go of the outcome.

One of the best pieces of advice Dr. Rankin offered was, "Accept the diagnosis but not the prognosis." By believing my actions could make a difference, I gave myself the gift of optimism and hope. I gave myself the gift of peace by letting go of the outcome.

As a recovering control freak, taking action was the easy part of the process. I threw myself into learning as much as possible, reading books and medical articles, watching videos, and taking online courses. Accustomed to setting goals, deadlines, and targets, adopting new habits was comfortable.

The hard part was letting go of the outcome. I tried using the *Serenity Prayer*, but it didn't resonate. Then I remembered Tosha Silver's book *Change Me Prayers*. I gifted my copy to a friend but remembered enough to make up my own.

Divine healer, change me into one who trusts all that happens is for my higher good. Change me into one who is comfortable living with uncertainty and the unknown. Change me into one who can flow with the Universe and let go of the outcome.

This became my mantra whenever fear crept into my consciousness. Still, learning to give up control remains challenging, requiring constant attention to stay in the present moment.

> 3. Tomorrow is not promised. Live your best life, lavish your gifts abundantly, and share your love before it's too late.

We've all heard the adage, "We make plans, God laughs." That came to life for me when I got my cancer diagnosis.

I always assumed my life span would be at least as long as my parents.' My mother was twenty years older than me, so when she passed away at age 89, I figured twenty more years were in my future.

The cancer diagnosis changed all that. I had to look in the mirror and ask: *How do I want to live the rest of whatever time I have left? How do I want to be remembered when I am no longer on Earth?*

One thing I knew for sure: I didn't want to live the rest of my life pleasing other people at my own expense, wallowing in self-blame and pity.

When I retired, I planned to take a gap year to travel around the world, scouting sacred places for writing retreats. Everything changed when COVID hit, and my mother became terminally ill. There always seemed to be a reason I couldn't take the trip, write the book, or plan the retreat to share my gifts with others who needed them.

My condition didn't require immediate treatment. I was placed on "watch and wait," which initially brought an agony of worry and uncertainty. But I learned to make the most of this blissful time without treatment to do all the things I placed on hold.

In October, we're taking a long-anticipated scouting trip to Portugal to find the perfect site for my next retreat. I invited my nephews and niece to a Thanksgiving holiday at a mountain resort in Virginia. My next birthday will be spent with close friends in St. Augustine to be dazzled by 3,000 Christmas lights. If my condition deteriorates, I may need to cancel some of these plans, but that's what trip insurance is for!

My plans are not all fun and games. There are dreams I want to fulfill while I still have time. They include finishing my fictionalized memoir about the 1970s, leading more retreats, and deepening my spiritual practices.

Recently, a close friend of more than fifty years passed away unexpectedly. I spent a week in hospice with her after she suffered a severe stroke that left her unable to leave her bed. At first, she couldn't speak at all. I carried on a one-sided conversation, holding her hand to keep it from twitching, hoping she could hear.

"We've been through lots of ups and downs together," I said, "but mostly I remember the good times. Searching for sand dollars on Sanibel beach, chasing seagulls so Auntie Mary could get a good sunset photo, making leis for President Obama's inauguration ball. You've been a loyal friend, and I love you dearly."

To my surprise, she gasped through her oxygen tube, "Thank you. I love you."

My friend had a long and distinguished career as a trial attorney with many awards and accolades. She signed up for my memoir writing course several times but never wrote her life story. As I sat with her in the hospice room, I couldn't help but wonder how many people she could've helped with her story.

THE TOOL

This section will guide you through the process of writing your legacy letter. What is a legacy letter?

Imagine getting a letter from a parent or child explaining what they love about you. Imagine getting a letter from a student or client telling how you changed their lives. Imagine getting a letter from a trusted colleague sharing the lessons they learned from working with you. That is a legacy letter. It's an opportunity to pass on your wisdom to future generations and to express love and gratitude to those you care about.

Have you ever pondered the legacy you'll leave when you're no longer on Earth? Most of us don't until death is staring us in the face. Facing mortality can provide a guidepost to living life to the fullest in the present moment. Here is what I've learned through my experience facing a scary cancer diagnosis.

The way you live your life is your legacy in the making. Writing your legacy letter now serves as a reminder to live in alignment with your values. It will nudge you back when you've taken a detour from your true path. In the end, you'll be remembered for the unique way you expressed your gifts to touch hearts and souls. Use it as your true north, and you'll leave a legacy of love.

There are three easy steps to writing your legacy letter.

1. Identify your audience

You may want to write your legacy letter to one individual, or you might have a dozen different audiences. What you want to say will depend on the audience, so you may need to write more than one letter. Your letters will be more meaningful if you have one special person in mind.

Not sure who you want to share your legacy letter with? Here are some ideas:

- Your spouse or significant other
- Your children
- Your extended family members
- Your professional colleagues
- Your students, clients, customers, or those you have served
- Your social, spiritual, or philanthropic community
- Your message to the world at large

2. Refine your message

You have lived a long life, and you have many stories to share. A legacy letter is not the place to write your entire autobiography. It's an opportunity to share something meaningful with the special person(s) you're writing to. Your message also depends on the purpose of your letter. Why are you writing to this particular audience, and what is important for them to know about your life?

Some of the topics people seem to find important when facing their mortality include:

- Documentation and preservation of family history
- Your values, beliefs, and life lessons
- The love and gratitude you feel toward your audience
- Your accomplishments, challenges, and life purpose

- Asking for or giving forgiveness for past mistakes
- Your regrets and what you learned from them
- Guidance, comfort, or inspiration to loved ones who are grieving
- Your hopes and dreams for leaving an impact on the world

3. Illustrate your message with stories

Nobody wants to read a dull sermon on the meaning of life. They want to know and understand you on a deep and personal level. They want to feel in their hearts what they meant to you. The best way to accomplish this is by telling stories, anecdotes, or examples that resonate and bring back fond memories of the time you spent together.

One easy way to choose stories to add depth and meaning to your message is by using a mind map. Just write your central message in the middle of a blank page, then free-associate ideas and stories that come to mind. Connect them with circles and lines to produce a visual roadmap of how your stories tie together into a coherent whole. Then, use your mind map as a loose outline for your legacy letter.

One more thing. Your legacy letter should reflect your real personality and character. Let your inner voice shine. If you're always cracking jokes, write with humor. If you love to wax poetic, write in verse. If you prefer visual art to words, illustrate your letter with drawings or photographs.

When you let your unique voice and personality shine through, you'll leave a legacy that inspires and enriches the lives of those you care about.

Would you like a template and sample legacy letter to guide you? Sign up for my newsletter and grab your free copy. https://www.lauriemorin.com/legacy-letter-template-and-sample/

Laurie Morin is a best-selling author and story doula, helping people birth their life stories into being. Have you always wanted to write a book and have a thousand ideas but don't know where to start? Laurie's gift is helping you parse through the tapestry of your life to identify the story calling you to be told right now.

Laurie's first book, *Shero's Journey*, is about her journey to live more authentically by giving up people-pleasing. It includes writing prompts and deep questions to help you unearth the challenges standing in the way of your dreams and vision.

She is working on her second book, *Chasing the 1970s*, a dual timeline fictionalized memoir about the parallels between the 1970s and 2020's political and cultural landscapes.

Laurie believes everyone has a story worth telling. Her *Jumpstart Your Memoir* program provides a roadmap for beginning writers, and her Writer's Circle provides ongoing support for people committed to writing a book. She also leads Culture and Creativity retreats for people ready to nurture their creativity in a sacred setting.

Laurie lives in Wilmington, North Carolina, with her spouse and two spoiled senior dogs, Blondie and Buddy. When not writing, she likes to walk on the beach, garden, and travel to cultural and sacred destinations. She has a white belt in Nia and is studying the ancient art of Qigong.

Connect with Laurie:

Website: https://www.lauriemorin.com

Facebook: https://www.facebook.com/laurie.a.morin

LinkedIn: https://www.linkedin.com/in/authorlauriemorin/

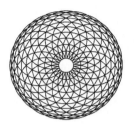

At times, it seems like a cruel game.
Caring for someone personally can be very intimate
and or intrusive. It can feel like your heart
is being stomped on.

~ Susan Thompson

CHAPTER 7

SELF-TALK FOR CAREGIVERS
HOW TO SHOW UP
WITH COURAGE, GRACE, AND EASE

Susan Thompson

MY STORY

Do you resent the person you are caring for?

Caregiver burnout is real!

The sun isn't up yet, and my sleepy eyes refuse to open. The morning goo has them nearly stuck shut. The alarm is rudely buzzing. Ignoring it becomes impossible. I resent the notion proclaiming it's time to arise from my warm, comfortable bed way too early. The pit in my stomach reminds me this isn't negotiable. I'll muster up all the courage to face another long, frustrating day.

I'm a caregiver, not a career I trained for or even set out to embark on.

I love and have compassion for people, especially my family members. I'm always there for those in need because my heart tells me it's the right thing to do. I couldn't live with myself if I put my needs above a helpless soul.

I don't want to get up, but she's waiting for her coffee and breakfast. I must dig deep into my psyche to find bravery. The kind of bravery needed to engage in the difficult situations coming my way.

The bible states that God can tell how we love him by the way we treat others—words to live by, so along with a morning prayer, I head next door to my cousin's home. She has end-stage COPD. Her stick-like figure weighs 74 pounds. She spends most of her day hooked up to a plethora of breathing machines.

She coughs up thick yellow globs of mucus and spits them into a paper towel, which I gather as I clean her bed—a paper towel graveyard. More disgusting is when her dog chews them up all over her room. I get to glove up and dispose of the contaminated material.

In this position, the sacrifice is overwhelming.

My needs are on hold, and I don't enjoy being in limbo as she decides what she wants me to cook. The criticism I received for what I served the day before leaves me cautious.

I think to myself, *This seems like a cruel game.*

"Too much butter on my toast, and it's too dark. My coffee is too sweet, and it needs to be warmed up," she speaks, and it wears on my nerves. Seldom is the warm-up ingested. Again, a cruel game or an attention-getter. Either way, I try to tell myself to look at these things lovingly and appreciate how needed I am. Sometimes it's tough to do. I feel inadequate.

How do I gather the strength to camouflage the resentment of what is expected? Knots in my stomach form as I think this.

It's time for breakfast. The anger swells up in my gut as she contemplates her options and choices.

Meal preparation can be excessively challenging. When current medicine side effects include a dry throat, choking becomes regular and frightening. "This needs more broth; it's not wet enough," I heard when I made a special soup for lunch. One day, broccoli is awesome; next time, she doesn't care for it. "Not my favorite" are words that make me question my capabilities. Inconsistencies are a way of life for an ailing person and make the caregiver's job confusing. Many days, I'm unable to please her.

She likes to scream as though I've hurt her when I reposition her in bed or try to dress her. I'm very gentle and do my best to minimize pain. It's all I can do. I trust myself and know I'd never intentionally hurt her.

Now and then, I go behind closed doors and flip her a gesture. She doesn't see it, so no harm done. Just a bit of a release.

I'm sharing all of this for a few reasons. One, it helps me vent and feel a sense of release, and two, I want other caregivers to know that frustration is normal. You give up so much of yourself to practically live your patient's life for them. In many situations, if you weren't there, they'd die. That's a lot of pressure and responsibility for one to take on. Sometimes, you may feel like the sky is falling in, and there's no stopping it. You must be brave!

All situations are different, but through experience, I learned that the caregiver's feelings are second in importance, and if you're hoping for appreciation, you may not find it. You'll get hurt, angry, and taken advantage of, and many times, you'll want to walk (or run) away as far as possible. Just a little compassion and understanding coming your way would make tasks easier to accept.

Although the behavior seems unreasonable, understanding the patient's circumstances and putting yourself in their end-of-life situation can help soften the blow, allowing access to bravery. The fact you tried so hard to keep someone alive, only to switch gears and keep them comfortable while they die, creates a core-based frustration.

A heartfelt pain in your soul feels like gut daggers and reminds you of weaker times in your life.

Today was a day filled with cleaning up a large bowel movement. Disgusting, and the smell is overwhelming. I gag. I glove up and try very hard to not get shit on me. It's almost impossible, and the brown blob appearing on my glove weakens my stomach.

Most days are spent with the belief I can't do enough. I continue to try. The pain of the pinched nerve in my back and the UTI symptoms are a moot point and unable to affect my activities. My house needs to be cleaned! Due to the lack of time to spend with my animals, a rotten smell blasts me in the face as I enter my home. I don't have the time or energy to locate it. *Pew!*

I gather the strength to be cheerful and present when I'm beckoned. Inside I think of what this takes away from me and it conjures up forbidden thoughts. *If only they would get on with it and die. How will I feel after my loved one is gone? Will I wish for one more unreasonable request?* At this point, I have difficulty picturing a world without her. I long for the days when she could take care of herself, and I'm sure she does too.

I take long, deep breaths and pull up my big girl panties. Bravery does not come easy for me due to childhood traumas. Excuses may make it easier to understand but do not play into the skill set needed to face the un-faceable.

Another exasperation attaches itself to the caregiver role is the dynamics of the loved ones hoping to "cash in" after death occurs. The manipulation is quite immoral. Often, the caregiver is made out to be the bad guy.

Accusations fly left and right, coming mainly from those who haven't been present and know nothing about the day-to-day of the ailing. No dinners delivered or fill-in days offered, just hurtful criticism.

They are the reason I put up a gate.

The hospice nurse, a warm and loving soul, came for a normal visit; she explained to us about a program called End of Life Washington. It's a way a person can euthanize themselves. The combination of drugs is very expensive, and my client was extremely interested—so much so she ended up buying it. Now, it sits in a lock box, waiting for her decision (because it must be her decision) to consume them at the time she chooses.

When she has a bad day, she uses it to scare me. She will say, "Today is the day." Then she starts to feel better and changes her mind—another frustration and a play on my emotions.

During the many years of offering end-of-life care, I developed tools to help me cope with challenging tasks. My story is written to assist other big-hearted souls with creating their tools, using mine as a guideline.

I hope my experience will help you be proud to be a caregiver.

You are doing God's work.

THE TOOL

Begin prepared for anything the day might throw at you.

Start by being good to yourself. Relaxing the body, mind, and soul with stretching exercises and self-talk helps to put your mind in a ready state.

This could also include a walk, yoga, or an exercise of your choice. Moving the blood around helps to focus the brain. Staying focused is an important tool.

Self-talk can make all the difference. Tell yourself you're important and your feelings matter. Don't be afraid to speak up and let the patient know your response to a rude remark or a demanding tone was necessary.

I find it very helpful to put myself in their place. Facing each day as half the person you have been most of your life is frustrating. You now pee and poop on the bed, you can't dress yourself, and taking your dog for a walk is impossible. You need help with all daily tasks.

Imagine if it were you in this place. I can't say I wouldn't be difficult and angry.

Don't beat up on yourself if you need a break. Leave the room. Leave the premises if you must. You're allowed self-care and won't do anyone any good if you don't take care of you.

It will keep the confusion at bay if you can schedule and document everything. Clients can get their days, appointments, and medicines mixed up. They might use it as something else to blame on you unless you can prove you have your ducks in a row.

The best ammunition against accusations is a chart of daily happenings. Keep records of all medications, bodily functions, attitudes, and behaviors. You'll find this information useful when dealing with family members.

You will find it easier to ask them how they want things done instead of doing it your way. For instance, I use the laundry soap she prefers, and I cook what she asks for and the way she wants it prepared. Do not assume.

Understanding your frustrations is key. You're earning the right to be skeptical and feel overworked. There is no easy caregiving task.

Just sitting in the quiet with them may feel as though you are glued to the chair. If you get up, they want to know where you are going and why you are leaving them alone.

You get up anyway. You have the right to. You're not being cruel. "Where are you going?" they may ask as soon as your butt leaves the chair. Don't be intimidated or make up a story of somewhere important. If you need to go watch your soap opera or get a snack, be honest.

Being true to yourself is pivotal. Be strong, be brave, and stand your ground.

Handling the relatives and loved ones is another challenge and must be dealt with.

The rumors of 'who gets what' run rampant. Everyone has their opinion of what they deserve.

In my situation, for example, Cousin two says she wants to be included in the care and gets her feelings hurt when she's left out.

Lo and behold, when I included her, all she did was bark and express how her grandpa would turn over in his grave if he knew she wasn't inheriting the ranch. She was asked to leave. It's perfectly fine to send them down the road.

Be very careful what you tell others. If your clients can speak for themselves, let them. It's aggravating when you're scolded for interpretations of harmless conversations.

One such conversation went as follows: "Why did you tell them I'm frail?" She barks. "My health, or lack of it, is my business and not yours to discuss." Understandably, I want to tell her, "You are frail, and when your friends ask me how you are doing, I answer." They took my words and embellished them. Except, that would make her wrong and me right. Not acceptable.

If you're caregiving a family member you're familiar with, you may be aware of their difficult personality. This can help your ability to shrug off hurt feelings. Remember the good times.

Also, keep anti-wrinkle cream on your face because caregiving will change your appearance. You will age fast.

Get help if you need it. Ask for a break. Support is all around. Use it.

I constantly think *I love her and know I am there for her through anything.*

Going to your happy place will help with your disposition. Breathe deep and go into your heart. Try to treat them with love and realize they're at the end of their life, which is an unpleasant place to be. Show compassion.

You're the lifeline for those you care for. Bless you for putting your needs aside and administering love and kindness to those in need.

Susan Thompson resides in Snoqualmie, Washington. She has been the caregiver for multiple family members. Earlier in her life she was a certified nurse's assistant at local nursing homes. Dealing with several different personalities has given her the flexibility to understand the needs of her clients. The experience she has is priceless. When you meet "Susie," you will understand her heart and hopefully learn from her. She can teach you how to be the best caregiver for your client and yourself. Susie's careers all included some version of taking care of others. She worked for ten years as a job coach for developmentally disabled adults.

Susie also supports a horse rescue called Heartstrings for Horses in Granite Falls, Washington. The rescue saves orphaned Mustang foals. You can enjoy her stories about Sundance in her two other Brave Kids bestselling books: *Brave Kids Volume One* and *Volume Two*. A portion of the proceeds for her Brave Kids books goes to Heartstrings. A veterinarian gives hormone injections to host mares that nurse the orphaned babies. It saves their life. Susie is passionate about supporting the work the non-profit does. She has always been a horse person.

Currently, she resides at her cousin's ranch and works as her caregiver. She has four horses, one dog, and two cats. Along with her significant other, they keep everything manicured and happy. Besides caregiving, it's a dream life.

Connect with Susie:

Email: Susiethompson1955@gmail.com

Facebook: @SusanThompson

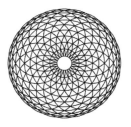

Celebrate the pelvic floor!

~ Julie Blamphin

CHAPTER 8

LEGS UP THE WALL
WAY MORE THAN KEGELS

Julie Blamphin

MY STORY

When you're in my world, we're going all the way.

Okay, not like that. It's like this—we're going deep into conversations, contemplations, yoga practice, and meditations. We tap into topics you typically avoid (but secretly can't wait to talk about).

Trust me, I haven't always found this easy. I used to avoid vulnerability at all costs. Check this out. To say I was anxious is an understatement.

It was the last night of my first wellness retreat. I was the leader of these ladies and had, thus far, retained a comfortable level of privacy with my emotions—until now.

They were asking personal questions, sharing thoughts on random themes, and taking turns around the table.

Only two more until my turn. I don't really need to share, do I? Ugh. Why do I already feel shame?

Here I was, in the gorgeous Yucatán of Mexico—the birds were singing softly, the breeze was sultry, and the vibe was as calm as any place on Earth—and my mind hopped around like a monkey in a tree, dreading this moment.

"Your turn, Julie! If you had any dream job, what would it be?"

There's no turning back now. Unclench your jaw. Stop sucking in your belly. No need to cry, Jul. Just take a deep breath and. . .

I shared (and didn't like it one bit).

Maybe you're thinking: *That's far from the most personal question ever!*

Fine, maybe not for you, but my answer includes some trauma.

When I was young, I wanted to be a singer. In recent years, this wasn't a dream job I actively sought, not that I'd succeed at it anyway. In 2013, I experienced a total loss of hearing in my right ear so my singing days are pretty much over.

In spite of all that, the moral of the story is that vulnerability is hard. Here's the unfortunate thing: Vulnerability can often bring up feelings of anxiety, and anxiety can lead to tension, clenching, and shame. According to the yoga tradition, we hold all these physical and emotional energies in our core.

Don't get me wrong. Tension in the core is important. These muscles tense to keep us balanced, upright, and safe from danger. Is being vulnerable actually dangerous? Obviously not, but our nervous system doesn't know the difference. Our thoughts affect our emotions, then the sympathetic nervous system—our fight-flight-freeze side of self—is off to the races.

"Emergency! High alert! Brace yourself!"

In this moment, the stress hormones release and wreak all kinds of havoc because our core clenches as if we're under attack. Core clenching can lead to poor posture, urge incontinence, constipation, and pain.

The core consists of fascia and muscles from just below the rib cage, all the way around the sides and back, and down (to the base of the pelvis) to include the 16 muscles of the pelvic floor.

As it turns out, my core has been clenching way too much and way too often ever since I was a child. Talk about tightness—I basically spent my entire childhood in a school of gymnastics (and I loved every second of it). Then I pursued even more adrenaline-rushing exercise and sports like soccer, track, cheerleading, swimming, diving, weight lifting, kickboxing, and skiing (water and snow). On top of that, I'm a doer. I love to get shit done. If I complete a few tasks before bedtime, I'll sleep like a baby. Check one more thing off the list? Yesss.

Oh my goodness, the pressure I put on my poor self.

Sometimes, less is more.

Not until I started feeling the effects of restorative yoga poses like legs-up-the-wall did I realize what my body really needs is just to chill the fuck out.

Just Because You Can, Doesn't Mean You Should

As a certified teacher of Pelvic Floor Yoga™, I've made a number of compelling discoveries. Through intentional vulnerability, chakra work, fascia release, and yoga poses like legs-up-the-wall, I manage my symptoms and give my body a freedom that's actually changed my life. Now I share this with as many women who will listen.

Like Wendy—she was at one of my sexual wellness workshops in 2018.

Ever since I founded my business *Stretch Your Spirit* in 2009, my mission still stands to this day. I seek to inspire women to feel joyful, stable, and sexy through movement and stillness. Think: quick wellness wins.

How do I do this? To be honest, it ain't easy. Here's why.

I'm an inspirational speaker, retreat leader, author, and yoga pro specializing in pelvic floor wellness and I've been paying attention. To be fair, I've got a good grasp on what women do, don't do, want, and don't want.

We women are compassionate humans, typically taking care of everything and everyone else, sometimes even more so than ourselves. How nice of us, right? *Whatever.* Now, please understand that compassion is kindness, and that's all good and fine, but often, we don't offer ourselves the same grace.

Why does this happen? Straight out of the gate, it seems our self-image is faced with a tough task. Call me crazy, but here's my theory.

We menstruate. Unfortunately, nobody tells us this is a sacred part of our life journey. Instead, it's *code red*. This time of the month—*the curse*—is so inconvenient that the only conversation around it is discontent. We dread our time on the rag. This typically isn't a time that we honor our beautiful bodies.

Pro Tip: Change the narrative. Be brave! Encourage the young females in your life to honor their beautiful bodies forever.

That all being said, in our teens, our sexuality is stunted. Sexual thoughts, feelings, and emotions are deemed inappropriate and met with judgment. We're usually told to keep it in check. We receive these confusing messages, they don't feel good, and this deeply ingrained negative perspective can lead to shame.

Shame sucks.

We then sashay our way into our twenties, thirties, and forties, and we're so knee-deep in kid stuff and/or careers; who's got time for rest? And what does *self-healing* even mean anyway? We're leaking, overwhelmed, pissed about the changes in our bodies, and feeling pain during activities that never felt painful before.

But we're busy, dammit! We're working from nine to wine. So what do we do?

We talk about it. Nope, just kidding. We don't talk about it because we don't even want to think about it. When we do, we cry.

So we settle for leak-proof panties, keep our secrets to ourselves, do our Kegel exercises a thousand times a day (and wonder why they don't work), say yes when we should say no and no when we should say yes, and pray every single moment that a magical fairy will appear with her sparkle dust to make everything all better.

Then we tip-toe toward menopause, and all bets are off. Some—okay, *most*—of us totally disconnect from our body's needs. We experience hair loss, hot flashes, brain fog, and rage, and our libido has completely left the building. Our estrogen plummets, and all of a sudden, we're stuck somewhere between Mommie Dearest and the Heat Miser, feeling totally whack, living an out-of-body experience for the rest of our lives.

Important Note: The "rest of our lives" is about *one-third* of our existence and that's a long damn time, dear reader. Let's get busy, shall we?

Mic Drop

"I was convinced I was a hopeless case."

So, at that workshop in 2018, Wendy walked in slowly with her sister. We introduced ourselves then they rolled out their yoga mats to have a seat. Her sister chatted amiably with the women on the mats nearby, but Wendy remained silent, smiling shyly. She looked nervous and perhaps even afraid. Maybe it was the big sign that said *Celebrate the Pelvic Floor.* There's always at least one who finds discomfort with that phrase. Like, why celebrate?

I started the music, dimmed the lights, guided them into legs-up-the-wall pose, and that's when I noticed her tears. I thought: *healing is happening here.*

After 15 minutes of stillness and some yoga breathwork, we moved through other poses and positions as I shared my knowledge of core and pelvic floor anatomy.

Along the way, Wendy quietly wept.

The Hopeless Case

The pelvic floor is our foundational core, aiding us with balance, bathroom habits, and sexual activity. It supports our internal organs and, according to the yoga tradition, is also the "seat of our stability." To maintain stability, it's just as important to stretch and relax these muscles as it is to strengthen and engage them. Typically, we're moving through life in a constant clench, or we're ignoring this area completely. One thing is for certain: not all pelvic floors are created equal. Some are doing too much, and some are doing too little. Here's the most important thing to remember: We *all* need to practice stability. The question is, can you guess how many women feel unstable?

Statistics show it's one in three, but I call bullshit on that.

"Pelvic floor disorders are more common than you think and can occur at any age. At least one in three women will experience a pelvic floor disorder in her lifetime..." (1)

Now, guess how many women are keeping this secret to themselves? I daresay a *lot*. My hypothesis is that many more women than "one in three" will experience pelvic floor disorder in their lifetime.

You see where I'm going here? Yeah, there's more:

"One in five women will need to undergo surgery to treat a pelvic floor disorder. Unfortunately, 30 percent of these women face the risk of needing repeat surgery…" (1)

Whaaat?

Yep, it's a thing. I can't tell you how many of you I've met who've had more than one surgery.

I love educating women on how to stabilize this space to reduce symptoms of leakage, urge, pain, pressure, and disconnection. When I tell them pelvic floor wellness means more than using lube and doing Kegels, they look at me like I'm nuts.

Note: In the 1940s, gynecologist Dr. Arnold Kegel invented a device to test the strength of the vaginal wall and pelvic floor muscles, and exercises to strengthen and engage these muscles. (2)

Brilliant! Although, here's the bad news: Kegel exercises could be doing your body more harm than good. The reason for this is twofold:

1. You may not have sufficient training.
2. Your body needs to be doing less (or *more* of something totally different).

There's a lot to unpack here! Rest assured, I reveal *all the juicy info* with my members (link below) and also share a bit about it in the Amazon bestselling book called *Hot Mess To Hot Mom: Transformational Tools for Thriving After Childbirth and Beyond*. My chapter in that book is called *Think Outside The Box: Five Creative Ways to Get Your Sexy Back*. (3)

Returning to the workshop.

It was time to share. At first, I thought Wendy would stay silent. Sharing our truth is hard! Trust me, I get it. Yet, the most amazing thing happened. A smile shone on her face that lit up the room as she said, "I'm so happy to learn about the legs-up-the-wall pose! It makes so much sense for my body."

Yesss. The power of this work makes my heart sing.

And then she said this:

"I'm so pissed that Kegel exercises are the only solution my doctor suggested. Plus, I've been doing them wrong all these years! I was convinced I was a hopeless case."

Ohhh Wendy, you're far from a hopeless case and you're certainly not alone in your thoughts.

Have you ever felt like Wendy, dear reader?

Has a medical professional told you that your pelvic floor issue is *normal*? I can assure you it's *not*. It's highly common, but that doesn't mean it's normal.

You can do something about it, and you can start today. Listen, sister – these are quick wellness wins! I won't promise that your issue(s) will go away, yet I *will* promise that you'll heighten your awareness of your pelvic floor and sexual wellness. Awareness offers hope, and hope is a motivator for healing.

No Turning Back Now

I don't know about you, but my intention is to feel fucken *great* 'til my dying day.

Are you with me on this or are you keeping your issues to yourself? Many women do that. Be that as it may, if you're keeping secrets, that puts you among millions of women who ignore the pleadings of their bodies.

Your pelvic floor is at the bottom of your torso but should *not* be at the bottom of your priority list.

Pro Tip: Listen to your body when she whispers because you *don't* want to hear her scream.

Research suggests that most women wait *six years* before doing something about these concerns. Some choose to live with it forever. These are the women who spend approximately *seventy thousand dollars* on pads, panties, then diapers instead of doing the work necessary to stabilize their muscles. Hmm, spend seventy thousand dollars or stabilize your muscles? Let's stabilize! At least, let's try.

But how?

Remember when I said that not all pelvic floors are created equal and that some are doing too much and some are doing too little? All true. I repeat: it's just as important to stretch and relax as it is to strengthen and engage.

We start with stretch and relax.

THE TOOL

Legs-Up-The-Wall Pose

Visualize this. When you're in this pose, your body will look like a capital L, with your back on the floor and your legs (yep, you guessed it) up the wall.

The perks of this pose:

- Relaxes your pelvic floor muscles
- Stretches your hamstrings
- Lowers blood pressure
- Calms anxiety
- Lengthens your spine
- Stimulates circulation
- Cultivates feelings of groundedness
- Reduces aching, swelling, and pain in your lower extremities
- Triggers the parasympathetic nervous system (aka. your "calm, groovy side of self")

A small pillow or folded towel can feel nice under your neck and/or head. Furthermore, if you feel pain while moving into the pose on the floor, simply practice it on your bed.

Set a timer for as long as you wish. Ideally, between ten and thirty minutes. Make sure to give yourself at least one minute to enter the pose and at least three minutes to exit.

On the floor near a wall, lie on your side in the fetal position with your knees bent and bum facing the baseboard. As you roll onto your back, scoot your feet up the wall. Rest your arms out to the sides (palms up) or lay your hands on your lower abdomen (palms down). Close your eyes and breathe.

After the timer sounds, exit the pose the same way you entered: bend the knees, scoot the feet down the wall, and roll to your side. Pause for ten normal, natural breaths. Plant your hands on the floor and push slowly up to a seated position. Pause for another ten normal natural breaths. Gently transition back into your day.

Modifications:

- Keep one leg straight up the wall, bend the other knee, and bring that ankle above the opposite knee onto the thigh to open the hip into Figure Four Pose. Spend the same amount of time on the other side.
- Open both straight legs out in a big V into Straddle Pose.
- Bend both knees, bring the bottoms of your feet together, and open your hips into Butterfly Pose.

Once you've established a ritual to relax and stretch your core and pelvic floor, it's time to learn how to engage and strengthen. For this, I invite you to stay with me. That work is more in-depth and necessitates more detailed instruction.

I've worked with hundreds of women since launching *Stretch Your Spirit* in 2009. From sacred circles at my retreats to business networking events to email questionnaires, I've gained a perspective that fuels the fire behind my work. Yes, my research reveals that general concerns include core strength, insomnia, and pain, but the tip top concerns among women are sexual disconnection and pelvic floor wellness.

This is real life, sister. Come practice with me! To get started with a quick wellness win, here's a free video for you: www.StretchYourSpirit.com/Top3Tips

REFERENCES

1. The University of Chicago Medicine, https://www.uchicagomedicine.org/conditions-services/obgyn/urogynecology/pelvic-floor-disorders

2. Wikipedia, https://en.wikipedia.org/wiki/Arnold_Kegel

3. *Hot Mess To Hot Mom: Transformational Tools for Thriving After Childbirth and Beyond*, https://www.amazon.com/dp/B0CW4PX3VJ?dplnkId=d60fdad0-9038-43f0-8d8b-b7d9c1f70a6e&nodl=1

Julie Blamphin's career path began in 1980 in her mother's school of gymnastics. She was 12 years old, teaching stretches and strength poses to kids in the Special Olympics.

She's a yoga pro, speaker, author, founder of *Stretch Your Spirit*, and currently uses her racy vibe and groovy energy to inspire women to feel joyful, stable, and sexy through movement and stillness. Her work often touches on taboo topics, always highlights hope in healing, and is certain to tickle your fancy.

Her recent speaking gigs include The Leading Lady Podcast, The Dr. Kinney Show, Midlife Rise and Thrive, the 2023 -and- 2024 WE LEAD Women's Conference, Embody Your Body, and a long list of top podcasts and YouTube channels. She's co-author of *We Lead: Building Connection, Community, and Collaboration for Women in Business; Hot Mess to Hot Mom: Transformational Tools for Thriving After Childbirth and Beyond*; and a contributing writer for AARP The Ethel, LIVESTRONG Magazine, Baltimore Banner, and Pelvic Health Support Canada.

Julie can whistle like a champ, is obsessed with cartwheels and alone time, and loves to dream in Spanish.

Follow her on social media:

www.Facebook.com/StretchYourSpirit

www.Instagram.com/StretchYourSpirit

www.Linkedin.com/in/JulieBlamphin

To book Julie to speak and learn more about her and her work:

www.StretchYourSpirit.com

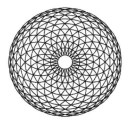

Your voice, like a bird's chirp, a stream's flow,
or a bee's buzz, offers the world a unique vibration.
Share it, shine it, sing it.

~ Colleen Avis

CHAPTER 9

SING LIKE THE WORLD IS LISTENING

POWERFUL SOUND PRACTICES TO RECLAIM YOUR JOY

Colleen Avis

MY STORY

Born Brave.

Clearly, I am the prettiest girl in line.

Like a superstar waiting for the curtain to be drawn and the applause to welcome me to the stage, I stood up tall and adjusted my shoulders. With a wiggle of my hips and shimmy of my shoulders, a slight pulse of nervous energy shifted.

Yes, I am ready.

As I waited, my tiny six-year-old hands found the rhythm of the holiday music piped in from the mall speakers while warmly nestled in my "for special occasions only" white rabbit fur muff.

I was dressed in my blue caped jacket, fuzzy hand muff, polished Mary Jane patent leather shoes, and bright white tights, which accentuated my knobby knees and disrupted my skinny stick legs.

I am ready!

"Hello, Santa!" I jumped eagerly into his lap. Not wanting to miss a moment, I wasted no time and spared no details as I read him my list clearly to ensure I wasn't disappointed on Christmas morning.

Polaroid flashing complete, photos shaken dry, list whispered, and holding the cellophane-wrapped miniature candy cane gifted to me by Santa's elf, my mom waved: "Your turn is over Colleenie Cabeanie Macareenie; Santa has a long line of other children to visit."

My mom's words meant something quite different to me. Her voice was a signal, my cue to begin! It was my time to shine bright; that was my real reason for being there.

Neither Santa, my mom, nor the long line of twitching children and their parents (frantically keeping bows in place, knee socks pulled up high, shoes on, and kids off the floor) knew what was coming next.

A-hem.

A-hem.

Aaaaa-hem.

Clearing my throat to prepare my vocal cords and get the audience's attention.

I sang my heart out. Loud and clear.

Every.

single.

line.

"Rudolph the red-nosed reindeer had a very shiny nose, and if you ever saw him, you would even say it glows."

Twice.

Hurray Colleenie Cabeanie Macareenie! How the audience loves you, you'll go down in history!

As a parent who has stood in those agonizing, long, snaking back-and-forth lines, I'm aware the clapping was meant to motivate me to move along, maybe. Maybe it was an expression of their admiration. I'm going with that!

Bravery and confidence were plentiful at a young age—abundant and endless, actually. During my childhood years, stepping into action was just the way I approached life: leading with my heart, doing what felt right without question, and always doing what was fun. I could do anything. I was beautiful inside and out (everyone was), and I lived fully without worrying about how it would be perceived.

Sure, some moments felt nervously electrifying, but they passed quickly and inspired me like the energy pulse a butterfly must feel as she pushes her wings open wide for the first time.

Share Your Gifts.

When I was 13 or so years old, I stood on stage at church, accompanied by only an acoustic guitar, and sang at Easter Mass.

Retrospectively, I realized a stage felt vulnerable, but singing inspired me and always felt purposeful.

These gifts are to be shared!

Sing!

While nervousness, pangs of anxiety, and perhaps stage fright exposed themselves now and again, they were shifted and adjusted with a quick wiggle and a few deep breaths. Being myself was exciting.

At Easter Mass, singing "Were You There When They Crucified My Lord," I didn't fully grasp the emotions others or I would experience. But when the tremble of nerves appeared, I leaned in and embraced all the feelings being collectively shared.

Follow the Fun.

"Absolutely no cameras or pictures behind the scenes!" The guide, wearing his crisply pressed Walt Disney staff shirt, firmly announced from the front of the bus. Pulling into the performers-only gates, I began to tap my fingers with calm specificity and hum my solo performance, visualizing the necessary musical pauses and inflections.

Walking onto the Disney stage as a high school freshman to perform "It Don't Mean A Thing If It Ain't Got That Swing" felt exhilarating.

A trip to Florida with my chorus and months of rehearsing my solo performance was a dream come true.

"So brave," everyone told me. "How do you not forget your lines in front of all those people? So brave." Brave or not, I felt alive doing my thing and following the fun!

Wiggle wiggle wiggle, humming the tune, you got this.

Something Shifted.

When does a wiggle not shift the fear? It must be a subtle process because I can't think of a moment when I felt my bravery fade away.

Where along the way did insecurity dim what lit me up? When did fear and failure trump fun?

My story of childhood abandonment and the reality of social pressures may undoubtedly provide some insights and answers to these questions. Yet I was surrounded by love and was always encouraged and supported, maybe even too much sometimes. She did allow me to sing Rudolf—twice! *Thanks, Mom!*

Maybe *when* is irrelevant.

My thoughts shifted to worry and fear of being seen as silly or not good enough at some point. Small moments chipped away at me, allowing "You won't fit in" and "Others are much better than you" to trickle in and create the loudest stories. Those shifts happened over time, slowly perhaps, because I wouldn't have consciously allowed "Let's just fit in" to take over!

So, there I was, often doubting myself, caring what others thought, dimming my light, limiting what I expressed, knowing my place, and shining a little less so as not to be judged, noticed, or compared.

Not Feeling Brave.

As a high school senior, I played Rizzo in the musical Grease.

During practices, I sang confidently, singing like I was performing for Santa again, this time with teenage hands tapping the rhythm and zero nerves. I sang my heart out. Until opening night.

A decade ago, a wiggle and shimmy would shift the nerves to fearlessness, but tonight, my voice was what wiggled. Shaking like a

Polaroid picture, looking for any escape in a "for special occasions only" fuzzy muff.

Whether I was good or not, I often lost myself in the movement, the sense of grounding and settling, and the feel-good connection that flowed while singing. I loved the spotlight, looking out into the audience and connecting through the primordial vibration of music.

I don't know if I have ever done anything super brave. Bravery feels somewhat objective to me. Like, brave to whom? Brave in what situation? Isn't bravery relative? Some days, I think simply getting up in the morning and taking on the day is darn brave.

Yet, somewhere on my path, I stepped away from love and into fear. *Ugh.* That made me feel unanchored and disconnected from others.

That doesn't feel any sort of brave; it feels disappointing and fragile.

I realized I didn't possess the skills needed, and maybe that wisdom unfolds later in life—in the teenage years for some, young adulthood for others—when these kinds of things happen. That seems to be what it was for me.

My old people-pleasing self took some time to reenter the bravery and comfort of being myself. Just the other day, a friend said to me, "I love how you have found your path, embracing what serves you and what's important to you."

That hit home. I cried. Being seen, no longer exhausted, and "following the fun" filled me with tears of joy.

Are You Brave?

How many times do we say "yes" when we want to say "no?" How many boundaries were crossed so someone else could have what they need? Or how about the number of times we say nothing because our opinion isn't the popular one, so we stand there and listen without action denying our inner voice? When do we hold onto friendships where we feel taken advantage of?

The singing and the freedom of my voice were muted.

I allowed this to happen.

The Imposter.

Entering the professional world, I vividly recall wearing my aunt's hand-me-down crisp navy blue fine wool Max Mara suit. It falsely empowered me to stand a little taller. I hid behind its beautiful buttons, on the outside, a picture of confidence and capability.

But this tall, confident exterior was an imposter because, on the inside, I was 100% thinking, *how did I get this job,* and *when will they find out I'm not good at all this?* I lived on the edge of those thoughts on constant replay and reminding myself to *just fit in, work harder, more hours!*

I perfected self-preservation and mastered hiding my true light, guarding and protecting my fears from others at the expense of my happiness. *Phew, ego protected.*

This type of fear and hiding narrows our thinking, limits our creativity, and prevents us from expressing our unique beauty to the world.

Time To Be Brave.

At some point, I got tired of my imposter.

Exhausted.

Really, what-the-Hell-exhausted.

Stepping boldly into exploring what following the fun meant to me now and singing out loud again became my focus. I lost track of what brought me joy; it was time for a not-so-subtle shift. *Sing more, not more acting.*

My shift back toward bravery started when I became a mom—at least, this is one moment when I was aware of it. I want my son to know he's worthy and that he can be humble, unique, and confident in this world.

Reclaiming confidence and bravery was a process—a twisty and messy path, one I'm most grateful for.

The Healing Power of Vibration.

> *"The brave may not live forever,*
> *but the cautious do not live at all."*
>
> ~ Anonymous

As I finished this chapter, I stepped outside to listen to the morning bird songs and allowed their frequencies to inform and balance me. For a few moments, I closed my eyes to find more presence with nature and leaned into the chirping clarity and a soothing sense of grounding.

While we're all uniquely beautiful, like waves in the ocean, we're also beautifully connected in a collective conscious energy. I believe when we aim to be in alignment with our true nature and keep an open and curious mind, we're in the best position to receive and ultimately serve others.

My bravery journey is about a newfound connection with sound and vibration; it continues to be a curious exploration I cherish. Vibration through song and chanting and nature's primordial sounds are my go-to tools.

They're available to all of us. Nature provides a constant stream and symphony, and you hold all the ability and knowledge you require to fully explore and embrace the healing power of vibration.

On another healing path, one that required me to release anger and fear, I began to practice Primordial Sound Meditation (PSM). Then, experiencing how frequency, sound, and vibration nourished and calmed my mind, body, and soul, I awakened to how other parts of my life shifted too.

Mantra meditation, throat chakra work, singing, and chanting were the practices that dared me and inspired my inner voice and confidence, guiding me back to the fearless girl I knew I was.

My confident rhythm and bold commitment to self felt more aligned with each chant, each note, and each moment I allowed myself to feel and was curious about vibrations.

These primordial, nature's first sounds remind me of the larger collective we're all part of, what I call sacred space. Imagine the ocean represents the infinite universe, and each wave is an individual or creature. Each wave freely expresses its unique self, rising to its crest, and then returns to the collective ocean, affecting and intertwining with all the other waves. Like each wave, our primordial sound vibrations are connected and affect and influence all that is around us.

Simply put, when we choose to accept or give more good than bad vibrations, we receive wisdom and healing power. Our minds, bodies, and souls shift toward, embrace, absorb, and reflect the good vibes!

I invite you to experiment with a few sound experiences that have guided my journey back to bravery. These will support your journey and empower you to lift yourself and others and enjoy greater alignment.

THE TOOL

Primordial Sound Meditation

The practice of Primordial Sound Meditation (PSM) connects us to the ancient wisdom of universal vibrations. Over 5,000 years ago, Vedic sages documented nature's vibrations in relation to lunar cycle changes. Today, modern science and this ancient wisdom allow us to calculate our personal mantras using the time and location of one's birth.

These mantras allow us to connect with our soul unaffected or influenced by labels, what we've been told to do and not do, family beliefs, or societal expectations.

Our mantra offers a tool that guides us toward a profound sense of peace, connection, and permission to accept our true nature. The vibration, repeating the mantra, and connecting with the collective sacred space (the ocean) allow infinite possibilities and curiosity to guide us.

Try these steps and begin the practice:

- Find a place where you can be still and undisturbed for a few minutes.

- Allow your body to settle and your thoughts to slow down.

- Take a few deep breaths and soften into the seat beneath you.

- Begin the meditation by asking yourself four soul questions (the invitation is to ask and release; the answers will find you when the time is right):

    o Who am I?

- o What do I want?
- o What is my purpose?
- o What am I grateful for?

- Begin to repeat the mantra *So Hum*. Gently and silently repeat *So Hum* for three to five minutes—longer if you like.

- Releasing the mantra, end your meditation by repeating four affirmations.

  - o Joyful and energetic body
  - o Alert and reflective mind
  - o Loving and compassionate heart
  - o Lightness of being

- When you're ready, gently open your eyes. Take a few minutes to wiggle your toes and fingers and begin your day again.

To deepen your practice, set up a time with me to learn your personal Primordial Sound Meditation mantra. https://calendly.com/colleenavis/subtle-shift-appointment

Throat Chakra Chant

The throat chakra, or Vishuddha, is the energy center associated with communication and self-expression. Of course, there are many ways to engage with and open your chakras. One powerful and simple shift for the throat chakra involves chanting "HAM."

Try this chant for a few weeks and notice shifts that open blockages in expressing yourself and foster self-expression.

- Sit up tall, inviting a straight spine. Close your eyes and allow your attention to connect with your breath.

- Allow your body and mind to settle. Notice your breath flowing from your nose to your lungs and returning. Guide your attention to your throat.

- Focused on your throat, invite a beautiful color blue into this space. Continue to breathe with awareness here.

- On an inhale, allow the lungs to gently fill, and on the exhale, open your mouth, creating the vibrational sound "HAM" (pronounced HAUHM).

- Gently breathe in, filling your lungs, spine straight, and exhale "HAM."

- Repeat the chanting for a few minutes or as long as feels comfortable.

- Return to your day or shift into the primordial sound meditation above.

With consistency, this practice will support you to speak with clarity and honest expression. It offered me one of my most powerful transitions from not speaking up to speaking with compassion while honoring my personal beliefs and feelings.

Singing and Chanting

Returning to singing and chanting reconnected me with the joy and freedom I felt as a child. Whether it was singing my favorite songs or chanting powerful mantras, these practices helped me regain my voice and confidence.

The simple act of producing sound, feeling its vibrations, and mindfully allowing the associated vibrations to resonate through your body can help break down insecurities and limiting thoughts.

Yes, sound baths and other sound healing practices are powerful, too. I love attending sound baths and receiving the therapeutic benefits that calm my mind and nervous system and promote my overall sense of well-being. I encourage you to try one in person or online. You can also begin receiving sound healing that you create from your own sound right now.

Step outside and listen to the birds, walk in the woods, and listen to nature perform for you. Whistle and sing as you walk along. One of the easiest ways to enjoy vibrational healing is to sing in the shower, hum in your car, or whistle while you work.

No stage is required; just sing and allow the resulting increased blood flow to pulse through your body, delivering greater endorphins (your body's feel-good chemicals), and know you are shifting your neural pathways. Scientists at MIT and NIH agree.

Singing and chanting, simple, subtle shifts, elevate your mood and change the way you respond to stress, fear, and uncertainty. That's brave!

I didn't realize it at the time, but the power of vibration helped me dissolve fears, clear blockages, and awaken the fearless spirit within me again. Just as I found my way back to bravery, you, too, can reclaim your inner strength and live a life filled with joy and confidence.

Want more on stepping into your brave self? Check out my free Bravery Assessment. I designed it to help you reconnect with your inner strength, identify areas for growth, and empower you to live a more authentic and joyful life.

Find it here and follow the fun!

https://www.colleenaviscoaching.com/howbraveareyou

"It is never too late to reclaim the connection to yourself and your true purpose; happiness and balance are obtainable, and you deserve it!"

Colleen Avis is passionate about supporting others in their journey to feel their best and live a harmonious and balanced life. A certified Chopra Integrative Life Coach, Ayurveda Health and Mindfulness Mentor, and Yoga Instructor, her approach embraces the whole person and believes all our spaces - mind, body, and home - are beautifully intertwined.

Colleen co-creates with and guides her clients toward wholeness and purpose while untangling limiting beliefs, unhealthy patterns, and unconscious conditions.

Her clients say working with Colleen feels like finding themselves again and helps them see they are not their stories, and obstacles once viewed with frustration, fear, and disappointment, offer opportunities that guide their transformation.

It all starts with meeting clients where they are now and knowing that subtle shifts create impactful and sustainable transformation. Everyone is unique and building their wellness "toolkit" is at the core of her approach and proven through her personal and clients' experiences.

Her approach is holistic, unique, nonjudgmental, and offers an informed perspective. Colleen knows her most powerful tools are the ones she has integrated into her life over the last decade by transforming through her own experiences and openly sharing her life lessons, struggles, and transformative tools with her clients.

In addition to her coaching and mindfulness work, Colleen is an award-winning author and the co-founder of The Kula Well (www.thekulawell.com), an organization designed for women to support themselves and be in service of human trafficking survivors in Kolkata, India.

Connect with Colleen:

Website: www.colleenaviscoaching.com

Instagram: @colleen_avis_coaching

Facebook: www.facebook.com/colleen.avis

LinkedIn: https://www.linkedin.com/in/colleen-avis-78a244/

Free Bravery Assessment landing page:

https://www.colleenaviscoaching.com/howbraveareyou

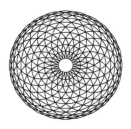

You might feel like the darkness has swallowed your light,
but your light is an eternal flame,
not even death herself can take it away.

~ Michol Mae

CHAPTER 10

CREATIVELY CULTIVATING EMOTIONAL STRENGTH
WRITING YOUR WAY TO RESILIENCE

Michol Mae

MY STORY

A few failed attempts and three suicides later, creativity and emotional resilience were the keys to survival.

A skinny, blonde thirteen-year-old girl sat at the edge of her seat next to her mother in the airport terminal. Her mother shifted uncomfortably, her hands folded in her lap and said, "Okay, let's go back home."

The scene leading up to this event replayed in the girl's head. The screaming and crying, her trying to grab a phone to call anyone and tell them she was given two hours to pack and was being shipped away. Her mother ripped the phone away and hovered over her in a rage. *She rages more since my stepdad left. Even my own mother is willing to pack me up like a doll and send me away like I mean nothing.*

She straightened her back, looked into her mother's matching blue eyes defiantly, and said, "No, you wanted me to go; I'm going."

She arrived at a three-bedroom apartment bursting at the seams with people. The designated tenants were her father, his wife (her mother's sister), her older sister, her grandmother, and two brothers. Also present were another sister, her mother, and several cousins.

I don't fit in with these people. It's like we're from two different worlds. No one here knows me. I'll just disappoint them, too. How's this going to work?

Her sister spoke up, begging her parents for the skinny little girl they called Mick to come live with her. "I'll share my room and all my things!"

She took her sister by the arm and whispered, "I wished on every star to bring you back!"

A few months after that, her mother called.

"I have to tell you something important; I need you to listen. I have cancer. I want you to come back home."

"You're just trying to manipulate me to come back; you're not dying."

Mick told the counselor, "My mom hits me; she tried to break my arm. Twice."

"Why would you tell them that? They think it's me!" Her sister's mom asked after a phone call from the school.

It wasn't long after that she was packed up and shipped back to her father. *Once again, I am a burden. I don't fit in here or anywhere.*

She slept on a couch in the dining room and lived out of her two suitcases; her denial about her mother's condition persisted.

"Your boyfriend said you're going to be just fine," she told her mom on a visit

"He's wrong; I'm dying, and I want to know what to leave you."

"I don't want anything because you're not going to die." Mick retorted.

She returned to New York, her mother's words echoing in her mind; she was torn.

If I go back, will she try to break my arm again? I'll have no freedom. Will I have to take care of everyone again? Will the house and my sisters all be my responsibility again? I'll have to be perfect. But here I have been assaulted, I have been taken advantage of, I have been raped. Maybe it would be better for me to go back. I don't fit in here either. But I won't have my freedom. True, but I'll be safer. I don't fit in anywhere, and no one really cares, but Mom's always been there; she's always cared. I should go home. This isn't home.

The phone rang, and she knew something was wrong; she felt it.

"Hello?" She answered

Her mother's boyfriend filled the silence, "I'm sorry, I'm so sorry, your mom isn't going to make it through the night. She's nearly comatose and isn't responding."

"You told me she was getting better! You told me she was going to be okay…." she continued screaming into the phone, brushing at the tears streaming down her face.

Her family came out to console her, someone handed the phone back to her, "Talk to your mother."

"Mom, I just want you to know that I love you very much. They're taking really good care of me here, so you don't have to worry about me," she lied, knowing what was needed.

Her mother tried to talk to her; small sounds escaped, but no words. That night, she captured all her emotions in a drawing as she felt her mom leave. States away, she knew before the phone even rang.

I am alone in this world. I have no one to turn to. I should have gone back. I could have taken care of her. If I went back sooner, she would still be here.

An Excerpt from *My Mother's Demon*

Silly, it seems that I would want her back,
But her temper didn't used to be all that bad,
If I could have her without the demon,
I would be glad as ever to call it even.

Two 15-year-olds sat, grieving, and talking about things no one wanted them to talk about, along with the standard teenage drama. That night, Mick snuck into the bathroom and rummaged through all the items in the medicine cabinet.

I don't want to take anything with a prescription—her grandparents will need those. But if I take everything else, I'll go to sleep, and I just won't wake up.

She woke up the next day from her first serious attempt. She pulled the sleeves down over the light scars on her wrists that everyone thought were just for attention. She touched the scar on her face from where she cut it with a razor after an incident with an 18-year-old man.

All this pain, is there no way I can escape it? I wish it were me instead of my mom; she was the only constant person in my life. Now I am truly alone. No one understands.

Mick became more reckless, lashing out at a bully in school. When he came up to her and punched her in the face, she pulled her hair back and laughed, "You hit like a girl; how did you miss one!?" The teachers pulled them in opposite directions.

I'll defend any of the misfits like me against any bully!

This landed her in the counselor's office. Again. This time, the counselor leaned over the desk sliding her a Maya Angelo journal book, complete with quotes. Shortly after, her English teacher encouraged her further into writing.

I went from an honor roll student to just trying to survive my own mind, but maybe this will help, at least with my grades.

Words spilled out on the pages in front of her with no effort at all, taking the form of stories, poetry, and reflective thought.

"It takes me hours or days to write a poem, and you do it in minutes." Her sister pouted. "You have a gift."

"You can write letters to your mom of all the things you wish you could say. You can write letters to anyone still living; you don't have to send them. You can burn them, tear them up, or keep them depending on how you feel, but it's important to get the feelings out," the therapist said.

Her father laughed, "She doesn't need help; she's just seeking attention."

He would think that. He doesn't understand. No one understands. Everyone keeps telling me to get over it. For everything. But this helps. I can escape into other worlds, I can write my own worlds, I can get all my feelings out.

About thirteen years went by, and Mick continued to write her way through troubling times, but her favorite thing was to stay as busy as possible.

One day, she stopped by to see one of her cousins, who was more like a sister. They sat at the top of the stairs chatting. It was clear her cousin was sad, so she sat with her for a bit, just talking. Her cousin was a poet as well, published and featured in the same anthologies as Mick had been.

She will be okay. I'll check in on her.

One night on the way home, Mick thought: *Maybe I should stop by. I'm driving right by, but I know I can't just have a quick conversation. If I am too late it might cause a fight when I get home. I'll stop by tomorrow.*

The next day, the phone rang. Mick was in the store getting food for dinner. The shaking voice on the other end told her that her cousin had taken her own life. She was stunned, sobbing, and paralyzed.

Why didn't she call me? What if I had stopped by like I planned? Why her and not me?

An excerpt from *I Love You My Cousin My Sister My Friend.*

> This loss aches deep within my heart,
> So very deep that it tears me all apart.
> With all of this anger and sadness, I cry,
> But these tears can't bring you back to life.

After experiencing and watching the aftermath of her cousin, she made a vow; *If ever I think these thoughts again, I'll call someone, I'll reach out. I'll not inflict this pain on those who love me.*

But will I remember that there are people who love me?

A couple of years later, she was out with someone she thought she could trust. Turns out she couldn't, but in this case, an otherwise tragic choice saved her life.

She reached out to her ex, "If something happens to me, I need you to take care of the cats for me; promise me."

"Nothing's going to happen to you; you'll be fine."

She reached for the muscle relaxers and water. She was sweating; something was wrong; she couldn't make sense of anything. She just kept taking them—one for each leftover bottle of water. She lost count as she got in the tub, hoping to soothe her body.

Maybe I won't wake up. I can't do this. I can't take anymore.

Later, when recounting the story to a friend, he said, "Everything you're describing to me is exactly what happened to me when I was roofied. I had the same symptoms when I went to the hospital. I tested positive for being drugged. I think the muscle relaxers saved your life."

About five years later, another young adult girl in the family attempted to take her life. She was struggling with drug addiction that she hid from the family. It was an unsuccessful attempt, but it wasn't the only one.

Around 2012, Mick got a call from Child Protective Services to take in two children. "Let me be clear," the voice on the other end of the line said, "If you don't take them in, we will prosecute their mother for neglect, and we will put them into the foster system."

"My hesitation has nothing to do with the kids. I love them, and of course I'll take them. . ."

I'll raise them as if they're my own. I never want them to feel like I did. I want them to feel loved and wanted. I'll take a break from dating for a few years and focus on them.

After a few years, she decided it was finally time and took a chance on love. One night, while out with friends for her birthday, he got upset. Her friends led her to the dance floor when he was going to ask her to dance. "You know how hard it is for me to ask you to dance. You didn't even think about that, did you? You just left me there. You're so selfish."

He continued the litany of everything wrong with Mick. She felt herself falling into that familiar despair.

You made a promise to reach out. It's the middle of the night. I can't call anyone now, maybe instead we can figure out the root of this issues so it doesn't happen again.

This became a pattern. A regular struggle that most wouldn't like to admit.

Excerpt from I Didn't Tell Him

I didn't tell him that the times he berated me
until I wanted to fade into nothingness

Often led to times I felt too much and not enough
and wanted to cease to exist.

I didn't tell him that I have the most debilitating
social anxiety I've ever known or that the free-spirited girl
who would laugh and sing just about anywhere was gone.

In 2019, her boy turned 15. In the months preceding his birthday, he was moody, from great moods (usually dependent on a girl) to broody. In May, Mick heard his sister scream. She ran frantically down the stairs and grabbed her robe, knowing and not knowing at the same time. He was gone. She hugged his sister and closed the door. In shock, she called 911. They offered her illogical hope, giving her instructions. Part of her screamed: *But he's gone.* The other part hoped against everything that she could bring him back.

What if I checked back in last night? What if I didn't yell at him for skipping band? Why didn't he come talk to me? Why couldn't it be me instead?

"I have to tell you something, but I don't want to," her friend said on the phone, "She's gone, she took her life and video recorded it on Facebook. Are you okay?"

Her friend was talking about that 15-year-old girl who sat with her before her first serious suicide attempt.

"I'm okay. Are you okay?" came the reply from Mick.

Her boy, her cousin, and her estranged friend all made successful suicide attempts.

There were three, and one of them wasn't me.

An Excerpt from *Unthinkable*

Leaving those who survived
in the wake of your earth-shattering decision,
To try and pick up the pieces with much indecision.
The aftermath of your choices echoes through our lives,
Each of us now has all we can do to desperately try and survive.
Forever, we will be changed by your actions.
Lost, broken, incomplete, and in desperate need of compassion.

According to the National Institute of Mental Health in the United States alone, suicide is the eleventh leading cause of overall death. There are nearly two times as many suicides as there are homicides. Suicide is the second leading cause of death if you're 10-14 or 25-34. It's the fifth leading cause of death if you're 15-24 or 35-44.

At the time Mick lost her boy, it was the second leading cause of death for teen boys, a fact no one talked about, so most parents were unaware of how serious the risk was. She later learned her boy had talked others out of suicidal thoughts just as she had done when she was a teenager.

Why didn't he survive like I did? Why didn't his attempt fail like mine? Why didn't I see it? I lived through it; why didn't I see it?

The year following the grief was so dense and dark it seemed impossible that there would ever be light in her life again.

Maybe I'll wake up from this and it will have all been a nightmare. If it isn't a nightmare, maybe I won't wake up. I can't inflict this kind of pain on my family, but I am in so much pain; this life's nothing but pain. Everyone will be better off without me. My boyfriend has pointed out I am burdening others with my grief. I'm a burden to him and everyone else. I wish I didn't have to live.

These were some of the thoughts she felt before she re-engaged with her creativity and writing. After re-engaging in writing, meditating, and other creative endeavors, she could process emotions and sit with them. She could get curious about them and get to know them. Instead of running from them or busying them away, she gave them a microphone and a pen and said, "Help me understand." It was then that she understood the true power of combining curiosity and creativity. With so much suffering in the world, it can't hurt to have another tool and the mental health toolbox.

THE TOOL

There are a multitude of studies that show the benefits of meditation and art therapy. I use a combination of these to process emotions and thoughts. While audio is not necessary, you can find supporting audio here: https://www.ladymaeimpressions.com/how-to-be-brave

Automatic or free writing is uncensored, unedited, raw writing. You allow the words to come through you and flow onto the page or the computer. The words don't have to make sense, they don't have to have an order, and there's no right or wrong as long as you keep writing. I found a timer is helpful for these exercises.

Phase 1: Preparation.

Grab something to write or type with.

Grab a timer (most phones have them).

Get comfortable (I like to put the fireplace on the TV and light some candles).

Phase 2: Visualization: A little fun with your favorite color.

Imagine your favorite color. How would you describe it to someone who has never seen color before? Imagine what that color would feel like if you could touch it. What would that color smell like? Imagine yourself talking with your favorite color. Imagine it starting to take form; what does it look like? Be curious. Ask questions like, where do you come from? And what do you need?

Phase 3: Write! Set a timer for five minutes.

Write everything that comes to mind while considering the questions above. If your mind wanders, that's okay; write down those thoughts, too!

Phase 4: Visualization: A little fun with your least favorite color.

Imagine your least favorite color. How would you describe it to someone who has never seen color before? Imagine what that color would feel like if you could touch it. What would that color smell like? Imagine yourself talking with your least favorite color. Imagine it starting to take form; what does it look like? Be curious. Ask questions like: Where do you come from? What do you need?

Phase 5: Write! Set a timer for five minutes.

Write everything that comes to mind while considering the questions above. If your mind wanders, that's okay. Write down those thoughts, too!

Phase 6: Review. Compare and contrast.

Read and review what you wrote for each color. Did they take shape? What did they look like? Where did they come from? What emotions did you discover? What do they need? Over time, you might cultivate a place to speak with the colors and emotions of your life in a positive and meaningful way.

You can do this exercise with any color or emotion at any time to explore them.

Michol Mae is the founder of Lady Mae Impressions, bestselling author, award-winning poet, educator, renegade artist, and musician. An intuitive, she weaves wisdom, experiences, meditation, shamanism, sound, energy healing, and her many crafts into her programs, poetry, music, and novels.

Her mission is to bring awareness to emotional intelligence, suicide, and mental health by encouraging creativity and curiosity as necessary tools for the toolbox. She shares her journey openly hoping it helps others avoid mistakes and heartache or heal that which couldn't be avoided.

Michol loves all furry friends, and you'll find her cats, Mac Lir and Cheeky Neeky, on her social media. In her "spare" time, you can find her writing, riding her motorcycle, spending time in nature, and practicing her many crafts. She shares the tools she uses to heal and find peace on the path to joy.

Connect with Michol:

Website: https://www.ladymaeimpressions.com

https://linktr.ee/ladymaeimpressions

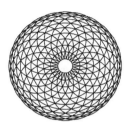

Life is a precious gift that I will not squander.
I boldly embrace this treasure with a heart full of love,
gratitude, joy, and reverence.

~ Janette Stuart

CHAPTER 11

HEALING
WITH YOUR ANGELS

RELEASE SURVIVOR'S GUILT AND THRIVE

Janette Stuart

MY STORY

I had pancreatic cancer in 2019, and Kim, my best friend since kindergarten, was diagnosed with the same disease a year later.

How could we both have such a grim diagnosis?

A doctor I didn't know until the fateful morning of my diagnosis gently held my hand and whispered the shocking news that I had cancer: pancreatic cancer, to be exact. In 2019, the survival rate was 8%.

I heard of one other person who had pancreatic cancer, and he passed away a week after diagnosis.

Scary indeed.

How can this be?!

How can I tell my elderly parents, as they've already lost a child?

Will I ever see my son again?

Will I live to see my next birthday?

As we drove home in stunned silence, these and many more questions swirled around in my head.

I never thought I'd have cancer. I always thought I was healthy. I walked 10,000 steps a day, never smoked, rarely drank alcohol, had extremely low cholesterol, and drank green smoothies.

Boy, I was in for a surprise when my energy dwindled to zero, and I could barely walk to the next room without considerable effort. I thought I was just overdoing it. I'd just completed my fourth book and helped plan our parents' 60th wedding anniversary.

I rested as much as possible and soon needed to cancel all my activities. That fancy new, expensive calendar system I purchased was getting pushed aside and was soon replaced by my oncology calendar, two months at a time.

After my diagnosis, I sought the best oncologist in the area. He said my case was borderline as to whether I could have a potentially life-saving surgery known as the Whipple procedure due to the tumor's proximity to a main artery.

I began with chemo two weeks later, which was difficult for me. I felt sick twelve out of fourteen days, spending most of my days resting on the couch after sleeping 10-12 hours per night. I was sensitive to cold; even touching room-temperature cutlery or faucets was painful, and the cold shot straight to my head and felt like the dreaded brain freeze.

Food didn't taste right either, and I lost my love for my favorite drinks, water, and coffee. I soon lost my hair. Through it all, I trusted better days were ahead and sought ways to flourish.

So many people prayed for me and my family, and I felt the love, even on the bleakest days.

After eight rounds of chemo, my phone announced that my oncologist was calling. I answered the phone, thinking it was a staff person calling to reschedule something or perhaps have an insurance question. It was my oncologist himself happily announcing, "Congratulations, good news! Your tumor has shrunk enough that we're ready to move forward with your surgery. There will be no more chemo, and I'll be placing you in the care of the surgeon now."

While this was terrific news, my stomach reeled with the reality that I'd be looking at this extensive surgery in the coming weeks.

The Whipple procedure involves removing the head of the pancreas (approximately 50 percent of the organ), the first portion of the small intestine (duodenum), the gallbladder, part of the bile duct, occasionally a portion of the stomach (approximately ten percent), and sections of nearby blood vessels.

How will my life change post-surgery?

How much will this procedure and hospitalization cost?

Will I ever be able to eat pizza again?

Will I ever feel like drinking coffee?

Three weeks before my surgery, the angels gave me a divine download while sleeping to reframe the word surgery to *Operation Hope* and guided me to draw a healing journey map. This guidance was significant because I'm not an artist and trusted the angels' guidance to create what they showed me. I never would've dreamed this up on my own.

The following day, I drew what they guided, and it truly helped me feel more optimistic and at peace about the life-altering procedure and the journey needed to heal. It also included many powerful affirmations and blessings.

I took a copy of my healing journey map to the hospital, and the nurses asked, "Are you an artist?" Ha! I smiled, as drawing a stick person or a heart can be challenging.

You can create your own healing journey map, which is detailed in the tool section below.

I was ever so grateful for the miraculous results of my surgery, and my labs and scans have been excellent, too. I got my miracle and was on the path to vibrant health. Thank you, God and angels.

A year post-diagnosis, Kim's sister texted me that Kim was in the hospital and diagnosed with pancreatic cancer.

We were best friends since kindergarten, both the oldest of three, and shared a mutual dislike of eggs. She was the first person I ever met who disliked eggs, too.

Our families have been lifelong friends since our days as Brownies and Girl Scouts. We went through elementary, junior, and senior high together. I was a bridesmaid at her wedding, and our sons grew up together.

How could she be diagnosed with pancreatic cancer, too?

Some questions we'll never know the answers to in this lifetime.

Kim was fit, athletic, an avid cyclist, and beautifully stylish. She often rode her bike up our local mountain (Mount Diablo, elevation 3806 feet) for fun and thought nothing of cycling a hundred miles.

We had the same oncologist and the Whipple procedure at the same facility. Despite those similarities, everyone's journey with cancer is different.

She lived three years post-diagnosis, and now the survival rate is 13%. Still woefully low.

The last time I saw Kim was two days before she passed away. Her family called another friend and me to her bedside so we could say goodbye.

I was so honored, and it was one of the most challenging things I've ever had to do. I prayed for strength and the ability to be a beacon of love and light for her and her family.

I walked into that hospital room where she was lying there looking beautiful amidst the blinking machines and the hushed voices of nurses and doctors nearby. Soon, she opened her eyes and, with a smile, asked, "How are you doing?"

I lied and said, "I'm doing great now that I'm seeing you." But I was thinking: *My heart is breaking. How can I go on without her?*

My survivor's guilt was kicking into high gear, and I thought:

Why her?

Why does she have to suffer?

Why does she have to die?

Why did I survive?

I held her hand and softly caressed her hair and face for the last time, sharing what a wonderful friend she was and our great times over the years.

Her husband whispered to us that Kim told him she was at peace with transitioning because she could again see her beloved dad, who passed away the year before. This news helped ease my sorrow a bit at losing her.

I drove home those 40 miles in a fog of grief. As I shakily put my key in the front door, I thought: *My head is killing me. I'm going to throw up.*

I went straight to the couch, stretched out, and let the tears come.

My husband came home shortly afterward and knew I needed tender, loving care. He covered me with a weighted blanket, and I didn't move all afternoon.

The following day was our 40th anniversary, and we planned to celebrate by hosting a small family gathering at a local restaurant.

Will I feel well enough to have the party, or will we cancel?

How can I celebrate when my best friend was on her deathbed?

I felt nauseous, and my head throbbed the rest of the evening. I went to bed thinking I could cancel in the morning if I still felt awful.

I prayed. "Please, God, get me, my friend, and her family through this time of sacred passage. Please help me feel better for tomorrow."

My stomach and head felt much better when I woke up the next day. Although my heart still ached for my friend and her family, I felt good enough to proceed with our anniversary event.

Kim would want me to move forward with our anniversary party and celebrate the gift of my life. She'd be the first to tell me that life is for the living and to enjoy it all.

She was a master connector, always arranging for us to stay in touch, plan outings, and celebrate life's special occasions.

She was also an avid scrapbooker, carefully documenting and archiving each year. Her scrapbooks were works of art and often a source of remembrance, joy, and walking down memory lane together.

I will honor the precious gift of her life (and mine) by fully embracing and living every moment of my life to the utmost, bidding adieu with love to any survivor's guilt that may bubble up to the surface.

It's now five years post-surgery, and I'm happy, healthy, and thriving. I'm so grateful for the miracle of my healing and share my journey to give others hope. Yes, I miss her every day.

There are many ways survivor's guilt can strike. It doesn't just have to be a life-or-death situation. It could be surviving a downsizing at work or a natural disaster affecting your neighbors but leaving your home unscathed. It could be bringing a healthy baby to term while your friend miscarried or any other type of trauma you survived and someone else didn't.

We've participated in two pancreatic cancer walks in Kim's honor since her passing. It's a time of gathering in remembrance and honoring the gift of her in our lives.

At the event, the survivors are also called to the stage to honor and celebrate the gift of our lives. I walk proudly to that stage, honoring my miracle and knowing my friend is looking down on me with love and gratitude.

For me, this is how to be brave—release survivor's guilt, and thrive.

I have nothing to feel guilty about. Kim would be the first one to cheer me on.

If my story resonated with you, I'd love to hear from you.

You can bravely reach out to me via email at janette@angel-angles.com

Or visit my website at https://www.angel-angles.com/ to learn more.

Blessings of love, joy, and peace to you always, dear reader.

THE TOOL

Healing Journey Map, Meditation, and Affirmations

I received angelic guidance to create a healing journey map before my surgery (Operation Hope), and it gave me lots of positive reinforcement for healing. It included feelings I experienced, how I wanted to feel, steps or milestones along the way, several affirmations, gratitudes, and my final focal point of vibrant health.

Below, I've listed plenty of affirmations to assist in your healing journey, which you may want to include on your healing journey map. An affirmation is a short, positive proclamation of the truth you want to call forward. It needs to feel at least 50% believable.

Affirmations beginning with the words "I Am" are the most powerful. Speaking affirmations out loud magnifies their potency.

Gather your supplies to create your powerful healing tool, and allow yourself a few minutes to get still and centered so that you can create from your heart.

Supplies Needed:

• Paper or journal

• Colored pens, markers, or crayons

• Candle and lighter

• Water to drink

• Sacred space

• An open mind and open heart

To create your healing journey map, allow yourself the gift of quiet solitude, light your candle, take a few deep breaths, in and out, in and out, place your hand on your heart, and visualize a map materializing before you.

You may want to call on your angels, guides, teachers of light, or Archangel Raphael, whose name means "God heals." Archangel Raphael is associated with green, so you can focus on the color green or place a green crystal nearby.

When you're ready, draw a meandering healing stream across the width of your paper.

At the beginning of the healing stream, write about your feelings as you begin your healing journey. List your starting point. Mine started with the diagnosis.

Chart important milestones or steps along the way, and list how you want to feel at each one. List affirmations to assist with your healing process. Some of my milestones along the way were chemo, surgery, and being cancer-free.

List your goal or focal point at the end of your healing stream. Add how you want to feel when you complete the journey upon your healing stream. My goal or focal point was vibrant health.

When you've completed your healing journey map, color it as desired and place it on your altar or another prominent spot where you can see it regularly.

Give yourself plenty of time to integrate back into your day. Drink your water. You may need extra rest and hydration. Please be easy, gentle, and loving with yourself afterward.

Sign up for a free copy of my Healing Journey Map and audio meditation here. https://bit.ly/HealingJourneyMap

Affirmations for Healing

I am loved.

I am supported.

I am protected.

I am healing now.

The angels have my back.

Hope is the conduit for miracles.

Only skilled and loving hands touch me.

My friends and family support me, and I am not alone.

I anticipate the future with so much love and gratitude.

I receive the Divine Love and Light to heal.

I am steeping in Divine goodness and grace.

I surrender in trust, knowing that all is well.

I am getting the care and support I need.

My heart is full of love and gratitude.

I am vibrant and healthy.

I move forward in faith.

My every need is met.

I am whole.

I am healed.

I am complete.

Janette Stuart is a beacon of hope and joy who shines brightly in a world often clouded by uncertainty and challenges. As the Emissary of Joy at Angel Angles and Well-Being and Wonder, she's a best-selling author, angelic practitioner, and triumphant survivor of pancreatic cancer.

Through the thousands of angel card readings she has conducted, her gentle approach helps clients find clarity, direction, and divine guidance.

As the Angelic Practitioner Expert Guide at The Wellness Universe for the past several years, her monthly angel affirmations are one of the most popular blogs there.

Her courses, books, card decks, and events are gateways to peace, inspiration, and transformation, empowering you to shine as only you can.

Janette knew she'd be an author at age eight. She credits this to a great Christmas gift she received: a feathered pen and a locking diary. She shared her feelings, dreams, and desires within that sacred space. She has now self-published five of her own books and participated in nine amazing collaborations.

Janette is a native Californian who lives with her husband of 41 years in the Bay Area. Their love story includes eloping during a blizzard on a Greyhound bus, a grown son, and two grandchildren.

She's passionate about self-care because she used to put herself last for far too long, which left her depleted, resentful, and sick.

Get your gift: *Self-Care Strategies*, a 37-page booklet delivered to your inbox to enhance or begin your self-care practice. It's full of tips, tools, and techniques to help you treat yourself like a beloved. Visit https://bit.ly/SelfCareStrategies4U

Connect with Janette Stuart:

Website: https://www.angel-angles.com

Email: janette@angel-angles.com

Instagram: https://www.instagram.com/angel_angles_101/

Facebook https://www.facebook.com/AngelAngles11

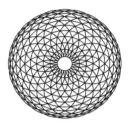

Why am I carrying someone else's baggage?

~ Michele Tatos

CHAPTER 12

YOUR GUIDES ARE WAITING!

A GENTLE APPROACH TO HEALING ANCESTRAL AND COLLECTIVE TRAUMA

Michele Tatos

MY STORY

I recently discovered a pain-free way to heal hidden trauma that has been secretly passed on to us—let your guides do it!

I can't believe the zen vibe happening right now! Wasn't this supposed to be super heavy and intense?

I'm locked onto the eleven serene faces of my workshop attendees as I guide them through the last of three hidden trauma-healing meditations. Their bodies are relaxed as if they just had the world's best massage, their faces are freaking glowing, and you can hear the peace and balance in their breathing. And, of course, Superdog, my spry twelve-year-old mini-schnauzer, is leaning lovingly against his favorite person of the moment. He can't resist soaking up all the good energy.

What a beautiful moment! Did I do this? Oh, right, it's the presence of so many guides in the room that is having this magical effect.

As people begin to open their eyes and stretch out their bodies, I'm dying to hear what they experienced.

"The bench in my personal garden was filled with guides! I couldn't see them, but I felt so many! It was wonderful; I felt love and joy!"

"I am not sure exactly what was healed, but I feel much lighter, and I felt loved and supported through it all."

"I am finally not in a fight or flight state. I can't remember how long it's been since I was actually in my body and fully clear-headed."

The comments during the workshop and in texts to me over the following days blew my mind!

I had an unusual amount of fear around creating and facilitating this workshop, which explored why trauma gets hidden or stuck, why it needs to be unpacked and healed, how to heal it, and what happens if it remains unhealed. It's a loaded and heavy topic. I didn't want to open doors that could make people spontaneously release and relive their hidden trauma.

"There is a more gentle way to heal trauma." My guides chimed in. *Phew, once again, saved by my divine team's wisdom!*

If you haven't met and worked with your guides yet, don't worry, you will.

Hidden trauma can come from a variety of sources: ancestral, collective, karmic, and direct. And it's okay *not* to look too closely at some of it.

I'm focusing this chapter on healing ancestral and collective trauma—burdens we carry for someone else. It's their wound, not ours, but the energetic resonance of the wound impacts who we are and how we move through the world.

Healing our ancestors' or collective wounds isn't just a gift for ourselves; it positively impacts present, past, and future family and community. How cool is that?

Ancestral Trauma

"Were you the one talking about generational trauma?" asks the woman sitting beside me at lunch. "Yep, that was me."

The woman looks at me for a heartbeat, then shares, "I recently learned about the term from my son's therapist, who said she believed my son's issues were a result of generational trauma that was passed on to him—from his mother."

This loving mother unknowingly, unconsciously, and energetically passed on her childhood trauma to her son.

Ancestral trauma (also called generational or trans-generational trauma) is when your ancestors' wounds have been inherited and are living in your DNA and your energy body.

This happens when your ancestors' direct trauma is not dealt with or healed, and the energetic imprint or vibration of the trauma lives on and is passed from parents to children to grandchildren. This impacts family patterns and behaviors, traveling through generations until someone decides to "take one for the team" and do the healing work.

No parent would consciously pass on their wounds to their children, but if we don't put in the work to heal ourselves, that is exactly what happens.

Collective Trauma

"Those who don't learn history are bound to repeat it" could be rephrased for our purpose into "Those who don't heal trauma are bound to pass it on."

Collective trauma is when a group, gender, country, race, etc., suffers a big enough, distressing, or disturbing event. Slavery, the Holocaust, displacement of indigenous peoples, war in the Middle East, the list goes on and on. The trauma vibration is so large it remains among the entire collective, living in their DNA and energy bodies until a group of brave souls decide enough is enough and take on the challenge of breaking the cycle, releasing, healing, and transforming the trauma energy into something peaceful. Think of the recent "Me Too" movement. All those brave women stepped forward, putting words to their suffering to begin the healing process on a massive level.

"Grab your shaman drum, put on your big girl pants, and let's go meditate!" commands my guides. I'm about to do the collective trauma meditation in preparation for creating the workshop I discussed earlier.

"I have only done one shamanic journey to date," I whine loudly to myself and Superdog. I have no idea why I've been given the drum directive, but I have learned to trust my guides.

I steadily beat my drum and head to my intuitive center (personal garden) to begin my work. Immediately, a new guide shows up! She was my ancestor, a shaman, and a respected member of her tribe.

I guess I know where this is going.

I really didn't. I gravely underestimated the level of intensity of the images I was about to be shown.

I saw physical, mental, and emotional abuse women have suffered. I saw rape, burning at the stake, fighting for the right to vote, and *Roe vs. Wade* being overturned.

All of this trauma lives in each and every woman—every single one.

Although women have gained more equality over the years, we're still not equal, and our wounds are tender. As I mentioned, the "me too" collective cry came up, as well as the collective sorrow stored in our hearts that has manifested in many as a breast cancer epidemic.

I'm not sure how long I cried, but I was a puddle by the end of it.

The second half of the meditation made it all worthwhile.

My shaman ancestor handed me a beautiful sparkling divine healing symbol to run through the collective women's timeline—past, present, and future. The timeline was rolled up and recorded at the akashic level, then the healed timeline and the symbol merged to become a pulsing healing energy that I brought through my internal akashic records, chakras, major organs, cells, auric layers, and then my grounding and shielding. Phew. I felt so much better after this powerful healing session.

I share this story with you to highlight how various collective traumas run through all of us and how, if we each do our part, we can begin to heal the collective.

I got up close and personal with these vivid stories to be able to teach this topic, but there is a **much easier** way to heal this!

In my tool section, I'll lead you through a guided meditation to help you clear ancestral and collective trauma from a healthy distance without having to witness and relive the pain like I did.

These next two types of hidden trauma are different from ancestral and collective because they are *your* wounds. I'm only going to touch lightly on them, as they tend to benefit from being healed in a more complex and engaging manner. That said, your guides can still support you through the healing process. Sometimes just setting the intention that you're ready and willing to end cycles and patterns that aren't serving you is enough to get the healing ball rolling.

Karmic and Direct Trauma

Let's talk about karmic trauma first, which is living in our energy body to help us learn specific lessons our spirit has chosen to take on. This can play out as repeating traumatic occurrences in our lives, sometimes over many lives, to provide us with opportunities to choose a different and more healing response.

Direct trauma is experienced by you in this life but can become hidden because, at the time, all the body's resources were being used to meet survival needs. An energetic signature is captured and contained within the nervous system and subtle energy body. The mind suppresses or dissociates from these memories as a protective mechanism. It's frozen and stored to be dealt with in the future.

There is so much more to be said on this topic.

I hope this introduction to hidden trauma has fired up your curiosity and inspired the question: "Why am I carrying someone else's baggage?"

Well, it's almost time to get to the healing part, but if this is the first time you're meeting your guides, you need a little more information.

What are guides?

Our guides are universal forces here to aid our spiritual growth and transformation. They're teachers and advisors and can be our biggest resource for healing.

They can appear to you as an angel, person, animal, mythical creature, ancestor, ancient god or goddess, otherworldly entity, archetype, cartoon character, or inter-dimensional being. How your guides appear to you can often be associated with your upbringing, religion, and life experiences.

Will I be able to see and hear my guides?

Everyone has the gift of intuition to some degree, but in some people, one intuitive sense may be stronger than the others. There are many ways in which people experience this, but I'm going to review the four most common ones.

When meeting your guides:

You may see a clear image of them (clairvoyance).

You may get a sense of, or a knowing about them (claircognizance).

You may hear messages from them (clairaudience).

You may feel their presence and get warm, cold, or tingly (clairsentience).

However it happens for you is just right.

Now, let's put this knowledge to work!

THE TOOL

Much of my healing work involves guided meditation. I created a ten-minute meditation in which you visit your intuitive center or private garden, meet your guides, and start healing ancestral or collective trauma.

If you're new to meditation, you may want to start by just reading the first section. The next day, read the first two sections, and the next time, read all three sections.

You can also visit my website at https://beatreewithme.com and listen to the recording.

Have a notepad and pen handy for afterward.

Time to do some healing!

Visit your garden

Close your eyes and get ready to take a few big, loud, releasing breaths.

In through your nose.

And out through your mouth.

Inhaling peace and calm.

Exhaling tension and stress.

Releasing and relaxing your entire nervous system.

Allowing your muscles to unclench.

Melting into your seat.

Take three more full breaths like this.

Now, let your breath just fall into its own easy and natural rhythm.

Get ready to go on a healing journey.

With your next breath, imagine you see a beautiful golden bridge in your mind.

It's a magical, sparkling, and peaceful bridge.

This bridge feels familiar to you.

You can't help but want to cross it.

This bridge leads us from our analytical center, where we spend most of our time thinking and planning, into our intuitive center, our source of inner wisdom, our heart wisdom, where we trust and just know things.

Imagine you're slowly walking across this awesome bridge.

As you reach the other side, you're entering into your own private garden.

You can feel the shift.

This safe and private garden is your intuitive center.

This is where your inner wisdom, your heart wisdom, lives.

Look around and take it all in.

Take a second to breathe in its beauty and grace.

What does it look and feel like?

Are there beautiful flowers and trees? If so, can you smell the roses, lavender, or pine?

Or maybe it's a quiet and warm beach? Notice the soft breeze or the salty ocean smell in the air.

Or maybe it's a peaceful desert.

Does it feel quiet and calm or a little bit too loud or cluttered?

Make it look and feel exactly how you want it.

Meeting Your Guides

With your next breath, take a look around in your garden, and you will see that there is a path with a brightly lit stone walkway, just asking for you to stroll along it.

Start walking toward this magical path, and keep walking as it winds its way through flowers and trees.

It's okay to stop now and then to smell the flowers or touch a particular tree branch.

You're suddenly aware that there is a waterfall nearby. You can hear it gently flowing. You can smell it.

You continue walking and notice that the waterfall is just up ahead.

The water is shimmering with all the colors of the rainbow.

There is an ornate stone bench in front of the waterfall.

There is someone, or multiple someone's, waiting for you, standing right next to the bench.

Now you remember them.

You recognize that loving connection you feel.

They've been with you your entire life! Of course, you know them.

They wave to you in welcome and motion for you to come join them.

They may be exactly what you expected or nothing at all like you expected.

There may be one guide or multiple guides.

Just trust that whoever is there to greet you is exactly who you are meant to be with today.

Do the healing work

Now that you've connected with your guides, allow them to lead you down a short path where you'll enter a large, bright, and open movie theater within your garden.

As you walk into the theater, they guide you to sit in the very back row as it's important to have distance from the movie screen.

Your guides have left you in your comfy seat and are heading up toward the screen.

Your guides will help you to heal trauma passed down from your ancestors or your collective.

We aren't just healing this trauma for ourselves.

As we heal in the present, it also heals our ancestors and community—past, present and future.

Take a deep breath in and out.

From your back-row seat, look at the screen.

Your guides are lighting up a copy of your energy body and your nervous system.

You can see what you currently look like as an energy being.

Your seven colorful pulsing chakras are all lined up with your central nervous system.

All the meridians and nadis, which are complex energy channels in the subtle body through which life force flows.

You might even be able to see the seven layers of your aura surrounding you.

Now, see or sense if there is any past trauma energy stuck anywhere in your energy template that's on the screen.

It will look dark or heavy, or it may feel sticky or sluggish.

Just look. You don't need to do anything. Your guides will do all the heavy lifting today.

Watch as your guides begin to flush divine energy through that blockage. The trauma may have impacted several different areas in your body so the flush may be through several blockages.

They're using beautiful divine harmonies such as acceptance, forgiveness, and unconditional love to clear out that traumatic event and get the energy flowing effortlessly.

You may receive some information regarding the trauma that created the energy block. You may not. It may just be too much to process right now.

Trust that even if intellectually you aren't receiving any information, intuitively you are.

Your higher self is receiving the information needed to heal so you can change your current behaviors and patterns that aren't serving you well in this life.

Once the guides have fully flushed and healed your blockage, the screen will begin to shrink down so that it can fit into a gorgeous, shimmering orb.

The orb now contains all the healing and lessons, with none of the negative charges.

Your guides will register the healing at the Akashic record level (a library of every soul's actions) and you'll record it at the body level (a library of just your soul's actions.)

Take an easy breath in and out.

Imagine the healing orb hovering right over your head while you're still sitting in the movie theater in your garden.

Let the orb gently descend through the seventh chakra at the top of your head and continue down through your remaining six chakras.

Let this beautiful healing energy fill your spinal cord and all those important nerves and ganglia.

Let it flow through your organs, fascia, bones, joints, and every cell in your body.

Through all seven layers of your aura.

When it is complete, let that amazing healing orb land in your heart chakra, where it can remain and continue to heal.

Allow your guides to escort you back through your garden to your beautiful golden bridge.

Slowly walk back across it to gently land back in your body.

Start to notice the temperature in the room.

Notice the sounds.

Wiggle your fingers and toes.

Open your eyes and give your body a good stretch. Welcome back!

Before you get up and start moving around, grab the pad of paper and pen and make any notes or drawings you like.

Michele Tatos is wildly passionate about the intricacies of the human energy body. She is a big believer in the magic of meditation and thinks working with your guides to heal can be absolutely transformative!

For over twenty-five years, Michele has been providing energy-rebalancing consultations and guided meditations. Her work focuses on aligning and harmonizing the chakras and energy body, and working closely with spiritual guides to provide you with information and tools to rebalance and heal yourself.

She spent fifteen years serving in the mental health field in San Francisco, including time as CEO of a mental health employment agency. She also worked with individuals of all ages with developmental disabilities. Her education includes an MBA, many psychology courses, even more energy and spiritual courses, and over 25 years of energy and intuition training.

If she's not hanging with her family, playing some sport that has a ball in it, or reading a juicy sci-fi book, you can find Michele blissfully walking on a trail filled with trees, talking to her dog, her guides, or any other creature that crosses her path.

She has been published in two bestselling Amazon books prior to this one.

You can find more information on Michele's practice at her website: https://www.beatreewithme.com/

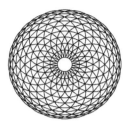

I am a frightened singer and songwriter,
and I want to be of service to you.

~ Glenn Schuster

CHAPTER 13

TRANSFORMING DESPERATION INTO COURAGE

BEING BRAVE IS EASIER THAN YOU THINK

Glenn Schuster, RN, LCSW

MY STORY

I trembled, hoping the blanket over my head would hide me from the monsters lurking in the closet and under the bed.

Fear was my constant companion for the longest time, keeping me tethered to a life of mediocrity, loneliness, and underachievement. I know what it's like to feel trapped in the clutches of self-doubt.

Running the five blocks from the Cub Scout meeting to home, I was sure I would be attacked by some hideous creature hiding along the path. It was always dark, and everyone knows darkness is where the demons live.

From my earliest years, I was an introvert, grappling with shyness and a constant fear of judgment. Small talk was challenging, and I often felt that my thoughts weren't worth sharing.

I remember my first date in high school. I had a massive crush on a girl who will remain unnamed. I took her to a movie and timidly inched my arm around the back of her seat, placing my hand on her shoulder and shaking. I wanted to ask if I could kiss her, but my fear struck me mute.

As I author this story, my heart is pounding, and my thoughts are racing with apprehension that my contribution will not measure up to my peers.

By my sophomore year of high school, I had fumbled and bumbled my way to a relationship with my future wife. I quit school in my senior year. *There's nothing more to learn at school!* My high school sweetheart graduated the previous year, and all my friends quit or were expelled.

I married in August 1967, and my son was born on April 6th, 1968. I turned 19 in May and voluntarily enlisted for the draft. My decision to enlist wasn't motivated by patriotism or a sense of duty to my country. I was very immature. *Going to Vietnam will be easier than being a husband and father.*

I arrived in Vietnam in December 1968. There was an excess of foot soldiers, and I was sent to a combat engineer unit near Phu Bai. I spent three months there building fire support bases in the Ashau Valley. When there was a shortage of foot soldiers, I was transferred to the 1st Infantry Division.

Following two weeks of indoctrination reinforcing the dehumanization of the Viet Cong and North Vietnamese soldiers, I arrived at my new unit. I was given the job of squad RTO (radio telephone operator). My squad was quite adventurous as we often took on the role of walking point for our platoon and company.

Before long, I started to doubt my decision: *OMG, what did I do? Why did I choose this?* My first month as an infantryman was tough as I got used to carrying ninety pounds on my back in temperatures exceeding one hundred degrees.

I woke up shivering and drenched as the monsoon rains persisted. The previous night was restless—swarms of mosquitoes feasted on me. I had one pair of dry socks left and took off my jungle boots to put them on. After weeks of trudging through rice paddies and mud puddles, I lamented the sorry state of my feet, which resembled raw hamburgers.

I put on my rubber poncho and then lit a piece of C4 underneath it to warm myself and dry my jungle fatigues. Anticipating the day ahead, I braced myself for the grueling prospect of traversing the Michelin rubber plantation for 10-12 hours. We were constantly vigilant for signs of the enemy, sincerely hoping not to encounter them.

Around noon, we stumbled upon a large North Vietnamese Army base camp. As we searched the area, suddenly, we were ambushed, and several of my fellow soldiers were hit.

Fear gripped me, but adrenaline kicked in, and I sprang into action. I provided cover fire for my squad leader as he ran toward an enemy bunker. I saw him toss a grenade into the bunker, destroying it. Luckily, most of the camp's inhabitants were away, so the battle was short-lived.

Later, I was awarded an Army Commendation Medal for my actions. The following is the official Army account of that day:

Army Commendation Medal with "V" device.

July 31st 1969

Republic of Vietnam

For heroism in connection with military operations against a hostile force in the Republic of Vietnam:

On this date, Private First Class Schuster served as a radio-telephone operator with his unit on a reconnaissance-in-force operation approximately two miles northwest of Fire Support Base Ramrod.

At approximately 1130 hours, the lead element discovered a regimental-sized base camp. As a sweep of the area was being conducted, the friendly force was suddenly subjected to intense automatic weapons and small arms fusillades from an undetermined size insurgent force.

Observing his squad leader assault an insurgent bunker, Private First Class Schuster disregarded his safety and placed devastating cover fire for his squad leader, which enabled the squad leader to silence the enemy bunker.

His courageous initiative and exemplary professionalism significantly contributed to the successful outcome of the encounter. Private First Class Schuster's actions are in keeping with the finest traditions of military service and reflect great credit upon himself, the 1St Infantry Division, and the United States Army.

The first week of November 1969, and I have approximately five weeks before I will be able to leave this hell hole called Vietnam. Once again, we walked through the Michelin Rubber Plantation in search of the enemy, hoping we wouldn't find them.

I'm so close to going home, and I'm afraid. *What if I don't make it out of here?* Abruptly, all hell broke loose, and another firefight took place.

Bullets are flying everywhere, and I'm wondering if my thoughts of death are about to come true. I'm an expert with my M-16 and only 50 yards away. *I know I've hit that son of a bitch at least three times, yet he won't fall. What the Hell kind of drugs is he on?*

The cacophony of battle has faded into an eerie silence—the intense skirmish lasted only about 15 minutes. I find myself trembling as I reach for a Marlboro, casting a wary gaze around to ensure the safety of my comrades. A sense of relief washes over me as I realize that none have sustained severe injuries.

Later, I was awarded a Bronze Star Medal for my actions. The following is the official Army account of that day:

Bronze Star Medal with "V" device.

November 7th 1969

Republic of Vietnam

For heroism in connection with military operations against a hostile force in the Republic of Vietnam:

On this date, Specialist Schuster was serving as a radio-telephone operator with his unit on a ground reconnaissance operation approximately four miles northeast of Dau Tieng.

At approximately 1500 hours, as the lead squad was establishing security, they observed three insurgents running away and placed suppressive fire upon them. Specialist Schuster disregarded his personal safety as he joined his platoon for an online assault.

As the friendly force advanced upon the insurgents, they were subjected to an intense hostile barrage of automatic weapons and small arms fire from the unknown size enemy force.

Continuing to disregard his personal safety, Specialist Schuster advanced and provided the communications necessary for coordinating the movement of the friendly fire teams.

His courageous initiative and exemplary professionalism significantly contributed to the routing of the enemy and the capture of enemy weapons, equipment, and documents.

Specialist Four Schuster's outstanding display of aggressiveness, devotion to duty, and personal bravery is in keeping with the finest traditions of military service and reflect great credit upon himself, the First Infantry Division, and the United States Army.

After being honorably discharged from the Army in June 1970, I struggled with significant alcohol and drug problems. I worked a dead-end job, and my marriage was deteriorating due to infidelities on both sides. In June 1971, I joined the United States Air Force, hoping to make a fresh start.

After completing training as a Radiologic Technologist in the Air Force, I eagerly anticipated the opportunity to use my skills in humanitarian efforts, such as aiding victims of natural disasters like floods and earthquakes. Unfortunately, those opportunities never materialized.

My problems with alcohol and drugs continued to progress, and by 1983, I was court-martialed for continued use of illegal substances and sentenced to four months of confinement.

During my Air Force career, I sold drugs to many of my subordinates and was fortunate I never got caught. Some of my friends who engaged in similar activities received lengthy sentences in Leavenworth Penitentiary.

Following my departure from the military, I started school at Rend Lake Community College and received an Associate's Degree in Nursing. Later, I continued school at Sangamon State University and earned a Bachelor's Degree in Family and Community Services.

Ultimately, I earned a Master's in Social Work from the University of Illinois. My educational successes would've never been possible had I not eventually addressed my ongoing addiction.

Fortunately, I entered an inpatient treatment program in October 1984. I was drug-free for six months, then had a short-lived relapse. I've been drug and alcohol-free since May 21st, 1985.

I worked in addiction treatment as a Registered Nurse and Licensed Clinical Social Worker for over 30 years. In May 2000, I moved from Illinois to Clarksville, Tennessee, and began working at Fort Campbell, Kentucky, for 12 years, treating soldiers with addiction problems.

Following that, I left Fort Campbell and went to work for the Veterans Administration, once again practicing addiction treatment. Many of the soldiers and veterans I treated also had PTSD and, during therapy, expressed feelings of guilt and remorse related to their actions during deployments to Iraq or Afghanistan.

Having become somewhat of a pacifist following my Vietnam experience, I frequently made these soldiers aware of organizations such as Veterans for Peace and Iraqi Veterans Against the War, despite possibly putting my job in jeopardy.

On one particular weekend, while working at Fort Campbell as a member of Veterans for Peace and Vietnam Veterans Against the War, I participated in a demonstration just outside the gates of Fort Campbell. We were protesting the Wars in Iraq and Afghanistan.

Some may call my actions foolish, but like those brave men who chose Canada versus Vietnam with no promise of returning home, I stood up for what I believed.

I have loved music since I saw Elvis on the *Ed Sullivan Show* as a child. When people ask me about my taste in music, my response is always the same.

"I enjoy everything from Frank Sinatra to Frank Zappa."

I like to sing, and I have a decent voice. Back in grade school, I was part of the church choir, but I was too scared to sing solos. Later on, I joined another church choir. The choir director told me, "You have a good voice," and encouraged me to do a solo. I reluctantly agreed and ended up trembling like a leaf during my performance.

In 2016, I attended an acupuncture class and met Stephanie Urbina Jones, a singer and songwriter. I've always been a huge music fan, so I looked her up online when I returned home.

The next day, during a class break, I sang one of her favorite songs to her on a whim. To my surprise, she invited my wife and me to a private concert at her house, and I even got to sing with her and some other folks.

Shamanic breathing came up during our conversation, and I hesitantly accepted an invitation to try it. Before the breathwork session began, I sang a song I had written, and once again, I found myself trembling.

However, nowadays, I rarely shake when I sing and often volunteer to perform instead of waiting to be asked. Some people have been impressed by my original songs and suggested I should record them. Unfortunately, no one has offered to cover the recording studio fees.

I'm still essentially an introvert but can be an extrovert when needed. Today, I no longer fear expressing an opinion. I don't worry about being judged for my words. As a therapist, my words have often been worthwhile and helpful to those in need.

THE TOOL

I learned there are no quick fixes in life. Band-Aids are temporary, and when they wear off, an unhealed wound remains. I hope the following suggestions will assist you in your quest for courage.

- Consider therapy.
- From the Four Agreements by Don Miguel Ruiz:
    1. Be impeccable with your word.
    2. Don't take anything personally.
    3. Don't make assumptions.
    4. Always do your best.
- Never stop dreaming; with time and persistent work, dreams do come true.
- Know you are loved.
- It's your choice.
- You can **F**uck **E**verything **A**nd **R**un or **F**ace **E**verything **A**nd **R**ecover
- **JUST DO IT!**

Glenn Schuster, aka Singing Wolf the Rainbow Shaman, is a published author, retired Licensed Clinical Social Worker, and Registered Professional Nurse. He has dedicated the last 39 years to the healing arts and personal and spiritual growth. His healing work has focused on treating people with addictions and PTSD.

Glenn is a Certified Toltec Sacred Journey Facilitator, Minister Of the Healing Arts, and Shamanic Usui Tibetan Reiki Master.

Glenn co-founded Kokoro Sacred Healing with his wife, Amy Takashima, LCSW. Kokoro Sacred Healing is a mountain retreat center outside Franklin, North Carolina. He loves facilitating Toltec Sacred Journey Breathwork and weekend workshops on Family of Origin and Shadow work.

Glenn enjoys reading, gardening, communing with nature and riding his motorcycle. Glenn also loves to sing and is a neophyte songwriter. He dreams that one day, he will write and record a hit song.

Glenn is also available for individual life coaching via Meet or Zoom.

Connect with Glenn:

Email: glennschu2003@netscape.net

Website: https://kokorosacredhealing.com

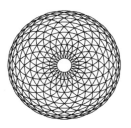

The fear of telling is worse than actually telling.

~ Val Meola

CHAPTER 14

BRAVE VOICES
THE SECRETS WE'RE DYING TO KEEP

Val Meola, President of RAACE Foundation, CSA Advocate

MY STORY

"Shhh. It's a secret."

In her four-year-old voice, "What is it?"

"It'll make you sexy."

"What's that?"

His hands make the shape of an hourglass.

Hmm? I guess that's good?

Hesitantly, "Oh, okay."

And thus, the grooming began.

This is the 50-year-old secret I thought was too shameful and hideous to allow myself to think about, let alone tell anyone. I was dying to keep my secret of 12 years of abuse, and it was, in fact, literally killing me.

Emotional tides held back behind a stone jetty made me ill with silent, caged anger; suicidal ideation coveted my sleepless nights; gorging on food, sex, and material goods was never enough. This secret was malignant; my mortality was fragile.

My family taught me the art of keeping secrets in my early years.

"Here's $20 for being a good girl for Daddy. Don't tell your mother."

After she threw an aluminum pot at me that hit me in the head, "Don't tell your father."

In first grade, I told my teacher that my brother hit me with a broom. Because she talked to him about it, I got a beating and was told, "You don't repeat things that happen at home."

The shame that came with secrets taught me to lie.

My mother asked, "Mr. George was touching kids on the back steps at the bowling alley. Did he touch you?"

Blushing slightly and turning away, I gave the safe answer, "No." *Liar.*

"I'm surprised it wasn't you."

I felt my heart thumping, and the shame covered me like a stinky old blanket that lay on our basement floor as I slithered away to the upstairs of our small row house.

What did she mean by that? What does she know?

At my grandparents' house, we played in the unfinished basement, and my uncle played the same games as my father. My grandmother hollered down the steps, "What are you doing down there?"

"Nothing." *Liar, liar.*

I was scared to tell anything—not about the sexual, verbal, or physical abuse, not about my pain, nothing about being bullied at school and in the neighborhood, and certainly not about my sadness and loneliness.

Putting on the show was my special talent. My wedding day seemed so perfect by all observances. I walked down the long aisle on his arm and gladly let him give me away. I convinced myself that this was symbolic of my freedom from him. And later that day, I danced to the traditional *Daddy's Little Girl.*

I feel so sick. Just keep smiling; they're all watching.

The pictures in my wedding album, perfectly posed as a perfect day, are a reminder to me of how sick I was before I began my healing journey. It's a bit embarrassing, but I keep them as my reminder of what it's like to be silenced.

Shortly into my marriage, my husband, father, and three brothers became friends. They shared many common interests, like hunting and fishing. It was irritating to me to see this bond between this man, who I knew was a monster, and the man who loved me more than anyone in this world. I had to tell Michael the truth. I tried to think of a way to let him know, but the words just weren't there.

How does one start a conversation like this anyway? It's not something you blurt out at the dinner table.

Here I was keeping a secret from the one person who loved me no matter what. I couldn't let this develop into the father image he never had growing up.

Michael is safe. It's better to tell him sooner than later. The blow will be less if I just tell him now.

It was an early night and we lay snuggled in our new waterbed. *Tell him. You can tell him. Just say it.*

A few deep breaths later, I muttered, "I have something very bad to tell you."

His brow furrowed, "Okay, what is it?"

"It's horrible. I don't know if I can say it."

"Can't be anything so bad that you can't tell me."

With tears falling down my cheeks, "I'm just so embarrassed."

His brows lifted, "Did you fool around?"

With a nervous chuckle, "No, nothing like that. It's not about you."

Crying hysterically, "It's about my father." "Umm," I'm gasping, "umm, umm." *Breathe.*

By now, his body joined my sobbing, slumping form, "What? What is it? It's okay."

"He, uh, uh, molested me, uh, when I was little."

"You've gotta be fucking kidding me. I'm going to tell that sonofabitch to stay the Hell away from you."

"No, please, please, don't tell him that I told you. Please don't tell anyone. Please. I'm okay. I don't want anyone to know. It's so hideous. Promise me you'll never tell anyone."

His voice becomes calmer, "Okay. But for you, not for him. Is this why you have crying nightmares?"

"Yeah, sometimes."

He never asked questions after that for fear of triggering me. I rarely made another mention of it.

How do I answer the questions they're too afraid to ask?

I continued believing I was fine.

I'll never let what those monsters did affect me.

Thirty years, two kids, and a grandchild later, my thoughts still ran wild with imagination as I toyed with the idea of disclosing my secret. All of the worst-case scenarios played like scratched vinyl on my mother's old Victrola.

I'll be judged. Hate. Rejection. Liar, liar. It will hurt the people that I love. I'm going to destroy relationships. People will look at me differently. I'll be pitied. It's my fault, and everyone will know it. I'll have a nervous breakdown and be sent to a psych ward. The kids will lose their grandparents, aunts and uncles. I don't want to hurt my sister. Mom will blame me. Mom will commit suicide.

Repeat. Repeat. Repeat.

If I open the locks on this dam, the flood waters will sweep away everyone in its path. The safe shores would be engulfed in the raging rapids that can't be harnessed. And I will remain alone and broken even more.

Quite unexpectedly, the secret couldn't be contained. This thing kept double-bolted in the closet was some kind of alien that clawed its way from inside my gut. I'm scared, but I can't stop the regurgitation. I overhear small bits of me escape.

Stop, this is dangerous.

I don't know what's happening, and the sutures on my lips don't repress the sounds echoing from my throat. I can't silence this little girl who is now awakened from her dreams that she will be okay.

My best friend Kathy was staying with us, and Michael was on a weekend fishing trip. She knew me well enough to know that I was unusually mopey that day. "Hey, Val, what's going on? Are you okay?"

"I'm fine." *Sorta.*

"You don't seem yourself."

"Yeah, I don't know why it's bothering me today. It's sorta about being molested when I was little."

"Ohh, no." Her big hug was all I needed then.

Some weeks later, after another late-night discussion, I wrote the poem *The Monster's Game* and shared it with her. That was the night I curiously searched the web for information on incest.

Anonymously, in an incest survivor group, I found a safe space to begin my journey of healing. My words whispered into the wind of some unknown universe, and she saw me. She was like me, a sister who knew my pain because it also belonged to her.

How did these strangers know me better than the people I've known my whole life?

Like an addict who needed a fix, each night for the next year when all was quiet, I retreated to my computer to join my cyber friends. I wept with my sisters as we reminded one another that we were all innocent children. It's so easy to believe that for them, but it didn't apply to me.

You could have stopped it. You let it continue for too long. You're the one who allowed the others to do the same. You should be ashamed.

I did want to hear those affirming words. I wanted to believe it.

Anonymous healing voices:

"That happened to me too."

"I feel that way, too."

"Wow, you were just a baby."

"At four years old, you wouldn't know the words to say what was happening to you."

"You were groomed."

"Freezing and leaving your body happened to me, too. It's called disassociation. It's a common survival mechanism."

"Once you've been groomed, it's easier for another creep to do the same."

"That shame doesn't belong to you; it belongs to those men who abused you."

"It's okay to be angry with your mother, too. She's not in denial; she's delusional. She was supposed to protect you."

"Forgiveness is up to you. You don't have to forgive him. Just forgive yourself."

"Molestation of a child is rape."

"We don't compare our abuse. Our pain is not measured by the extent of the abuse. Being violated one time can have deadly consequences for some."

"I understand. I see you, and I'm here for you."

"You're a survivor."

"You're resilient."

"You have helped me, too."

I hear all of this, but why can't I get rid of this shame?

At last, this little girl, who was *not* a whore, was acknowledging her own pain, anger, and suffering. There's relief in feeling so sad.

Although I was able to share most of my story with my new sisters, there were events I couldn't bear to write in plain English. This is where I turned to poetry to obscure the ugly truth in rhymes. I collected this poetry, created from a year of pain and healing, as the content for my first book, *The Monster's Game*, a memoir of my life and tribute to my sisters.

There's not a specific moment where the voices in my head shut down, but I rarely hear them now. When I do, my sisters are always nearby with a kind word of encouragement. "That shame doesn't belong to you." *I know!* Smiling.

Telling strangers was no longer enough. I needed more. I needed to know that my real people would support me.

Copies of my book had arrived and of course the easiest one, Michael was the first to read it. "This is great. There's a lot in here that I never knew. I'm proud of you."

The second copy goes to my bestie, Kathy.

"Here it is," my heart pounding as I positioned it in front of her on the table. *I guess it's too late to take it back.*

She lifted it, looked over the cover, and returned it to the table. "I'm not ready to read this."

"That's probably a good thing. It's pretty heavy."

Thank God. I'm not ready for you to read it anyway.

Just a couple of weeks later, we were sitting around a blazing fire pit to take the chill off the early autumn night. The bottle of wine on the small table between us was almost empty. Our usual chatter had stopped. I hadn't noticed the silence.

"I read your book."

I leaped up and started walking in circles, and with my hands covering my face, I cried, "Oh my God. I'm sorry. It's hideous." *I'm going to be sick.* I fled to the bathroom.

I can't go back out there. What have I done? Breathe. Go back. No, go home. What am I going to do now? She knows everything. She must think I'm a terrible person. Breathe. Think. Breathe. This shame is not yours.

When I returned to the fire pit, I felt like a baby as she hugged me and I cried until I couldn't. Then there was a calm spirit that brushed across my torso that said, *it's going to be okay.*

She still loves me.

More than a year passed before I requested a family meeting with my children and their spouses. That same old record played in my head. *This will destroy them. But then again, if they find out another way, it'll hurt them more."*

We sat looking at one another on the red sofas and leather club chair that formed a U-shape in the family room. I grabbed the remote to turn off the TV as the room filled with anticipation of what I would say. I lifted the two copies of *The Monster's Game* from the coffee table and passed them to each couple.

"Umm," I paused. "I have to tell you guys something, and it's pretty bad." The tears were already trickling down one cheek. My deep breathing slowed, and my heart raced.

My voice quivering and barely audible, I slowly divulged the story, "When I was little," pause, "Poppy molested me."

"What!?" echoed from the four of them with their brows lifted and their mouths agape.

My daughter spoke first, "I wondered why you were always so mean to him. Now I know why."

Oh, I was mean? I didn't even notice.

"I'm sorry to drop this on you all, but I feel like I have to get it off my chest. It's been a secret for too long."

"Mom, you don't have to be sorry. I'm glad you told us."

"I also want you to know so that you can protect your babies. You need to understand that this can happen anywhere by people that you least expect."

"We certainly didn't expect this. Poppy is always so nice. Who would've ever thought he did something like that."

"How long did he do it?"

"Many years." *Too many.*

"I'm sorry, Mom."

"We will support you any way that we can."

My son-in-law was sitting next to me and cried, "I can't understand how anyone can do this." I touched his shoulder, and he touched my heart.

We didn't talk much afterward. It was late, so they drove off to their separate homes to mull over this disturbing news. The next day, I received messages of love and support. Some of them stayed up late to read the book.

It wasn't until after my mother's passing four years ago that I'd be able to tell my three brothers and be totally free from the secret. I decided never to tell my mother. I started this journey in my 50s and vowed not to go public while she was alive. I did it to protect her.

Why am I trying to protect the person who didn't protect me? Am I really protecting myself?

The truth is, as fiercely as I believe she loved us all, I'm not sure what she would've done if I had told her. I'm not sure I could handle her taking his side or continuing to live in denial after being forced to see how broken I was. Would she have blamed me or called me a liar? I'll never know and there is a degree of regret still.

I divorced my father after my mother's death. I chose to never confront him.

I don't want to hear, "I'm sorry." Forgiveness is not mine to give.

He died last year, and I didn't attend his graveside burial. Many who don't know what he did will judge me. I'm at peace with that.

The voices of guilt and shame are mostly silent. The monster no longer has permission to rob her of self-worth, esteem, and ultimate happiness. The monster is dead.

The fear of telling is worse than actually telling. Nothing close to what I had imagined became reality. Those who loved me gave me unwavering support. Those few who would judge, call me a liar, or just hate, don't really matter. This was finally about me, not them.

I don't feel judgment or anxiety when I speak my truth to anyone who will listen. I'm no longer standing alone at the top of that dam. My family, friends, and new sisters are standing next to me.

I've had the privilege of meeting survivors from around the world. My new power of speech has opened the door for other survivors to share their stories, some for the first time. Friends and families of these survivors thank me for helping them understand how CSA has affected their loved ones. I'm grateful for these experiences that make the journey to this place worth the tears.

THE TOOL

Survivors know that voice in our heads that tells us we're the guilty ones and that we should be ashamed or embarrassed that this happened to us. Thrivers tell that voice to go to Hell.

We all have it within us to thrive. There's that one person we can trust with our secret, whether it's an anonymous person in an online chat group, a love partner, or that best friend who gets us better than anyone. We have a voice, and no one can silence us except ourselves.

This sounds very simple, but it could be one of the hardest things you do. Trust that the rewards far outweigh the risks.

Begin your journey by writing a poem, a letter to your monster, sharing a journal entry or telling a trusted friend or even a stranger. It's your choice how you'll unleash this demon festering like a malignancy inside of you.

Let your kinder self acknowledge that you were an innocent child. You didn't have the words to tell or the power to stop it. The grooming was intended to keep you silent. Throw that shame down the toilet and nurture that child within who is so sad and angry that the monster stole her childhood and impacted her life on so many levels. She deserves to be free. You deserve it.

If you're still thinking about all the bad things that can happen from telling your story, just remind yourself that the fear of telling is worse than actually telling.

Whose life will you save? Maybe your own, and just maybe, many more.

To receive your free copy of the *Power of Prevention Guide* from RAACE, please visit our website and become a RAACE Hero.

Val is the author of *The Monster's Game, A Poetic Look into the Child Behind the Mask of a Survivor*, written under the pseudonym littlegirl413.

She is the Chapter 9 author in, *Stop the Silence®: Thriving After Child Sexual Abuse, a Collaborative Book of Thrivers'* stories led by Dr. Pamela J. Pine. She is also a contributor in the anthologies *Letter to a Monster* by Caroline de Chavigny and *Purple Sparks* by Stephanie Y. Evans and Sharnell D. Myles. She was featured in multiple issues of *Memorabilia* magazine in 2014.

Val is certified in Child Trauma and Protection and has been utilizing that education to further her work in CSA advocacy and prevention.

Her current position as President of Race Against Abuse of Children Everywhere (RAACE) is giving her a platform to educate others on this silent epidemic and stop the abuse of millions of children around the world.

As a speaker, she hopes that her voice resonates with other survivors, teaches all who care for children and warn the monsters that they can no longer hide.

Connect with Val:

Facebook page: The Monster's Game

Email: vmeola@protekhealth.com, valmeola@raace.org

RAACE Website: RAACE.org

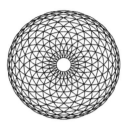

"You carry your ability to be happy with you."

~ Grandma Sheila

CHAPTER 15

RADICAL HONESTY FOR LIFE-CHANGING CONNECTION

BECOME AN EMPATHETIC STRANGER AND EXPAND YOUR COMMUNITY

Leslie Engle

MY STORY

Them: "Tell us a little bit about why you're interested in this job."

Me: "Well, I'm currently pulling myself out of soul-crushing, terrifying, life-threatening postpartum depression. So…"

This probably isn't how most people answer this question in a job interview, particularly with the organization's founders. But I had nothing to lose. My 14-year career was timing out, my marriage was in trouble, and my mental health and my children were the only things I could prioritize if I wanted to survive. So, for the first time in a long time, I decided to lead with the unfiltered, radical truth, deciding that the messy, complicated, and challenging parts of my life were just that—parts of my life.

And while I didn't share this insight into my life to get the job, I got the job. And every day since then has been a step forward (and sometimes several steps back) in the journey towards living a more authentic life.

What got me to this point? Shame. I was so incredibly tired of shame—shame of mental illness, shame of troubled relationships, and shame of being unhappy when, on paper, I *should* be happy.

I was diagnosed with clinical depression when I was 22. I was in a loving relationship, ate a healthy vegan diet, and was successfully training for a marathon. I did all the *right* things. But I felt like shit. I was annoyed at people I loved, and the things that once brought me joy no longer did—a common story that was, fortunately, very simple to diagnose and manage. Despite one scary six-week stint on a medication that didn't work, I found a path to being well with therapy and antidepressants.

I spent the next decade or so being well. I stayed on the medication, got married, and found a beautiful and fulfilling career in international education. I moved to a new city and built a new community of friends. But if I'm being honest (this is all about honesty), the deepest truths began to get harder and harder. It was hard to say that *maybe* the job and organization and career I loved weren't right for me anymore; *maybe* my marriage was becoming a friendship; and ultimately, *maybe* motherhood is a beautiful, fulfilling clusterfuck that fills your soul while striping your identity, leaving you to face a stranger in the mirror.

When I was pregnant with my first child, I lived in a constant state of semi-panic that I was going to be struck with any and all variations of postpartum mood adjustment disorder (PMAD), given my personal and familial history. *What if this baby breaks me? What if I can't care for her? What if I don't love her?*

And the fear was ultimately stronger than anything that actually hit. Becoming a mother rocked my world and changed my orientation to nearly everything, but it didn't impact my mental health in any lasting or concerning way. My daughter became the center of my days (and nights), and, as every parent warned me, I experienced a new level of love—when your heart lives outside your body.

Four years later, when I was pregnant with my son, I assumed I'd be in the clear. I was in a different place in life. I held it together through COVID in New York City with a husband working in emergency medicine and a two-year-old, helped keep my then-organization afloat through a financial crisis, and felt deeply connected to my pregnancy in a way I hadn't before. I reveled in third-trimester insomnia, sitting on the couch watching *Schitt's Creek* and holding onto my sweet boy inside my belly, keenly aware that this would be my last baby and that the clock was ticking on our time together, just the two of us.

When it came time for baby boy to make his way into the world, it went exactly how I wanted. I labored at home while tucking my daughter into bed, then groaned on my hands and knees while watching my go-to reruns. I was supported in delivery by a dear friend and had the unmedicated birth of my dreams—into the hospital at 11:31 PM, baby out at 12:01 AM.

And though it all went to plan, I also thought I would die. Something inside of me broke open during those 30 mins of delivery. Part of it was, of course, the physical pain, but the emotional and mental piece of it changed me forever. It forced me to grapple with my physical mortality while also showing me that, *holy shit, I can do very hard things.*

In the weeks after baby was born, I was on autopilot (as most new parents are)—the lack of sleep, screaming, and around-the-clock feeding. Once I was past the six-week postpartum period, I felt relieved. But then, one night, while holding a two-month-old baby, I had a deeply specific and pervasive thought: *My kids would be so, so much better off if I were dead.*

My heart breaks for any person who has ever felt this—for people who have felt this for weeks, months, and years of their lives. And for people who had nowhere to turn when this feeling overtook their body, mind, and soul. Because that's what it does—it overtakes you.

It breaks you.

Because I had dealt with depression for years and seen it up close and personal with friends and family, I was in the incredibly lucky circumstance to recognize this moment as a moment—to know my mind was fucking with me. I immediately sent a message to my OBGYN and dear friend saying, "I need some help." And then I sat on the couch, shaking and sobbing, nursed my baby, and watched as David and Moira Rose went wine tasting.

In the weeks after that night, I got help—a lot of help—the sort of help often only afforded to people with a lot of privilege in this world. I saw a postpartum psychiatrist covered by insurance, had my medication adjusted, and continued to be afforded paid parental leave.

I knew I was lucky to be okay. But I was still broken.

During this soul-cracking time, I got a new therapist (an LCSW who was perfect for me in every way) and was challenged weekly to say hard things. She taught me that saying the thing aloud, even in an empty room while sobbing uncontrollably, can release the feeling that we have to hold everything all by ourselves. So, to a blank wall, I could say: "I hate being a mom right now. I don't want to be married. I hate my career. I'm lost." And I said them again and again, in the shower, to the wall, and in the mirror. Because I knew letting those words out into the open would mean that someday, somehow, I'd say them to other people and wouldn't have to carry it alone. Because we can't live like that. We aren't meant to live in our heads carrying our own burdens.

A couple of months into seeing my therapist, I told her, "I'm interested in a new job." She's the sort of therapist that rarely, if ever, gives advice. And she had yet to show shock from anything I told her. But this momentarily floored her. She went silent and gave a, "Hmm, let's think about this together."

"I know the new job is a risk. It's a startup. I'll be the sole employee. It's a pay cut, and there's no confirmation or backup plan if it doesn't work."

While those facts all alarmed her quite a bit, as I was still struggling with postpartum depression and my marriage, it was the basis of the work that really got her. I would work directly with a mother who had lost her 25-year-old son five years before by fentanyl poisoning. I would be a fragile mom to a baby boy and work with a mom who was grieving the loss of her son.

For my therapist, this was basically a hard no.

"Do you think you're in a place to hold space for other people's grief? For other people's hard emotions?"

My short answer was *no*. My longer answer was that somewhere in me, I knew that this was right. I connected so deeply with the family who started the organization, and being a part of their shared, active grief project felt like something I could throw myself into and make a difference in.

When I watched Jodi's face in the Zoom interview when I told her I struggled with depression and motherhood, I saw someone who showed compassion and had the worst possible thing happen in her life. She knew on some level that I hoped never to know just how deep grief can be. She was someone who long ago said, "Fuck it" to playing a part and pretending to be happy when she wasn't.

Because life happens. People break.

And with community, people heal.

THE TOOL

Say the damn thing, hear the damn thing.

At Sprout Society, our organization is dedicated to combating loneliness and bringing people together. There is much research on the best ways to do this—peer support groups, community gardens, intergenerational friendships, etc. One and half years in and we've tried several of these ideas and will continue to try several more. But the one thing we've found that works time and time again is simple: show up and listen.

Breaking this into two specific and distinct parts, I'll share how to *say the damn thing* and how to *hear the damn thing*. Both are integral to building community, friendships, relationships, and, ultimately, healing.

So first, *say* it. Whatever it is you're holding in your heart at this exact moment that brings you fear, shame, or anxiety—say it aloud. Let the air in the room grab hold of your words and begin to take away their power. They are just words, and this is just a moment. So say it.

Next, say it to the person who most needs to hear it: yourself. In the mirror, again and again, say the thing. Look at yourself, your beautiful, bold, radical self, and say it. "I don't like being a parent right now. I want to quit my job. I need to break up with my partner."

Finally, say it to someone not impacted by it. Say it to an empathetic stranger. You're just testing out how the words feel when they fall on someone else's ears. The first person who knows you want to quit your job doesn't need to be your boss. It doesn't need to be your partner. It can be the barista you chat with in the morning, the Uber driver who takes you home, or a random person in a coffee shop. Just say it aloud and let the weight of it be shared and fill the space between you two.

Each time you say it, it will get easier and easier to say. The words will start to become natural, and with repetition, they'll get lighter and lighter.

Now, of course, this didn't magically fix whatever problem you're facing. There are many more steps between admitting to yourself that you want a new career and *getting* that new career, but the first one is truly the hardest. The part where you have to love yourself so deeply that you're willing to disappoint other people. The part where you shake off the shame of quitting something, leaving someone, moving on. The part where you have to be the bravest version of yourself you can be.

On the other side of this exchange, we as social beings are uniquely equipped to *hear the damn thing;* to be an empathetic stranger. Learning how to be an empathetic stranger and practicing it each and every day is the single thing that has contributed most to my own healing and my fulfillment with Sprout Society.

My therapist's question about whether I could sit with other people's grief was valid and important. A month prior to that, the answer may have been no. But after I took the time to say my own baggage aloud— my own fears and shame—I had the space to hear it from others.

I feel honored to hear the words someone needs to say and know I don't need to fix them, that I could never fix them. Working in a job that exists solely because a family tragically lost their beloved son or brother means that the very existence of that job is based on a problem that can never be fixed.

Each of us has the opportunity to do this every single day. When we ask a stranger, "How's your day going?" we have the power to show with our words, our expressions, and our energy that any answer is fine. They can be having a shitty day because shitty days happen. And sometimes saying, "My day is shit," can release just a bit of that shitiness.

So, after you practice saying your thing (and the future things that will come up) practice being able to hear it. Being able to show up in the world as an empathetic stranger and someone people can say their hard truths to will change the way you interact with people and grow your community in ways you've never been able to imagine.

Leslie Engle is the Executive Director of Sprout Society, a nonprofit that is focused on combating loneliness and building community. One of their guiding principles is that we all need *less bullshit, more connection.* All of their programming is directed at bringing people together, virtually and in person, to ensure that nobody needs to go through life's peaks and valleys alone. Sprout Society has a program offering called Empathetic Strangers: Both on the phone and in real life, trained empathetic strangers show up to *hear the damn thing.* Sprout Society team members can often be found sitting behind a folding table on a busy sidewalk and offering a listening ear without judgment and without advice—just listening.

Follow along with Sprout Society's weekly program offerings on their website at www.sproutsociety.org and on instagram: sproutsocietyorg.

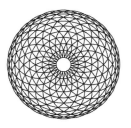

Honesty is the shield of strength and the sword of truth.

~ Bradford W. Tilden

CHAPTER 16

YOUR BRAVE SPIRITUAL UPGRADE

MANIFESTING MAGIC DURING ANY CHALLENGING CONVERSATION

Bradford W. Tilden, CMT, MM, UWT

MY STORY

Do you believe in magic?

Holy shit! I could be turned away at the border!

The severity of this situation suddenly hit me. Exacerbated by the horror story my host just shared with me about her interactions with the Canadian border patrol officers, I clutched my passport tighter and metered my breath. In the driver's seat, Sandra, my host, drove us onward inexorably toward the answer to the terrifying new question: *shall we be granted passage?*

I'll tell them I'm just visiting. It's no big deal. Right? This will be easy. Right? Nobody needs to know I'm on a business trip to teach a few classes.

My body lurched back and forth in the passenger seat of the well-driven 2011 blue Ford Escape as the car swerved out and back into our lane. Sandra steadied the wheel with one hand as she reached and fumbled open the glove compartment with her other hand to extract her passport and immigration documents well ahead of our arrival. Luckily, in the small border town of Oroville, Washington, no other cars were on the road at this early evening hour.

"Here's what we are going to do," Sandra decreed. "I'll do the talking. If they ask, you're here as my guest doing a *free* talk."

Sandra and I met through the Amazon bestselling anthology book, *The Energy Medicine Solution,* published in 2022. We both knew I was there to teach three certification classes over three weeks.

"Okay," I hesitated, preparing to be not quite truthful.

A silent anticipation hovered over the vehicle as we approached the border.

My chest tightened.

Play it cool.

The border patrol officer approached with a clipboard snug to his chest. His uniform fit him comfortably. He lowered his face to the driver-side window and routinely asked for our documents while darting his eyes about the vehicle's interior.

Once Sandra explained our relationship and the reason for our trip, the officer looked me in the eye and inquired.

"What brings you here today?"

"I've been invited to give a free talk at a Metaphysical Center in Penticton, British Columbia," I flatly reported.

The officer looked me in the eye once again, this time for a little longer. He scribbled something down on his clipboard, gave Sandra back her passport, and handed me mine along with a yellow slip of paper with an "X" written on it. He pulled himself back to full stature and, with a gesture of verdict, pointed.

"Pull through and park in that garage on the left. You (to Sandra) remain in the car. And you (looking at me) go through that door and give that paper to the officer inside."

Gulp

The garage looked deserted in the twilight as we pulled in. It was built to hold about seven full-sized campers with a ceiling height to accommodate. Sandra's mid-size SUV was dwarfed by the dull, off-yellow lights illuminating the space from the rafters. The sun disappeared behind the nearby mountain range but had not yet set completely. There was still hope.

"Stay here." A flare of optimism shot through my voice. "I got this."

I paused to look back over my shoulder toward the car as I pulled the heavy door to the processing center open. Inside, Sandra appeared to be staring into blank space, perhaps contemplating the consequences of what might befall us—perhaps praying. With a deep breath, I entered the building.

Inside felt as deserted as the garage. I was alone. I looked around at the bleak, dated bureaucratic ambiance, grey poured concrete floor, tan glazed brick walls, and lightly stained wooden countertops arranged in a long "L," bifurcating the large open floor plan between travelers and administrators. There was no glass barrier separating the two sides of the counters. My eyes settled on a solitary wooden bench that matched the color of the countertops. A massive silent clock mounted on the wall made the passage of time obsolete.

My shoes squeaked on the floor as I traipsed toward the area labeled "Intake," leaning over the counter, expectant.

Just stick to the story. You're here to give a free talk. Breathe. You are doing nothing wrong. Be strong. You can do this.

A door across the room burst open, and a different immigration officer emerged. The pint-sized woman plodded her way through the maze of cubicles and kiosks toward me. Her hair was pulled back tightly in an unflattering ponytail, and her uniform swallowed her up. Her arms swished as if they were wearing swimming floaties. The motion agitated the badge on her constricted breast.

Here's someone with something to prove.

Straight to the issue, she took the yellow slip without looking at it.

"Why are you here? Who are you with? Who's hosting you? What's the name of the store? How long are you here for? Where are you staying?"

The quick succession of questions broke through my defenses like bullets, riddling the bucket of my story with holes. I physically staggered back from the assault. Ungrounded, unprepared, unarmed, I stuttered my desperate replies.

"Go have a seat," she snapped, satisfied.

Bewildered, I staggered toward the bench not sure what just happened. I closed my eyes and breathed. In that moment I took responsibility for my poor actions and decisions. I was unprepared and dishonest. I was facing *real* consequences.

*This border patrol is no joke. I **must** get through. I **cannot** be turned away. I have too much riding on this!*

Clicking sounds from a computer keypad started chirping through the space like gossipy little birds.

What's she doing?

The clicking abruptly stopped. A chair wheel squeaked. Urgent footsteps.

"Come here, please."

I opened my eyes. The officer was back at the counter, grinning, ready for the next round of interrogation. I approached.

"You haven't been completely forthright with me, have you?"

"No."

The cat's out of the bag.

"What's the real reason for your trip?" Her voice winding up, ready to punch.

Honesty. Complete honesty. Be completely honest.

Without honesty, you cannot have integrity, and without integrity, the foundation of all spiritual principles collapses within you, and you're disempowered. Honesty is the shield of strength and the sword of truth.

"I'm here to teach a few classes."

Disarmed, her eyes widened at the unexpected truth.

She continued, "I found your website. It says you charge $600 per person to teach up to six people."

"Yes."

"So, you're coming into *our* country and taking *our* money without paying taxes?"

Well, if you put it that way, that does sound illegal.

"You didn't think to file for a work visa for this trip?"

"I didn't know I had to."

There was a moment of silent exchange between her probing and my innocent eyes.

"Have a seat, please."

We parted in opposite directions.

This isn't good. I have to do something.

Back at the bench, I called for an emergency assembly.

"Higher Self, personal guides, angels, masters, help me now!"

With a straightened back, feet flat on the floor, and palms face up in my lap, I activated my Universal White Time distance healing powers for the singular purpose of getting into Canada.

My crown opened. Blasts of energy filled my body from foot to finger. Colors swirled behind my closed eyelids as the force of White Time flowed forth.

"Love, Love, Love, Esé, Esé, Esé. . ."

Chanting silently, I sent healing to the situation. The room faded away. The bench faded away. Time faded away. I was one with the pure force of total love.

★★★

Esé is an extraterrestrial word meaning 'total love.' It's taught in Universal White Time healing. UWT has existed in this Universe since the beginning of time. The oldest, wisest, most advanced ETs, light-beings, and angels understand and work with some form of UWT. I describe it to my students as cosmic Reiki, but it's much more expansive than that.

UWT comes in at a much higher frequency than all other energy healing modalities on Earth partly because of its unique origin from beyond our universe. "White" Time implies *all* time as one unit, past, present, and future, empowering the practitioner to work outside the confines of linear time. UWT contains the forces of unconditional love and divine light, providing the strongest protections available against negative energies and entities.

Many ET contactees are confidentially taught UWT Healing, including one woman named Channie West. In 1993, the higher beings permitted Channie to teach this knowledge to others, becoming the first Ambassador for Earth for UWTH. Since then, it has spread worldwide from her home country of Sweden. There are two branches: energy healing and gemstone healing, each with four levels of training.

I was introduced to UWT in 2006 by the head UWT gemstone healing teacher for the United States after following cosmic breadcrumbs that led me to her home in Aptos, California. After receiving a UWT gemstone treatment, I quickly understood its power and potential. Within one year of studying with her, I became one of the leading UWT gemstone healing teachers in North America. I've written about this encounter in *The Energy Medicine Solutions*, Chapter 19.

UWT became a huge part of life. It also saved my life.

In 2010, I was hospitalized for what appeared to be late-onset bipolar disease. For three months, I was pumped full of psych meds that did nothing to improve my condition. I went from a healthy 145-pound 30-year-old man to a 78-pound skeleton in less than 90 days.

Fearing the death of their son, my parents fought for a new doctor who discovered CMV was attacking my brain the entire time. The virus's toxic waste products caused symptoms of the mental disorder. After successful radiation treatment, my body and mind began to mend. I survived AIDS, but my real battle had just begun.

I entered a crisis of faith. Who was I? What did I believe in? What was real? When had I started slipping into delusion? I compared myself to Icarus and believed I was abandoned by God.

The psychosis denied me the right to fight for my own life. I needed to prove to myself I was strong enough. I created my own crisis by suppressing the trauma and self-medicating with hard drugs.

Addiction proved quite the adversary. I struggled for years with the cycle of relapse. Far into my dark night of the soul, I implored the Universe for help. Help arrived in an email from one of my UWT students about the "New Initiation," a powerful spiritual upgrade Channie disseminated for UWT teachers and practitioners.

I found a certified teacher online who performed the spiritual upgrade on me via Zoom. This was the beginning of my true spiritual healing. My life immediately began to improve. Reconnecting with the inner knowledge of the power to have a positive influence over things, I developed inner strength, determination, and resistance to drug use. Hope and faith were gradually restored. I'm now gratefully clean and sober in large part thanks to UWT.

Back on that bench, I found myself using the same force that saved my life and pulled me out of my darkest period to positively influence the outcome of this situation.

"Love, Love, Love. Esé, Esé, Esé. . ."

"Come here," a voice barked, yanking me out of my healing trance.

The officer perched behind the check-out counter waved a thick printout of documents, ready to throw the book at me. I glanced at the giant clock on the wall.

Fifteen minutes had passed.

Surrounded by my entire legion of guides, I approached her, radiating all the love and light I could muster from my entire being.

"Here's what's going to happen. We're turning you away from the border. You need to go to a different office and file for a work visa, then bring that back here. The process can take up to a month for approval."

She looked at me for a reaction. I beamed more love and light toward her.

"That just won't work," I replied. "Is there any way I can get across the border today?" I beamed love and light directly into her eyes.

Her face relaxed a bit, and she let out a tiny sigh.

"Let me see what I can do."

She withdrew to her computer while I regrouped at the bench.

Have faith. I will get through the border. No room for doubt.

"Love, Love, Love, Esé, Esé, Esé. . ."

I sat motionless with my eyes closed in complete surrender, channeling healing energy. Time passed. The phone rang. I heard the fragment of dialogue ". . .plus I don't want to deal with the paperwork. . ." Finally, I heard,

"Come forward, please."

I opened my eyes. Thirty minutes had passed.

"Good news. We are letting you through. There is an obscure clause in the immigration law stating you don't need a work visa if the event you are holding is less than five days in duration. Because your three classes are each less than five days, you are, in fact, not doing anything illegal."

I couldn't believe it. But then again, I could. I then silently closed my healing powers.

"Thank you for this healing. Thank you for this healing. Thank you for this healing."

I thanked the officer profusely, grabbed my passport, exited the building, got into the car, and beamed triumph to my perplexed and concerned friend, who patiently sat there the whole time.

With a sigh of relief, Sandra started the engine, backed the car out of the garage, and crossed the border into Canada.

THE TOOL

You have the potential within you to create real magic in your life by shaping the outcome of events in your favor without harm, aggression, or forcefulness. We spend our lifetimes building defenses to ensure our survival and to protect us from emotional pain. But these defenses hurt us in the long run, evidenced by the reactive disposition of most people. The escalating conflicts within our own lives and in the collective yield no rewarding fruit, only barren battlefields.

Sometimes, we become so enmeshed within our own walls that we need help from a higher source. Spiritual upgrades provide an acceleration of spiritual growth. They serve to remove obstructions that shield us from our total divine self, our true self. And that's not just ones we've created in this physical incarnation; it's also blockages in our souls. When we're born on this planet, we have amnesia of our past experiences and our past lives. That amnesia, in a sense, is a blockage. We have many blockages for different things, and it's all part of our process of unfolding and awakening in this lifetime to connect with and develop our purpose.

By removing blockages in your aura, you can access more of who you really are. This manifests in your life in different ways as a spiritual awareness. This sophistication allows you to be more present, peaceful, and joyful while less stressed, triggered, confused, and angered.

I've provided a link with a discount code at the end of this chapter if you'd like to receive a spiritual upgrade from me.

Here is a powerful five-minute exercise you can use to cultivate spiritual awareness and inner peace anywhere, anytime. It will aid you in remaining peaceful and positive in chaotic situations and challenging conversations.

- Find a comfortable position, either seated with feet flat on the floor and palms face up in your lap or standing with arms by your sides, palms facing forward. This is a power position of divine surrender.
- Inhale deeply and exhale completely three times, making an audible sound.
- Start a timer for five minutes.
- Send three grounding cords down to Mother Earth's core from your feet and the base of your spine.
- Draw up a wide golden ray of light from Earth's core through your base and lower chakras to your heart chakra.
- Take down a pure white light from the central sun of the universe through your crown and upper chakras to your heart chakra.
- Combine the gold and white light to create an iridescent sphere in the core of your heart chakra.
- Expand this sphere in all directions until it completely surrounds your body and energy field.
- Add the thought: *This is my sphere of healing and protection only beings and energies of love, light, truth, and manifestation may enter.*
- You may now call upon your higher self, personal angels, guides, archangels, ascended masters, etc., to be present with you.

- Meditate while focusing on your third eye and heart chakra.

- Add the silent mantra, "Love, Love, Love. Esé, Esé, Esé. . ." [pronounced "essay"] at least three times, and as often as you like.

- When the timer goes off, gently come back to your body. Thank any beings who were present by saying, "Thank you for this healing" three times.

- Notice how you feel.

By adding this to your daily practice, you will cultivate inner strength and shift quicker into inner peace and gratitude even in the most difficult situations. By changing your inner vibration, you positively influence the external world, including others' behavior toward you. It seems like magic, but it's a simple universal principle. After all, change *always* starts from within.

Many blessings to you on your path of spiritual becoming.

Visit https://crystalmusichealing.com/how-to-be-brave-spiritual-upgrade and use the discount code HTBB50 towards your first order of a spiritual upgrade.

Bradford W. Tilden MM, CMT, UWT is an internationally best-selling author, composer, pianist, and master intuitive vibrational healer. He specializes in sound healing, crystal and gemstone healing, and Universal White Time Healing. He is one of the leading UWT Gemstone and Energy Healing teachers in North America. He graduated *magna cum laude* from Amherst College in 2002, attended the Globe Institute of Sound and Consciousness in San Francisco in 2006, and received a master's degree in music composition from UMASS, Amherst in 2014.

Bradford founded the Lemurian School of Intuitive Natural Healing in 2008. The mission of LSINH (pronounced "*listen*") is to develop one's intuition while opening up to the power of sound and crystals to become an effective healer for oneself and the world. It is derived from the knowledge of the ancient Lemurian civilization, as revealed to him by his UWT master guides, past-life remembrance as a Lemurian priest-healer, and through his work with Lemurian seed crystals.

His musical compositions and live sound journeys are powerful, divinely orchestrated collaborations with higher beings. Bradford channels authentic angelic, galactic, and shamanic healing frequencies through his voice. His music is available on all the major streaming platforms and at https://bradfordwtilden.bandcamp.com

Bradford brings the greatness out in people through inspiration, education, and activation of the divine potential within. Visit https://www.CrystalMusicHealing.com to learn more about UWT, LSINH, and all the different types of healing services and products he offers, including spiritual upgrades. He will travel anywhere in the world to teach. Contact him for commissions, podcast interviews, or to host a class in your local community. Book a free 20-minute consultation here: https://calendly.com/crystalmusichealing/20min

When he is not hiking or running around with his shirt off, you can find him talking to his crystals at home in Cheshire, CT.

Connect with Bradford:

https://linktr.ee/bradfordtilden
https://Facebook.com/CrystalMusicHealing
https://instagram.com/BradfordTilden
https://youtube.com/MuseOfAquarius
www.linkedin.com/in/bradfordtilden

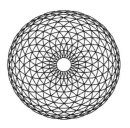

There is a difference between ceremony from the heart and ceremony that bleeds your blood into the sacrificial bowl. Be clear on what you are saying "yes" to.

~ Angel Rohrer

CHAPTER 17

BOUNDARIES OR BITCH?

MASTER YOUR SACRED NO FOR ULTIMATE EMPOWERMENT

Angel Rohrer

What is the difference between boundaries and bitch?
Are there shades of grey between dark and light witch?
My soul needs to feel protected by me
In the dark, my eyes are initiated to see
Yet, in all energetic realms, it turns into "we"
Do not think I can't see what you do
Your gaslighting and dominating, covered in "woo"
I hold Archangel Michael's hand in the night
I said no, with all my might.
Take your darkness elsewhere, love
He passes me his sword,
slashing demons below and above
The truth shall be revealed, as I step into the light
I hold Archangel Michael's hand in the night

MY STORY

The sacred grounds of the Teotihuacan pyramids are bustling with thousands of people as they eagerly gather for the sighting of the eclipse. Our group gathers in a circle in front of the pyramid of the moon.

Prayers are conjured with divine masculine and feminine energies by the facilitator.

"…preparing all the masculine energy here within us, within this planet, within the heart and the mind of the men here, to receive her as she is now, in her true rise, in her true grandness again. Never to be diminished, never to be shadowed again.

He lets her pass in front of him as the queen. As the true queen. The true mother that came before all. We carry this journey within us, the grand reunion. Prepare now…."

Blinding light reflects off the black obsidian blade; the next thing I know, I'm spread eagle, lying on the hot, hard, dusty altar floor, attempting to re-enter my physical body.

What the fuck is happening?

My eyes attempt to adjust to the rays of sunlight penetrating from the scorching eclipsed sun. *Why is everyone being killed? I didn't give you permission to kill me!* I see penetration on an energetic level as the witch attaches her womb to my husband in a full kundalini orgasmic channel.

My heart shatters as the digestion of what I'm witnessing sets deep within my soul.

I'm literally laying on my back with the entire group at your feet while you complete the divine feminine and masculine union, with my husband, on the eclipse.

You said we were sisters! How could you be so ruthless! How is this happening?

As the moon greeted us with its presence that evening, my soul brother, John, brought his healing hands to my heart.

Fresh tears ran down my cheeks as his deceased brother, Peter's essence joins us in the room. *Willow White Wolf is safe with me now, love; it's time to start a new storyline.* The last shard of my heart shatters with love. *If I could only hold you one more time, how do I exist on this planet without you here?*

My hands reach up to John's shoulders as his head comes down to join our third eyes. "I love you" escapes from my lips, between my heart shattered sobs.

John's physical body shifted as he lifted his third eye off my brow, "Just chill, you're alright," he whispered, patting my shoulders and turning to address my husband.

I love you too, Dear. My body relaxes into Peter's etheric words: *You are never alone. Allow the death and enjoy all the magic it will bring to you in this next cycle of life on Earth.*

Remember, I am right here with you, always.

In that moment, I recalled the first time Archangel Michael physically revealed himself to me in 2008, shortly after a brain injury.

Rolling over in deep slumber, a feathery bone slides off the side of my cheek, waking me to the presence of Archangel Michael standing beside my bed. *What is happening? Why did you hit me in the face?* This large presence lets out a deep chuckle, "That was your own wing that slid across your face, love. We are in the process of re-attaching your wings, and you woke up in the middle of it," he replies matter-of-factly.

My jaw stays open as I slide out of bed and stand directly in front of this magical being. He stands as still as a statue, gazing into my eyes as I breathe in his magnificent essence.

My eyes fixate directly in front of me, landing at his golden solar plexus. Admiring his stellar physique, my quivering hands connect to his heart, and I lift my head to meet his soft gaze. His eyes shift into twinkling lights of amusement as my nimble fingers trace down his chest and ripped ab muscles.

My goodness, you must be nine feet tall, I ponder as my fingers follow the smooth indents that lead to his hips.

Closing my eyes, I take a deep breath in, time stands still. I open my eyes to an empty room. He was physically gone, yet there was a tangible knowing that I'd never be alone again.

★★★

Knowing and experiencing that connection within, that you're never alone, is essential when you're experiencing PTSD symptoms after a betrayal.

Relational betrayal hits deep. Not only is it an intentionally deceptive act, but it violates the fabric of soul-level trust offered to the humans you choose to create with, be it a marriage, friendship/family, or business partnership.

Traumatic experiences leave everything distorted because you're left questioning if any of what you experienced was real.

This level of violation causes a great rupture to your foundation of safety and security, often causing you to lose faith in love, in the people surrounding you, but more so in yourself. You stop trusting your own instinct and intuition.

I learned the hard way that certain humans will take advantage of your gifts and siphon your energy from your heart if you let them.

Hear that again, fixer-pleasers.

Humans will take advantage of you as long as you let them.

For most humans, this is unconscious. They're just going along with their storyline, trying to survive. When they "teach" awareness and spirituality, there is a knowing.

This teacher drops seeds into the circle, watered with dark intent, assuming that nobody will question her ways.

"Remember, when I'm in my channel, it's not me performing the ceremony."

- *If you can't control yourself in your channel, does that mean you have no discernment?*

- *Permission is required for penetration in the 3D world, or it's called rape. Is permission needed for merging in the 5D world as well?*

- *Does that mean all humans can do what they want to whomever they want, and they're not responsible for their physical actions if they're channeling?*

- *Where is the radical responsibility in that statement?*

- *Does that mean you're dangerous if you're not accepting responsibility for what your body does in and out of ceremony?*

"It was divinely orchestrated! It had to happen!"

Did it? Did it HAVE to happen the way it was orchestrated?

Yes. The divine masculine and feminine needed to merge in that ceremony, on the eclipse, agreed.

As I practice the 5th Agreement (Be skeptical, but learn to listen) by my teacher Don Jose Ruiz, I ask myself: *What situation is more powerful to complete this ceremony for the collective consciousness?*

Twin flames who have committed to a life in service together, have a deep storyline already, and have made the sacred commitment of marriage to one another.

OR

The siren who kills the wife and steals the innocent sailor as her lover.

As I spun in my own haunting questions that evening, navigating a nervous breakdown, the answer came the next morning when most of the participants in that ceremony were ill, purging from both ends.

There is a difference between ceremony from the heart and ceremony that bleeds your blood into the sacrificial bowl. Be clear on what you're saying "yes" too.

If the ceremony does not feel good, there's a chance you were fed upon.

Black witches use energy from the emotional atmosphere and other humans. They need to create an atmosphere of trauma to make humans release emotional energy for them to feed off for their own selfish purposes.

This spiritual war demands your connection with the Divine.

It is your greatest weapon.

Of course, sometimes healing is painful, the medicine, your medicine, must go deeper than the poison.

Both faith and fear demand you to believe in something you cannot see.

You now have a choice.

Even though I want to find meaning behind the pain they're projecting, if I tell them they're hurting me, and they keep doing it or gaslight me to play the part they want in their storyline, the only thing for me to understand is that I'm not safe here.

Like many women, I've had deep sister wounds all my life that I've worked hard to unpack and heal.

Betrayal trauma is a soul-level violation. This one took me to my knees, changed my brain chemistry, and brought me to the depths of my soul.

We must sharpen our sword of discernment and be unafraid to speak what we see, even though to some, it may look like judgment and being "not spiritual enough."

Do not get sucked into the new age trap of awakening souls.

Part of the controllers' agenda is to destabilize sacred unions because this is the greatest threat to a system that thrives on the addiction to suffering.

The infiltration or attack on divine union isn't hindered because you're spiritual.

I believe the attack on sacred unions is even greater within conscious communities because it veils itself under spiritual glitter and unhealthy boundaries.

Everything does serve a purpose, however.

As healers, we're taught to dig in the dirt and find the gold of our experiences.

My gold out of this experience brought me a greater discernment of invisible boundaries and a deeper knowledge that some people are quite happy where they are in life and choose to wield their magic in dark ways.

People will gladly take all the parts of you that you offer for free.

They will also gladly take the parts you don't understand are being taken.

It's up to you to say no, ask for reciprocity, and put boundaries in place to protect your energy.

Owning your power can sometimes come off to others as aggressive.

Are you coming off that way?

Or are you being gaslit into submission by their own will and power?

Taking radical responsibility for your actions is where the healing begins.

I don't walk away to teach people a lesson. I walk away because I learned mine. I'd rather adjust my life to their absence than adjust my boundaries to accommodate their disrespect.

It takes strength to forgive someone who wasn't even sorry.

It takes even more strength to challenge their ways and share your experience.

To challenge those who say, "Are you doing this for revenge?"

I've experienced this type of betrayal a handful of times in my life. The gift this woman gave me was asking me the first question of our "flared nose-to-nose."

"If you didn't want me to kill you, then why did you let me? Why did you give your power away?"

It was in that moment that I knew deep within my bones that she was working within a storyline I wasn't willing to create with her, one that didn't harbor trust and respect—a storyline based on "take." With this information, I knew the only peaceful way to end this connection was to disconnect entirely.

Understand, some humans weren't put here to evolve.

They're here to remind you of what it looks like if you don't.

Discernment is when you don't have to reach the end of a lesson to learn it.

Manipulation is when they blame you for your reaction to their toxic behavior but never discuss the disrespect that triggered you.

The narcissist wants the authority of a queen with the accountability of a toddler.

As you experience patterns, you learn, notice them sooner, collect tools, and you will start to naturally choose:

- Healing over coping and trauma bonding

- Affection over attention

- Boundaries over tolerating disrespect

- Connection over attachment

- Prioritize mutual support over codependency

- Intimacy over enmeshment

- Internal self-love over external validation

Unconditional love for yourself means withdrawing your attention from the conditions you don't love.

Stop expecting people who aren't on your energetic frequency to understand or receive you. You'll never have to go out of your way to prove yourself or be seen or heard by your soul tribe. Those meant for you will naturally align—no force, no stress. Trust this.

Everything is reversible and healable in a higher realm of existence, and when you merge within that field and anchor it back to the physical realm, magic, and miracles are possible and experienced:

- No matter what you've faced that has been from the depths of darkness.

- No matter what spells are conjured from the dark arts against you.

- No matter what was thrown at you to deter, detour, and destroy you.

- No matter what dark web of black spell seduction you stepped into.

- No matter what false mother came in to poach with jealous hate claws and arrows.

Take back your throne.

Return their hate, return their projections.

Get comfortable using your Sacred NO!

You have now found your Priestess within
your dark veil initiation is now complete
as you awaken to the Pure Light and Regal Queen within you.

SHE is not designed to give.

SHE is designed to multiply what she is "given."

Those operating from their ego will be stripped of their power moving forward.

Only those operating from the heart will now lead us.

Ecstatic consent (*Fuck yes!*) is needed from all parties before collaboration takes place, in life or ceremony.

Consistency is king!

Emotional safety is established through consistency.

Consistent communication.

Consistent care.

Consistent responsiveness.

Inconsistent patterns and unpredictability cause the nervous system to retract into survival instead of expanding into surrender.

As a queen, this is a threat. Allow your king within to provide protection and security.

Love cannot survive in unsafe spaces. Safety is a prerequisite of love.

Choose people that bring calm instead of chaos to your soul.

Helping the wrong person can throw you off track. You cannot save everyone, and you're not supposed to save everyone. Some deserve to be where they are.

Use discernment before you pour your attention into someone.

Always ask, "Is this someone who deserves my help or is in a place to receive my help?"

It's not judgy to protect your own energy field first.

It's not selfish to protect your marriage.

It's necessary to choose your nervous system first and then your partner's.

"My experience was that of Hansel and Gretel"
~ Seth Rohrer

Being able to discern who to help and who to interact with means you first have to connect with your own Divine essence. The Mirror Room tool was how I did that.

THE TOOL

I've been blessed in this lifetime to find humans learning to embody the energy of Archangel Michael. However, the first person I really saw it in was myself.

I found this essence in the mirror. I can remember talking to myself in the mirror when I was young, before I knew this was a powerful connection tool. This place was natural for me and went deeper with my time and energy spent in the gymnastics world, where you had to watch yourself on film, in the mirror, and be watched by others.

Reflections became a part of my daily life.

After experiencing such a breakdown of trust and trauma with this teacher, I found myself heading back to my own mirror room, where the most profound and powerful healing always happens.

The Mirror Room

Mirror work is a high-performance way to challenge and release programming or agreements that you or society placed upon you.

It takes courage and dedication to meet yourself in the mirror, more than most tools, because it's your beliefs and dreams that teach you how to love yourself!

Most humans on this planet fear looking in the mirror. It's the last thing they want to do. That right there is an invitation to lean into that resistance and reveal what's underneath.

It's easy to continue your negative thought processes if they just stay in your head, but as soon as you verbalize them and include verbalizing them to yourself in a mirror, it shatters that belief system.

Are you really stupid?

Are you sure you're crazy?

Why are you so sensitive?

Why are you saying such mean things to yourself?

Would you let someone else say such things to you?

Do you actually believe that, or are you parroting something said to you as a child, and you took it on as truth?

The clarity from doing mirror work brings you back to your innate power. Your power lies within, and it always has.

You've been looking in the mirror and being your own tyrant most of your life. When you face the tyrant within yourself, those outside of you have no choice but to retreat.

Take back your sovereignty.

Reclaim your freedom.

Remember your power.

You are a powerful being of infinite possibility.

Once a day, minimum:

- Find a room with a mirror, quiet, with no distractions and no one around you. Look deep into your own eyes and say, "You are the love of my life." Repeat this to yourself a minimum of ten times and do your best to also feel gratitude for yourself and your body while you say these words.

- Journal what you see and feel each day as you do this practice. This will allow you to see the shifts over time, and it's a wonderful way to process and move energy.

- Be your greatest cheerleader. It's time to evict the tyrant! It's time to stand in your power and show the world that unconditional love won't be mistaken for weakness.

Unconditional love is, in fact, where your true power and freedom are found.

Survival mode isn't the gold medal of Earth school!

You truly do not have to settle at this level of life. Own that you want more; you are reading this book, aren't you? Clearly, you're looking for something.

Your high performance in sports can also be transferred from sport to life.

Yes, authentic living is also a high-performance specialty on Earth.

Mastery of Self happens on all levels, not just your physical body.

Remember, you are the love of your life!

Want some help?

Here's a free Mirror Room guided meditation just for you: https://www.rohrerevolution.com/offers/qo54LPDe

Angel Rohrer is the bestselling lead author of *Bytes of Light, Evolving Leadership for the Spiritual Entrepreneur*, Bytes of Light Podcast Host, and co-founder of Fire Heart Consulting.

She is a former high-performance coach in the power tumbling and trampoline world. She comes with 25 years of national-level experience training athletes of all ages and genders. After retiring, the last ten-plus years were spent focusing her coaching skills in the holistic community, becoming a Crystal Reiki Master teacher and deep tissue massage specialist. She began coaching and healing those looking to wrangle their shadows of life as well as healing their physical body.

Ancient medicine has always been calling, and she spent 30 years mastering breathwork and moving energy through Kung Fu martial arts, as well as apprenticing with the Ruiz family (Author of *The 4 Agreements*), Toltec Shamans of the Eagle Knight lineage, and honoring her own Celtic shamanic roots.

A master healer and shaman, Angel assists you in reclaiming your power, focusing your intent, and creating a life once thought impossible by most.

As you walk your path through all that currently holds you back, you are not alone. Inner work does not mean lonely work. Angel is also available for one-on-one work where the training will be specialized toward your highest growth, highest personal power, and truth. Or join her power journeys to Teotihuacan, Mexico, Peru, and the Rocky Mountains of Canada.

Connect with Angel:

On website: https://www.bytesoflight.com

On Facebook: https://www.facebook.com/bytesoflight

On Instagram: https://www.instagram.com/angel.rohrer/

On YouTube: https://bit.ly/4dVrUYm

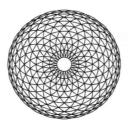

I was beginning to see clearly that staying calm around high emotions and not getting hooked on irrational arguments was my superpower.

~ Tiffany Thomas

CHAPTER 18

THE UNSEEN SUBTLETIES OF ABUSE

SAFETY PLANNING YOUR WAY TO FREEDOM

Tiffany Thomas, CADC-II, LMFT

MY STORY

I can't believe this is how my relationship is turning out. I'm suffocating. I couldn't breathe—I was crying too hard. I locked myself in the bathroom, curled up on the floor, and sobbed. *I wish I could die.*

I quickly approached my 35th birthday. It was a defining moment, one that made me reflect on my life and how I wanted the rest of it to look.

What happened to that fun, outgoing, happy woman I used to be?

I felt depressed, hopeless, and like a prisoner in my own home. I woke up to the alarm, listening for any sign of him in bed next to me. Stillness. Relief. *Thank God!* I ran to the bathroom without making a sound, hoping I could close the door quickly without setting off a bomb. It was the only place of solace. I spent too many nights on the cold tile floor, tears spilling out, struggling to catch my breath, wondering if I'd pass out from exhaustion next to the toilet.

I need to get out.

According to the World Health Organization, Intimate Partner Violence (IPV) refers to behavior within an intimate relationship that causes physical, sexual, or psychological harm, including acts of physical aggression, sexual coercion, psychological abuse, and controlling behaviors. 34.9% of California women and 31.1% of California men experience intimate partner physical violence, intimate partner sexual violence, and/or intimate partner stalking in their lifetimes, according to National Coalition Against Domestic Violence.

IPV ranges from emotional abuse, such as name-calling, manipulation, and humiliation, to physical abuse. In between, you may experience stalking, threats of harm, invasion of privacy, controlling behavior, extreme jealousy, and financial abuse, among other types of abuse.

My relationship didn't blow up overnight. It sunk into quicksand, one morsel at a time, so slowly I didn't realize I was disappearing until it was almost too late to get out.

When I met John*, he was charming, charismatic, successful, good-looking, and generous. During the early months of dating, I noticed extreme reactions to situations, but they weren't directed at me, so I just tried to comfort him, not thinking much of it.

For a long time, I wasn't the target of disappointments, anger, and frustrations, but wanting to be a good partner, I tried to comfort him or calm him down when he was upset. When we went out to dinner, and the waiter didn't show up fast enough to take our order, John became enraged. My anxiety skyrocketed, anticipating the embarrassment: *Please don't get up and walk out this time. Stay calm, let him have his feelings, he'll calm down once he eats.*

John started to retreat from others. I'm a planner by nature and usually made plans for us with family and friends. When John and I agreed to go somewhere, shortly before we needed to leave, I would notice he hadn't budged from what he was doing. *Why isn't he getting ready? That's weird. Maybe he doesn't need to do anything but change.*

It's time to leave. Dread set in. *Again? What am I going to tell people this time?*

Time and time again, he yelled, "I'm not going! Don't you see I have work to do! Why can't we just do it another time?" At first, I didn't want to flake on the person we were meeting, so I begged him to come. "It'll be a good distraction from the week. I'll help you when we get back."

Other times, the morning we were set to have plans, I'd hear, "Tiffany, I need your help! If I can just get a handle on _____(insert the never ending list of things he was working on), we can go do whatever you want." I gave in—for months—always hoping that would happen, believing it would. I felt guilty if I said no. *What kind of partner am I if I don't help him?*

I tried to maintain the image of being in a happy relationship but started to accommodate and gave up what I needed for myself. I started negotiating with myself when I wanted to hike or go to the gym on the weekend. *If I give up what I want to do this weekend, I can help him finish and we can go on a date next time.* I felt so selfish if I did my own thing while he was struggling to complete a task. My entire identity became about accommodating him and his emotions.

Then began a slow erosion of who I was. I was caught in the web of keeping the peace but never doing or being enough. I was pinned between living my life as the ambitious person I was and feeling like I was a terrible partner.

When he did agree to go, the drive was unbearable. He'd be furious that he stopped what he was doing in order to leave. *Why isn't he interested in doing these things? Doesn't he want to spend time with me?* We argued the whole car ride as I tried to calm him down and manage my anxiety. *How do I make this better by the time we get there? I wish I could just turn the car around and bail. But I don't want people to know. We all have bad days. Maybe he just needs to vent, and then he'll be fine.*

This became a pattern. *Do I go alone without him? What will they say? What will I say?*

I love to experience new things and stay connected with my friends and family. If I stopped going out, they'd know something was wrong. So I pretended. I went anyway, by myself. "Where's John?" they'd ask. With a pit in my stomach, afraid they'd know I was lying, "He isn't feeling well," I might say, or "He got tied up with work." When they wouldn't push the issue, I immediately relaxed; *the secret is safe.*

I continued to follow through on my commitments to others, and John questioned my loyalty to him as a result. He reacted when I went to leave the house, even to work, and I noticed a new pattern. He didn't want me to leave. My superpower was activated—I started setting boundaries. "I'm not going to be late to work. This conversation can wait until later." That escalated his reaction until I felt like a caged animal that needed air to breathe. So I walked out, terrified of the phone calls or texts that would come moments later. *At least I can ignore my phone.* The more I maintained my sense of self, the stronger the threats became.

He threatened to call my family if I didn't do what he wanted and to not leave the room until I talked to him. I locked myself in the bathroom just to have space, a place where he couldn't get in. I slowly started to realize: *I can't live like this. This is torture. I'm trapped. How do I get out?*

We fought daily. The fights were so confusing. We started talking about one thing, but he changed the topic quickly, and I couldn't keep up. *I feel like a crazy person. What is happening?* I tried harder and harder to change so the fighting would stop. I tried different ways to respond, different approaches, a different tone of voice, or time of day. *Maybe I can text him; that way, he can have his reaction away from me. Maybe I'm not communicating well enough. I'll wait until he is in a good mood.* I apologized and took responsibility for things that weren't mine. Eventually, it became the only way to end a fight. I bargained a lot with myself: *It'll get better if I just get through another year.* I rationalized: *We all have bad days.*

There were moments of inside jokes, watching a TV show in common, or normal, calm conversation— temporary moments of relief, the calm before the next storm. It's why it took me years to leave.

We operated on opposite sleep schedules, with him staying up until the wee hours of the morning and me going to bed around ten. He started coming into the room and waking me up from a dead sleep to start a conversation with me, one that could have waited until the morning. *God, please just let me sleep. I'm too tired for this.* I went years without a full night of sleep.

Each time the door opened, I lay still, hoping he wouldn't sense I was awake. *Please, not tonight.* I held my breath, unable to sleep anyway.

As I started to pull away to protect myself, he went through my journals, drawers, and my clothes. I lacked any sense of privacy, but when he became upset at what he saw me write in my private journal, I thought: *That's what you get. Oh shit. What's he going to do next?* Terrified, my heart was in my throat.

It wasn't until I was in therapy that I started to recognize what he was doing was abusive. When I tried not to engage in an argument or explain myself in a more healthy manner, it enraged him more—he started putting his fists up. I was afraid he'd hit me, so I started recording our arguments with my phone. I started the recording and stated that he put his fists up; he responded, "What are you talking about? No, I didn't. Why would you say that?" *I need evidence if something ever happens.*

I tried walking away during arguments, but he followed me around the house and forced me to listen to what he wanted to say. "Come back here; you're going to listen to me!"

I started to verbalize that I wasn't happy in the relationship. I convinced myself that if I gave a good explanation of why, that would somehow soften the blow. I spent years trying to find a way to make it work but was more afraid of what would happen after I left, than of continuing to expose myself to what was already happening. It was another reason it took me years to leave.

Once I told him I was done, he punched and broke some of my belongings. One day, I walked out during an argument to go to work, and he followed me in his car: "Just stay home and let's deal with this! Don't leave!" I became terrified of my safety and his. *This is out of control. Someone is going to get hurt.*

I was helpless—hopeless. I couldn't trust my environment. I had nowhere to retreat; the house was my prison. I was drained, scared, and numb—survival mode. *You need to get out.*

I wanted to protect important documents and items. One day while he was gone, I paid for a storage unit for 30 days and put some of my belongings in there. If I needed to walk away, I could breathe knowing some things were untouchable. I knew there was no turning back after I took that step. I was on the path to freedom.

Only a few close friends and my therapist knew what was going on. Not even my family knew. They accepted John like a son, and I tried to protect him for a long time. But sitting there on my birthday, in my soul, I knew: *It's time to protect me.*

I saw clearly that staying calm around high emotions and not getting hooked on irrational arguments was my superpower, something that developed over time as a way to protect myself. I no longer had to accept that kind of behavior as my reality in intimate relationships, in a context where I desired to be cared for and loved.

Deciding to leave is *hard*. Figuring out how can be terrifying. You may be scared about how you will get through it, what others might think or say, or what is next. You may even feel frozen or paralyzed, like a frozen lake. When you start to realize you need to get out, that ice starts to crack and thaw. You receive movement and sensation back into your body, just like the fluid-moving water under the surface, no longer bound up, rigid, and fragile. You can now move and flow, feeling the signals of the body guiding you toward your next steps.

*not his real name

THE TOOL

Creating a thorough safety plan as you leave an abusive relationship can save your life. It's also vital for your own empowerment and deeply nourishing to your nervous system as it undergoes significant change.

The steps you need to take will vary depending on the unique circumstances of your relationship. In my situation, securing a storage unit for 30 days was a relief, knowing my valuables would be safe, and if I needed to leave immediately, I'd have access to those things when needed.

It wasn't until after I left the relationship and started working with a domestic violence program that I learned about all the resources available, ones that may have helped me to leave sooner. For example, you may be entitled to break a lease early if there is domestic violence. Or depending on your employment, you may be allowed to take a leave of absence to seek shelter or find safety.

Use the following recommendations as a way to start thinking about how you can leave safely.

Planning ahead

Create a new email address. You'll want a secure way to communicate with those closest to you where conversations won't be monitored. If you're looking into new places to live or need to save receipts or reservations, having an account of your own will be crucial.

Tell someone you trust. It can feel scary, embarrassing, or shameful to tell others about your abusive relationship, but confiding in someone who can check in on you and make sure you are safe each step of the way could be life-saving. Choose someone who wouldn't be likely to share information about you or be manipulated by the abuser. Write down contact information somewhere safe. Create a code word you can use to alert them that you're in danger.

Identify some places you could go on short notice. This may be a friend's house, a family member's home, a hotel, or a domestic violence shelter.

Gather your valuables, including documents. Pack a bag with essential items (ID, passport, birth certificates, etc.), money, medications, some clothes, and other important documents (tax returns and bank statements). Place this bag somewhere hidden but accessible, perhaps in the trunk of your car or closet. If you have a restraining order, keep a copy on you. Take out cash if you need a way for expenses to be untraceable.

Taking Action

Plan the best time to leave when the abuser isn't present or planning to be away for a longer period.

Make arrangements for any animals that need care. Some animal shelters offer temporary foster arrangements to help you during a transition.

Be careful about posting on social media. Remember that all computer and online activity can be monitored. Consider using a public computer at a library, internet cafe, or trusted friend's house. If you think your abuser has access to your iCloud or location on your phone, turn off the location before leaving.

Find support. Not everyone will understand the courage it takes to leave an abusive relationship. Some may wonder why you waited as long as you did, some might want to place blame, and others may tell you what you need or should be doing. Find what works for you. If something doesn't feel right, it's okay to take space to get what you need.

Find a therapist who is knowledgeable about abusive relationships, or locate a local support group for survivors. You may find Domestic

Violence educational groups valuable as a way to make sense of what has happened. Many of the options available can be low-cost or free.

If you have children:

Consult with an attorney to find out how to be protected. In certain instances, a Good Cause report can be filed, which may protect you from being charged with kidnapping. If appropriate, notify your children's school. If you decide to go to a shelter, they may be able to enroll your children in school so they don't fall behind. Make sure your children know how to call 911.

When you are planning to leave an unsafe situation, being practical and taking action is prioritized. Oftentimes, during an abusive period, we can go into survival mode, navigating each interaction as safely as possible, which leaves very little room to process what is happening on an emotional level.

It's not uncommon that once you're away from the abuse and abuser, the emotional experience catches up. If you start to have trouble sleeping, trouble focusing, memory problems, body aches, irritability, labile mood, changes in appetite, or other symptoms, your body is telling you it's okay to let it out, everything you have restricted to stay safe. If you start to notice a change in how you feel or your ability to function, please seek out help. Talk to your doctor or a counselor who can guide you through this transition.

Trust your instincts during this process. Creating and following a safety plan can significantly increase the chances of leaving an abusive relationship safely and beginning the journey toward healing and independence.

For immediate resources, contact the National Domestic Violence Hotline at 1-800-799-SAFE (7233).

Tiffany Thomas is a Licensed Marriage and Family Therapist as well as a Certified Drug and Alcohol Counselor with over 12 years of experience. Tiffany's journey in the addiction field led her to delve deeper into understanding the root causes of human behavior.

With a Bachelor's Degree in Human Services and a Master's in Clinical Psychology earned in 2018, Tiffany's expertise spans various levels of care within the substance use field, including detox, residential, and sober living. She seized the opportunity to broaden her horizons by working with survivors of Domestic Violence and developing trauma-informed care programs.

Tiffany is not only a dedicated clinician but also a mentor, providing clinical supervision to pre-licensed clinicians and crafting training programs on diverse topics. Her passion lies in community outreach, where she educates others on supporting loved ones dealing with Domestic Violence/Intimate Partner Violence and Substance Use.

In her private practice based in Los Angeles, Tiffany specializes in substance use, grief and loss, and interpersonal conflict. She envisions a world where people prioritize self-care and reconnect with their true purpose for a fulfilling and joyful life. Tiffany firmly believes that our relationships with ourselves and the world around us profoundly influence our sense of fulfillment.

Beyond her professional commitments, Tiffany enjoys a vibrant life, participating in soccer, exploring local and international destinations, hiking, and auditioning for exciting game show opportunities.

Connect with Tiffany:

www.tiffany-thomas.com

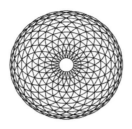

Limiting beliefs are like anchors we've unconsciously
tied to ourselves along life's journey. By being brave and letting
go of these anchors with healing rhythmic movement,
we open ourselves up to endless possibilities where
true potential awaits, ready to be embraced and unleashed.

~ Jane Ann Guyette

CHAPTER 19

ECSTATIC TRANCE

HEALING RHYTHMIC MOVEMENT TO DISPEL LIMITING BELIEFS

Jane Ann Guyette, CHt.

MY STORY

Rock-a-bye Baby in the treetop.

Why did we ever stop?

When babies cry, we rock, pat, and bounce them gently. When we rock our babies, we move with them to soothe them. When we move or rock our bodies, like babies, it soothes our souls; when we soothe our souls, we heal from the inside out.

The simplicity and effectiveness of rocking babies to soothe them remains timeless and universal. It's like a universal code that speaks directly to the baby's soul saying, "Relax, little one, everything is going to be alright."

About 21 years ago, we welcomed our daughter from India. Amidst the whirlpool of emotions accompanying our journey to India after years of applying and waiting, we were stressed, overwhelmed, and tired by the whole experience. The emotional and physical strain weighed heavily on us. Despite our initial apprehension, whenever we were exasperated, grandmotherly women would notice and just come up and hold their arms out to us, offering to hold our baby so we could eat and rest a moment. At first, I thought they were trying to take her, as we stuck out like a sore thumb with our pale, clueless tourist vibes. They rocked, patted, and bounced our sweet girl and insisted we eat while we could.

Movement is our body's first form of communication before we can talk, and our sweet little one needed constant rhythmic movement, to heal and transition.

The flight back home was quite amusing as we treated the entire airplane to an olfactory adventure as our daughter had explosive diarrhea. It was like being in a Dutch oven at 3000 feet for 11 hours. I'm pretty sure the pilot considered an emergency landing to escape the smell, but, hey, shit happens.

We finally deplaned, and the movement of people helped disperse and dispel the lingering scent. Scent is also energy, and just like we shook off that foul smell by leaving the plane, we can also shake off negative energy and feelings within ourselves.

"To be still is to be stagnant; to move is to evolve."
~ E'yen A. Gardner

Movement creates energy, and energy never dies; it's transferred from one place to another. What if you could kick those negative limiting beliefs to the curb with funky dance moves or channel your inner Taylor Swift and "shake it off."

You can shake it off!

Not flippantly like your parents told you to shake it off, but we can wholeheartedly shake off limiting beliefs, self-doubt, fear, shame, negative self-talk, past mistakes, and anything else that holds us back. Embrace your full potential by letting go and moving forward with renewed energy and confidence, like a dog shaking off water after a swim.

Movement heals by making us feel vulnerable, then empowered, and eventually transformed.

Rhythmic movement physiologically changes the brain. It affects the parts involved in communication, attention regulation, memory retention, and, most importantly, depression, body image issues, and anxiety.

Rhythmic movement also connects your body and your emotions. We can get so in our heads that it's nearly impossible to get it out with just words. We live in a world where the pace is getting faster and faster. It's time to slow down, and instead of controlling your body, let your body do its thing and release all those negative feelings, images, thoughts, emotions, and sensations.

Crossbody movements play a fascinating role in brain rewiring by fostering communication between the left and right hemispheres. When you engage in activities involving crossing the midline of your body, like reaching your left hand to touch your right shoulder, you stimulate neural connections that enhance coordination and cognitive function. This promotes brain plasticity, allowing the brain to adapt and reorganize itself, resulting in improved motor skills, cognitive flexibility, and emotional regulation. Regular practice of crossbody movements can lead to a healthier and more interconnected brain.

Imagination and visualization also play an important role. The concept of mentally rehearsing exercise provides benefits similar to actually performing it and is supported by several neuroscience and sports psychology studies. One prominent study by researchers at the Cleveland Clinic Foundation found that people who visualize themselves exercising could increase their muscle strength by up to 35%. While visualization alone cannot replace physical exercise entirely, it can significantly complement physical training and provide noticeable benefits.

According to the National Institute of Mental Health, 46.4% of adults in the US will experience some sort of mental health issue during their lifetime.

A deluge of confusion floods over me. All I can see is bright white light. *Oh my, where am I? Is this the other side?*

I try to speak, but nothing comes out.

I'm right here! They can't hear me. They seem concerned and walk out as I'm screaming.

Hey, don't leave.

I'm adrift, unsure of who I am or how I got here. Fear grips me, and I feel like a fish struggling to swim upstream. Once again, I took a long, lonely journey into the depths of my jumbled brain.

As I look around, the only thing I can move is my eyes.

I'm alone.

I faintly hear someone talking, but it sounds like a foreign language. My body wants to move, but it feels like I'm paralyzed. I want to move my body, but nothing's happening. I'm aware that I can move my eyes, and looking from side to side has started to cause tingling in my fingers and toes. I realize the rhythmic movement is particularly effective and that is so reassuring. Now, my mouth can move, but no words are coming out—only mumbles and groans. Throughout all of this, I feel my heart pounding loudly like it wants to burst right out of my chest. A while later, words begin to come, and feelings return to my body. I still don't know who I am or what happened.

"Do you know where you are?" someone asks. I don't. "Do you know your mother's name?" Nothing.

More time passed, and I was told I had grand mal seizures that they couldn't stop. Several medications were tried to no avail, and six hours later, my body just quit once drained of its energy reserves.

That made me think about how energy moves. As tired as I was, I wanted to move my body. I *needed* to move my body. Movement possesses the incredible ability to revitalize the body, mind, and spirit. When my body was seizing, I wondered: *Is there something lurking within that needs to be shaken out, washed away, or gotten rid of?*

> *"Movement is a medicine for creating change in a person's physical, emotional, and mental states."*
> ~ Carol Welch

This was not my first trip to the ER for seizures. In the past, following such an intense seizure, I was hospitalized for five days, and recovery took about six weeks. Gran Mal seizures take as much energy and the same amount of stress as running a marathon. This time, I was able to leave within 24 hours after an EEG was performed to be sure my brain was okay. During the EEG, they had me breathe deeply like I was running up a hill for three minutes consistently. During the breathing exercise, I was to move my eyes from left to right and sometimes up and down. While doing this I noticed a healing feeling in my brain that I can't exactly explain. It felt like sand sifting and shifting, rewiring, renewing, and restoring areas of my brain. A part of me, maybe my higher self, told me I had a new tool to use to heal—movement. I knew somewhere deep down that some part of me could speed up the healing process.

Starting afresh, well-versed in the journey ahead, I have a powerful tool that promises to accelerate my healing and release deep-seated trauma. I've discovered rhythmic movement is incredibly beneficial, so I am embracing rhythmic movement and music to heal. Because, let's face it, who doesn't want to shake it off and bust a move when life gets a bit too serious?

Whether it's writing, dancing, or just flailing around, if it makes you feel good and brings you joy, then movement is your body's reset button.

When my body felt like it was staging a mutiny, I knew it was time to break out my moves and show it who was boss. I'm not a good dancer and often compared to Elaine from *Seinfeld*, so I usually dance alone or pretend no one is watching. I have a little dance party, giving my inner sloth a wake-up call, telling it to hit the road. I find inspiration and motivation in drumming and trance-like music. It's my musical, magical potion that transports me into an "Ecstatic Trance."

What is your magic elixir of music and movement that gets you into the zone? Music is universal, but even a simple metronome can work wonders, tapping into that hypnotic rhythm that gets you in the zone. The only rule is to let go and groove to the beat.

With each rhythmic healing step, I sense the transformative magic of movement, from short strolls to lengthier walks. Guided by the rhythm of music, I'm drawn into my body, each step a catalyst for healing. Immersed in the dance of music and movement, I slip into a state of ecstatic trance, where healing vibrations penetrate every fiber of my being, soothing my soul and igniting a profound sense of renewal.

"Change happens through movement and movement heals."
~ Joseph Pilates

Mid-life crisis sucks!

I only started having seizures as a result of the stress due to infidelity in a 30-year marriage. I never had them before and haven't had them since my divorce.

I saw the signs and patterns repeating; I knew in my "knower," as many women do, that something wasn't right. Instead of trusting my gut and leaving, I decided to do what a good mother would do and stay for the children to make it work. We did counseling retreats and couples therapy, but his behavior didn't change, and having the person I loved the most in the world lie to me repeatedly was more than I could bear. After years of denial, depression, and heartache, my body finally gave up and started seizing. In that moment of despair, the seizures shook my world to the core, igniting a powerful awakening within me. Those turbulent years marked by betrayal and inner turmoil were undoubtedly the hardest times of my life.

Through our trials, we discover resilience, strength, and the profound truth that, sometimes, the greatest upheavals pave the way for the most profound revelations and transformations.

I realize every situation or relationship we go through teaches us that past experiences don't define our worth. Whether it's abandonment or neglect, relationships and situations help us realize our intrinsic value, inspire us to embrace our potential, and move forward with confidence.

We attract the people, places, and circumstances needed in our lives to become aware of and gently acknowledge and transform negative patterns and perspectives. Then, we can navigate away from victimhood and embrace the current of empowerment. Sometimes, the most powerful thing we can do is to walk away, but you have to be in a place to know your worth and value so you have the strength, wisdom, and support to do it.

Surround yourselves with people who support and encourage your health, well-being, and growth. Ultimately, it's up to us to take responsibility for our happiness and well-being so we no longer succumb to the lure of those willing to reinforce our belief in victimhood.

By seeking out positive influences and actively changing our mindset, we can attract more positive experiences, people, and opportunities into our lives. The key is to learn from our experiences, accept them for what they are, and, if they align with our preferences, embrace them. If the experiences don't align with our preferences, it's important to let them go and move on. Shake off what no longer serves you and make room for what does.

We're here to be human mirrors for each other and to discover more of who we are, individually and collectively.

One of the most powerful ways to discover more about yourself is with hypnosis. My favorite form is ecstatic trance, and I love it. It's all about rhythmic movement and blending the meditative aspects of hypnosis with the expressive freedom of movement.

When we think of hypnosis, many of us have images of Marvel supervillains and Kaa the snake from Disney's *Jungle Book*, but far from the swirling eyes and zombie-like mind control that we tend to associate with it, hypnosis involves transporting people into a state of intense focus or what I call ecstatic trance. The trance state is attained through rhythmic movement and focuses on solutions, empowering individuals to make positive, productive lifestyle changes.

In my hypnotherapy practice, I've seen a trend,
people cling to their limiting habits until the very end.
Sometimes it takes things falling apart,
to find the courage and know-how, to make a new start.
When things hit rock bottom they finally see,
It's time to move and change and set themselves free.

Movement can help us reach an ecstatic state of trance. Many cultures use dance and movement to enter this trance state, allowing them to set intentions for personal transformation, community change, and even global impact. Some examples are:

Sufi Whirling music: In Sufi ceremonies, music accompanies the spinning dance known as Sufi whirling to induce a meditative and trance-like state.

Pow-wows: Healing is indeed a key aspect of American Indian pow-wows. The traditional dances and songs performed and the sharing of stories help heal past traumas and strengthen cultural identity. They provide a space for support, understanding, and solidarity.

Djembe Drumming: Originating from West Africa, among the Manteca and Malinka people, drumming is known for its energetic rhythms and communal dancing, which can lead to trancelike states.

Didgeridoo Music: Indigenous to Australia, the didgeridoo is often used in Aboriginal ceremonies. Its low resonant tones and rhythmic patterns can induce altered states of consciousness during ritual dances. Just to name a few.

The beauty of movement and music is that they transcend age, ability, and physical limitations. They offer a universal language of expression and healing that anyone can tap into regardless of circumstances. Movement encompasses a wide range of activities, from simple gestures like eye movements to intense physical workouts. So, whether it's gentle stretches, a brisk walk, or an intense workout, every rhythmic movement contributes to our overall well-being and vitality.

Ecstatic Trance is not about the performance as much as it is about presence. It's about being fully present in your body, solely focused on yourself. Surrender to the healing flow of movement and music, sync with the rhythm, and become one with the beat.

THE TOOL

Ecstatic Trance

Never do this while driving a car or operating heavy machinery.

- Create a space where you can move freely without obstacles or interruptions. Set up a welcoming environment that enables you to fully engage in your movements and focus on the sensations and rhythms of your body.

- Start slowly with at least three deep letting go breaths to prepare the body and mind.

- Find some music that resonates with your soul. I prefer music with no words, but use whatever gets you in the mood to move and groove.

- Set an intention for what you want to receive from this healing movement and write it down three times.

- I usually use a sentence like; I desire, or I deserve_____ (fill in the blank with a positive statement). Use powerful words that focus on the solution you desire.

- Repeat the intention three times, either out loud or in your head.

- Now, move to the rhythm and listen to your body and how it feels as you move. Are there aches and pains? Discomfort? Do a mental scan from the top of your head to the tips of your toes, looking for any negative feelings, images, thoughts, emotions, or sensations that are stuck.

- Next, visualize the tension melting away as you exhale, releasing tension and tightness, flowing out of you like a gentle stream. With each breath, let your intention guide the energy, allowing it to flow freely through your body, releasing any blockages and restoring harmony. Gradually increase the rhythmic movement to a level that feels comfortable and manageable. Listen to your body and adjust the intensity of your movements based on your capabilities. By gradually building up the pace or intensity, you can challenge yourself while remaining within your limits and avoiding strain or injury. Find a flow that suits your fitness level and allows you to move easily and enjoyably. Perhaps, as I do, start with just eye movements, or maybe you thrive on intense exercise and adrenaline; finding the rhythmic movement takes your healing workout to a new level.

- Enjoy yourself and have fun while moving your body! Let go of any stress or expectations and focus on the joy of moving. Embrace the moment, and let yourself feel the pleasure of being active and moving your body.

- Be brave and try something new. Move to stay alive. The more you move, the longer you live.

"You can do anything you put your mind to"
~ Benjamin Franklin

Hypnosis extensively incorporates rhythmic movement and visualization to assist individuals in various areas, including enhancing sports performance, achieving weight loss goals, regaining lost senses, overcoming fears or phobias, and improving overall health and well-being. Hypnosis can help individuals tap into their subconscious mind to create positive changes and achieve their desired outcomes. If the idea of hypnosis and ecstatic trance speaks to you, let's embark on a journey together into the depths of your subconscious mind, exploring endless possibilities. I'm here to support you as we delve into the transformative experience, embracing the adventure that awaits in the realm of Ecstatic Trance.

Jane Ann Guyette is a certified hypnotherapist at Alive2Thrive Hypnosis, a best-selling author, dietitian, personal trainer, yoga and exercise class instructor, and Reiki Master.

She is a certified clinical hypnotherapist with extensive training and experience, specializing in self-hypnosis, weight management, anxiety control, and helping people find their purpose.

Her approach is genuinely transformative. By merging her intuitive abilities with hypnosis techniques, she guides people toward profound alignment of the body, mind, and soul for lasting transformation.

Jane is a graduate of the Clinical Hypnosis Institute of Michigan and a member of the Clinical Hypnosis Professional Group and the Michigan Hypnosis Guild. She presented on Heart Healing Hypnosis at the Michigan Hypnosis Conference 2023.

Jane owns and works as a clinical hypnotherapist at Alive2Thrive Hypnosis, in person and online.

She received her dietetics degree from the University of Wisconsin Stevens Point and has always been interested in whole health, including body, heart, mind, and soul.

Previously, she worked as a clinical dietitian at Henry Ford Allegiance (Foote Hospital), was a manager of employee wellness programs, and managed fitness centers. She is a great motivator and an expert hypnotherapist specializing in helping people make positive, productive lifestyle changes. Hypnosis is her passion while guiding clients to align their intentions and actions is her mission. Change your mind, change your life! Empower yourself and reach your goals! Your success is her mission.

Connect with Jane:

Email: Alive2thrivehypnosis@gmail.com

Website: Alive2ThriveHypnosis.com

Facebook: Alive2Thrive@intuitivejane

Youtube: Alive2Thrive InAbundance

Instagram: jane_trosin_

TikTok: Alive2Thrive@alive_2_thrive

Free self-hypnosis video: https://bit.ly/Janesself-hypnosis

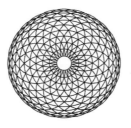

Understanding the difference between moments of personal courage and what others perceive it as is essential.

~ T.L. Woodliff

CHAPTER 20

OTHERS CALLED ME BRAVE, BUT...

HOW SACRED DANCE REVEALED MY TRUE FEAR

T.L. Woodliff

MY STORY

I hugged the mother of the man who killed my child.

That sounds like a profound moment of bravery, doesn't it? To walk across a courtroom aisle as everyone rises, exhausted, shoulders slumping as the weight accumulated through months of anger and worry is allowed release with the final sentencing; to sidestep through a sea of her family and friends—all there to support the killer—and reach out, turn her to face me, and wrap my arms around this woman I'd never met.

Brave.

The shock on her face is something I'll never forget, nor the soft moan of deep grief and guilt at the sight of me up close, inches away. We'd only glimpsed one another across crowded courtrooms or packed hallways. We didn't meet during the long hours spent in the hospital because only her son survived the carnage he'd created. Only she was gifted the chance to comfort her broken child after his DUI.

"How brave," some whispered. I heard them. Some part of my brain accepted the title. Whatever I felt in that moment must be *at least a part* of what it means to be brave. Right?

People called me brave when I reached out to sacred singers in Poland and asked if they'd visit the U.S. to share their magic in workshops, even though I'd never organized a tour of any sort, never dealt with the nightmare of visas and taxes or the hurdle of advertising such a unique experience.

"You're so brave. I wouldn't have the nerve to even write them." And again, I accepted the title. *This is what it means to be brave.*

Yet when the hallway of the gangplank shrunk right before my eyes as I tried to board a cruise ship for a getaway with my husband, the thought—*be brave*—felt utterly alien. Where was my reserve to boldly go forward? *That's what I do, isn't it? It's who I am. Everyone says I'm brave.*

I'd had bouts with claustrophobia in the past, but it never impacted my life. This time, I couldn't get on that damn ship. And it grew worse. Being in the car with someone else driving became a battle between my will and my tingling fingertips to open the door. Road trips, which we love to take, became exhausting. I was a tight string, and my husband's words of encouragement were met with a discorded snap. I needed to change.

Psychiatrist. Drugs. Hypnosis. Spiritual counseling. Sound healing. Meditation. More hypnosis.

"If we can find the root of it, you'll be free." But then again, maybe not. Claustrophobia has a genetic component for some—a hereditary trait that primes this pump of fear: *GPm6a*, a very unhelpful stress-regulated neuronal protein that causes claustrophobia. And it's hereditary.

Adding to that, the literal size of the amygdala is a part of the equation. Then mix in childhood trauma and the evolutionary benefits of fear—*Ugh.*

But I beat it. Twice. However, this phobia can return when events aren't repeated regularly for exposure. And the so-called "root cause" may be misidentified because the roots have twined together with a hundred events along with the genetic predisposition.

Plus, the rarely recognized ingredient of praise: a hundred moments of accepting the definitions of others. *You're so brave.*

You may ask, how can others calling you brave affect your actions? Ask a hundred people what it means, and you'll receive a hundred definitions.

We now know that if you say to a child, "You are so smart!" it may harm them. Yet, praise is intuitive—you want to encourage them and let them know you're proud. However, when the child later encounters problems they can't easily answer, they don't think it's this new problem that's at issue. They think:

"It's me. I'm not smart after all."

"They're all wrong."

Fraud.

This leads to avoiding anything that challenges self-worth.

We've learned that praising the *effort to find* the answer is better than focusing on some hidden measure of intelligence. This builds the belief that if you don't reach the answer in one way, you can try a different route—explore, learn, and try again. Instead of, "How smart you are!" we focus on, "I like how you figured it out!"

Being brave is the same thing. Understanding the difference between moments of *personal courage* and what *others* perceive it as is essential.

My claustrophobia has roots in many things. I was hit by a truck when I was six years old. I spent weeks in traction, flat on my back in a bed with one leg lifted in a metal contraption tied to the ceiling with constant reminders voiced each day:

"Don't move, Sissy. Be still," Mom whispered.

"You won't heal if you squirm, young lady," said the nurse.

"Quit wiggling your toes," snapped the doctor.

This was followed by months in a body cast stretching from my toes to my chest. And my childish mind said, "Don't move. Don't eat. You'll break the cast and have to start all over."

The hypnotists and psychiatrist (and me!) believed the debilitating claustrophobia primarily stemmed from the loss of my daughter, Yvonne. I had sharp moments of clarity working with both modalities. When I'm in a machine, be it an elevator, an MRI, as a passenger in a car, or flying, I can't escape to quickly reach my surviving children if they need me.

I need to be able to leave at any second!

I did the work. Exposure therapy works best for most people, including me. I rode up and down a tiny elevator four times a day for an entire month. You can't get more exposure than that.

Fast forward a few years. I hadn't been in one in ages. Without a second thought, I boarded one to check out a new office space. Yet when the doors closed, my eyes widened, and I clawed at the metal frames, trying to open them. By the time I reached the third floor, I was close to passing out. The panic was so sharp I hadn't even considered the panel of buttons right next to the door.

What. The. Hell. I already conquered this! Didn't I?

I dove deep, wanting to know more about how the mind recreates such fear. It was part of why I returned to school to earn my MS in psychology. I also earned certifications in healing therapies.

Still, it was a back-and-forth of conquering and backsliding, again and again.

Then, I decided I needed to isolate for a few weeks. I headed to Utah and visited the desolate wilderness of Coyote Buttes. Alone. I *adore* long drives and solo hikes. I stood on a bluff overlooking wild stone canyons with no sign of life in any direction for miles. It remains one of my most treasured memories.

That evening, I called a friend and tried to explain the wonder of such an experience. "I can't believe you did that. You're so brave to hike alone in a wilderness," she said.

After I put down the phone, I thought about those words. I went for a walk and pondered why they stayed with me. "You're so brave." I took a long bath, and the words kept circling.

I reread the research on the use of praise with children. Had the praise—brave—affected me the same way? I'm not a child developing a learning system. But had my understanding of what it means to be brave, and thus, how to overcome fear, been skewed by how I internalized such praise?

I know there is real magic when a human puts a pen in hand and writes. I decided to begin there. I picked three instances where people called me brave. I listed their name and summarized my feelings about the word *brave* being applied to the event.

Colleen = False

Amy = Ha!

Laury = Fraud

Ouch. Even I could see I was being too harsh with myself. But why? I walked with it. Darwin, Jung, and other great thinkers claimed their most powerful insights came when they walked in nature to ponder a thought. It's a powerful modality for clarity. But I had been walking for days.

I decided to switch things up. When I owned a dance studio, I'd taught a group of women a six-week chakra dance class, which somehow morphed into something more that lasted years. I combined my guiding voice with segments of free movement, group dance, and energy exchange.

One of the simplest and yet most profound exercises I created was to take a single focus and combine it with powerful music (innate human art form) as I crafted a story (innate humane art form) and dance (innate human art form.)

I hope you see the thread here. Our current society believes only a chosen few can sing, write, or dance. But these are a part of the human experience and belong to all of us! We intuitively created this combination because we were instinctively moving to heal ourselves in a group environment. Such ageless tools of healing arose around the globe.

I needed those tools once more. I chose powerful music. I lowered the lights to ritualize the space with candles and stones. I returned to my journal to explore one of the events that caused me to be so harsh with myself, the one where I wrote *false*: **I was brave when I hugged Mrs. Jones in the courtroom.**

I moved to the center of the sacred space I'd created and allowed myself to sink back into the feelings of the courtroom, to visualize the crowded space, the judge standing up to leave, the guards making the prisoners rise—all of it.

At first, I could only sway, my arms wrapped tightly around my core. Then, my right arm stretched to my left shoulder to cover my heart. *Brave*, I thought. But no. There was nothing about bravery in that moment.

I stood up and crossed that aisle because I saw a mother's face contorted with pain, with despair—an inability to accept this harsh, new reality. I saw in her face all the things I felt.

I was not brave. I visualized my friend saying those words to me. I understood at once that I was just a mirror. When she said those words, she was trying to see herself in my situation. *She* perceived it as a moment of bravery. But I understood as I swayed and then moved with greater freedom, allowing the music and the visualization to claim me; I had given her a glance at an experience she'd never had. I was the mirror in which she sought to see herself in my shoes.

In such moments of significant loss, it's common for people to offer extreme grace. Both my husband and I remarked on how everyday losses we all see, such as a dead animal on the side of the road, seemed to take on profound significance. Watching the news hurt. Seeing others in pain—anyone—felt wrong.

The word *brave* at that moment did not belong to me. I was simply in that state of grace that comes with profound loss.

I did this again over the next few days: short sessions with a single memory or one session with several experiences, focusing on when people called me brave.

This led me to accept how, in each case, *I was simply a mirror to the world.* No one else can see through my experiences. I could now release such praise. Without a doubt, I knew I'd perceive those words in the future as no more than a reflection of the speaker.

But that left me with a challenging question: What *is* bravery—to me?

I wrote down all the times fear caused me to change my course of action. But at the top, I wrote: *Fear Is Vital For Life. It's How We Evolved* in bold, all-cap letters. I made it more than just a heading. Women's intuition has saved more than one life. My ancestors jumped away from slithering things and survived. (Those who didn't jump didn't live to leave their DNA behind.) I was done with being cruel to myself.

*Cruise ship *Elevator *Car ride

I knew at once these were too vague.

*Door closing *Door closing *Door closing

Oh.

I danced *door closing* and the tears flowed! *Whoa.* I had no control over the door closing on my life with my daughter, Yvonne. I had no way of forcing that door to open again.

Then, I danced *control* and felt as helpless as a dandelion in a thunderstorm. Helpless. No control. Door closed. I lay on the ground and cried, and I realized in that raw moment what *bravery means to me: to look forward to opening a new door,* to be happy and excited for new experiences, and to embrace the idea of total and complete joy being available to me.

All of which felt disloyal and dishonest.

In this last year, I've tried to share my journey of dealing with the loss of my beautiful girl. I hit a roadblock while creating a video about the tools I used to step back into life after the loss. Hard stop.

So, I repeated the sacred dance and stepped into the circle with that one feeling. Once more, the word *disloyal* sprang out. Loyalty and justice are *huge* morals to me. Our morals shape our identity, so seeing this, I knew I was looking at a core belief. As I danced, it came to me: To be deeply happy after her death is to be disloyal.

Whew.

Okay. This is my starting point. A core belief has become tangled in pain. I need to dive into all the roots of loyalty and claim how they've shaped me. It's the start of my new journey. Doors open. *This is where I begin.*

My husband and I recently took a short road trip. The car door closing didn't bother me, and his being the driver didn't cause my fingertips to itch with a need to escape. I knew then that I had found my starting point on the journey to truly healing.

THE TOOL

Mixing the magic that occurs when the hand meets paper with the compelling recipe of music, poetry, and movement in a sacred space utilizes potent healing modalities humans have used for tens of thousands of years.

1. Create a sacred space. Ritualize the experience by giving it the focused, loving intention you would offer others: take a cleansing bath with Epsom salts, light candles, make sure you won't be disturbed, and use bells or scents to cleanse the area.

2. Play music that sings to your soul. Don't rush the choosing! Music you love may feel different when you are *in the moment*. As you move about the space to light the candles or cleanse, sample different songs and go with one that increases the feeling of *sacred*.

3. Choose three moments when others called you brave and add the equal (=) sign. It doesn't matter how big or small the moment. The fact that it comes to mind means it's been circling in your thoughts. Think of the event and write one word to sum it up. You might use a name, like I did. *Colleen* = ___. Or choose the actual event. For example, write *Stage* = _____ if the event was about singing or speaking in public.

   Visualize everything about the moment. Recall the humidity in the room. What sounds were most prominent? Where were other people standing or moving about? What shoes were you wearing? Add as many details as you can.

   Then say to yourself: *I was so brave*. Without pausing, write one word or symbol to summarize how it feels to define the moment as brave. For me, one answer was *ha!*—a laughable thought. I answered with exclamation points when the feeling rang true: !!!

4. Now, move to the center with the first response that *didn't* ring true. Allow your body to rock, then add arms and swaying movements of the head, hips, and chest as you utilize your body to link the emotions of that moment with the music. Sink into the memory and allow your body to express the truth. I did this for about three to five minutes, but you may want more or less time.

5. Write without pause for five minutes. My first false statement concerned being brave in the courtroom. Since it wasn't about bravery, what was it? I wrote extensively about what I saw in Mrs. Jones's face and body language and how it affected me. Another false statement was that I felt brave when traveling solo. Nope, not bravery. Adventure! I wrote about the freedoms of driving and seeing this beautiful country up close and in person. While I didn't define these as *brave*, I found joy in my unique personality.

   This is important. Even as I accepted that an act wasn't courageous, not to me, I often acknowledged a nifty aspect of who I am. This exercise helped remove a lot of harsh self-criticism. Spend as much time on this as you can. You may wish to stop here for a few days and bask in your own wonderful and unique juju.

6. Now, it's time to tackle the moments of fear. Write at the top of a new page: *Fear Is Vital For Life. It's How We Evolved* in bold, all-cap letters. Your goal is to explore how your unique sense of evolutionary-driven fear is adapting to your modern life.

   Dig down and be specific. I started with *car ride* but whittled it down to *door closing*, then *control*, until finally, *disloyal*. You may need to keep whittling to find the reason fear took control.

7. Look for similarities. That's the goal here: find what links them. Then, reread that heading, set aside judgment, and return to the center to dance.

This is your new starting point.

Terran Woodliff is a writer and spirit-dance facilitator. She has a BA in Literature and an MS in Applied Psychology. She is a priestess of the nature-based spiritual path Vega's Path Priestess Process, which focuses on archetypical energies combined with the power and beauty of the natural world. She is also a certified Farland Fiction Writing Coach and has co-facilitated writing groups and workshops for many years.

Alongside Dr. Ruth Souther and Stephanie Urbina Jones, she co-facilitates *Alchemy: A New Earth Priestess Mystery School*. She crafts handmade Burn Books to ritualize release, change, or reclaim life, along with handcrafted grimoire and journaling pens.

As an author, she publishes fiction stories, such as *Grimoires of the Galerè*, and writing support, such as *Assess Your Writing From The Inside Out*.

She is a contributing author and board member of Crystal Heart Imprints, an independent cooperative press that supports and guides authors in their individual creative projects and fun anthologies, such as *Mystic Memoirs*.

Examples of powerful music used in spirit dancing are linked on her website: https://themysticspen.com/

Contact Terran to facilitate Burn Book rituals or Dance Journaling as part of your next event: Terran@TLWoodliff.com

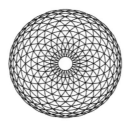

Family generations—God's gift to reteach us about the simplicity, wonder, beauty and continuity of life.

~ Barbara E. Hanley

CHAPTER 21

EMO SAGE SPEAKS!
COMMONALITIES ACROSS THE GENERATIONS

Barbara E. Hanley, PhD, RN

MY STORY

My 19-year-old granddaughter, Angela, gifted me with a sketch she drew. There were two figures surrounded by bright red stars. Upper left was Angela, a full-body tall figure dressed in black jeans wearing a tee shirt with the letters M, C, R, and a shock of dark curls with a splash of red covering most of her face, revealing only the right eye and cheek. She labeled herself "Me (emo)." Down to the right was me, only it was me from just my chest up, smiling, granny glasses and pearl necklace, sticking out of the ground. I was labeled "You!! (emo in spirit)." In addition to us, there were two skull heads with crossbones and two Hawaiian peace hand signs.

My immediate response was to request an interpretation of the letters "MCR" on her tee shirt and "emo," and received the following:

"MCR is my favorite band: My Chemical Romance! Emo is a little harder to explain, but not by much. Musically, 'emo' is short for "emotional post-hardcore," a music genre categorized by confessional-style lyrics (they are sad and angry mostly—think angsty teen!) with an upbeat tempo! The first wave emerged in the 90s, and then came the second in the 2000s (where MCR is from!). Some people also consider pop-punk 'emo' (but it's so totally not!). Socially, 'emo' also just refers to people who look and act like me: people who listen to the kinds of music I like are, well, angsty teenagers who wear a lot of black, are sad, and, like, rage against the machine."

How would you react? Do you think it's cute, or do you do a deep dive? I took the dive!

It intrigued me that although our contact was limited, we share no bloodline, and have had limited interaction, she picked up on a core characteristic that we share two generations apart—and 'emo' is a characteristic of Indigo children!

Indigo Children

Angela's message led me to look more closely at our family of 12 young people under the age of 20. I identified three Indigos by exploring their characteristics. *Indigo* is derived from the intensity of the blue in their sixth chakra (third-eye energy center), which extends to all the other chakras, as observed by individuals who perceive colors in the auric field. They also exhibit marked intuition, the major influence of the sixth chakra.

The term 'Indigo children' began receiving public attention about 25 years ago when parents and teachers identified students who seemed different from the norm. Various writers described them as highly individual, rebellious, angry, emo and Goth, truth-sensing, and highly intelligent with rapid thought processing. Other characteristics include intuitiveness, unusual psychic gifts, and wisdom beyond their years. They've been identified as the special children who are here as light workers to help usher in "The Age of Aquarius"—the global energy shift from the Piscean Age, which has been a pattern of control and rigidity, to one of harmony, warmth, and understanding.

While I haven't heard much mention of Indigos recently, in observing my family with myriad grandchildren, nieces, and nephews—the concept came to mind as I viewed the range of personalities. Several of the youngest seem outside the mold with their magnetism, sensitivity, high energy, and IQ. To illustrate, my 27-month-old grandniece, Sophia, attending our Christmas party, spotted my sister's quad cane, picked it up by its protruding straight handle, lifted it onto the large coffee table, climbed up, and started to loudly sing "Frosty the Snowman" into the black handle microphone!

As Indigos enter school settings, restrictions frequently exacerbate many of these characteristics, leading to their disrupting classes, their labeling as ADD or ADHD, and possibly medicating to control them. Further, some students may be labeled as having ODD (Oppositional Defiant Disorder). These patterns challenge both parents and educators.

Sophia's grandfather's experience as a child exemplifies such challenges. My oldest sibling, Bill, had a very difficult time in school, getting poor grades and had no interest in being there—likely ADD before it had a label. As he was drawn to electronics, at age ten, he took apart and fixed our neighbor's console TV, which two repairmen were unable to do. Later, he enrolled in a vocational high school to study electronics. Ten years after graduating, he was the audio engineer who designed, developed, and ran the audio system for Woodstock! He became known as the *Father of Festival Sound* because of his many innovations and the wide scope of his work in that era.

The Duality of Anger

Indigos' personality traits are complex and interactive. They have a fundamental underlying anger born from their frustration with having strong truth—sensing yet having no filter in speaking. They may blurt out first impressions of what is perceived as wrong or unjust, thereby creating problems at home, school, work, and in social situations. However, anger creates energy, and by learning to focus this energy, it can be used to create systemic or social change and to heal physical ailments.

For example, the injustice of Apartheid in South Africa spurred Bill to send audio equipment, facilitating the efficacy of the Anti-Apartheid movement demonstrations; he is still recognized and honored over there.

"Anger is power, and that power either pushes or inspires one to move and get things done quickly and with less effort. When committed to the greater good or help another, the power of anger transmutes into healing energy."[1]

---

1. P.M.H. Atwater, Beyond the Indigo Children (Rochester, VT: Bear and Company, 2005), p.106.

Indigos are born healers. It's instinctive for Indigo children to know how and when to touch when people are ill or injured and may do so spontaneously even with strangers. Many can see energy as well as aura colors. With such gifts, even young children can be taught formal healing energy healing systems or techniques such as Reiki or Therapeutic Touch.

The New Age

The societal change preceding the Indigo awareness was precipitated in the 60s with several movements that revolutionized our culture: the women's movement (including birth control and sexual freedom, pay equity, glass ceiling), anti-poverty, racism, and anti-war activities (Vietnam).

The Broadway musical *Hair*, with its anthem "Age of Aquarius," encapsulated most of these major shifts in the energy of American and world culture.

Astrology is the study of celestial bodies and their energies. Their movements regulate day and night, the transitions of the four seasons, and deeply influence the human psyche, soul, mind, and spirit. The changes in the psyche emerge first and proceed outward to influence the culture.

The Zodiac is an imaginary energetic belt in the cosmos containing the paths of most planets over 12 months. It includes 12 star groups displaying emotional and physical characteristics, divided into four groups denoting birth, maturation, decline, and restoration, as in the four seasons. Each sign also has a symbol denoting a main personality characteristic, such as Taurus' sign of the bull is descriptive of bull-headedness!

This annual movement of the celestial bodies influencing our inner and outer worlds, our moods, and our weather is named for the 12 signs of the Zodiac. There is also a major planetary cycle shifting the energy of the Earth called The Great Year, which reaches completion every 25,920 years. Through complex celestial mechanics, this movement on the Zodiac is toward the West, the opposite of the annual cycle. Both are divided by 12 for the 12 signs of the Zodiac and every 2,160 years, a major energy shift occurs on Earth. Therefore, the Great Zodiac cycle begins with Aries (March, the ram) on the first day of spring and moves backward through Pisces (February, the fishes) to Aquarius (January, the water bearer).[2]

2.Kabir Jaffe and Ritama Davidson, Indigo Adults (Wayne, NJ: New Page Books, 2009), pp.14-15.

Religion and Spirituality

Preceding the Piscean Age, the Arian Age was characterized by first chakra energy of aggression: expansion through will and war; the worship of many gods, and animal (and human) sacrifice in some cultures, leading to God's adoption of the Jews as His chosen people and the Ten Commandments as described in the Old Testament.

The Piscean Age 2160 BC to 0

The seminal change stimulating the transition to the Piscean Age is the birth of Christ and a new personal approach to one's relationship with God, culminating in the creation of a new religion, Christianity, as documented in the New Testament.

As a water sign, Pisces' characteristics focus on feelings and emotions. Operating through the seventh chakra (seat of intuition), it influences religion and spirituality. However, combined with the influences of the second chakra on family and inner child and the love and compassion of the fourth chakra, it allows for an emotionally based spiritual connection rather than an understanding.[3]

The overlap of two ages, as the old is waning and the new is increasing influence, is known as *the cusp*. This period may last from 100 to 200 years as the Aquarian Age energy affects the mood, beliefs, and paradigms, reshaping Piscean thoughts, emotions, and behaviors. Since the 60s these worldwide changes have been reshaping our psychology, religion and spirituality, societal structure, and civilization.

Religion and Spirituality

New Age criticisms of Christianity and Catholicism as overly rigid and controlling reflect how the institutionalization of Christ's message has distorted the breadth of His love message. Catholic Pope Francis is working toward inserting more emphasis on the love message yet is meeting resistance from the old-school orientation of many of the church hierarchy.

A major tenet of Christianity, particularly Catholicism, is that the original sin of Adam and Eve was transmitted to the souls of all their offspring through the generations.

3. Kabir Jaffee & Ritama Davidson, Indigo Adults (Wayne NJ: The Career Press, Inc. 2009), p.16.

The extent of the nascent New Age influence is their rejection of organized religion overall leading to decreased attendance in church services and activities. This is particularly problematic for the Catholic Church as Baptism is required for entry to the Church, participation in the other sacraments, and receiving the Holy Eucharist. Further, rejection of the concept of original sin is reflected in the decrease in Catholics baptizing their offspring.

One role of Indigos is to raise questions and offer interpretations more consistent with souls' desires. They recognize God-presence in each of us and the oneness of all His creation. Therefore, they're looking internally or in nature for spiritual connection.

The decrease in the number of people joining churches and attending their services is indicative of the prevalence of New Age thinking permeating the culture. However, even in this cusp period with its overlap of Piscean 2nd and Aquarian 3rd chakra characteristics, residual Arian warring activity persists around the globe.

THE TOOL

The Aquarian energy shift is propelling each of us forward to recognize, honor, and release our inner EMO. We face the challenge of serving, inspiring, and empowering those in our personal and community spheres. By enhancing our spiritual connections, we can unleash our potential to overcome challenges and achieve extraordinary results for ourselves, our communities, and our world!

I took an even deeper dive into the meaning of EMOS, which, for me, means:

Exceptional

Mastery

Of

Self

The bedrock of personal, religious, and spiritual growth – self-mastery - is meditation, including mindfulness, centered prayer, and meditative exercises such as Yoga, Tai Chi, and Qi Gong. On any level, it provides the quiet space to drop the stresses of our hectic lives and connect with our inner being. We do have the answers. Meditation's companion is gratitude – for our gifts and for the ever-present problems that bespeckle our lives. Gratitude helps us shift focus and reminds us of God's presence within.

One simple meditation technique is to recite this line from Psalm 46:

Be still and know that I AM GOD

Be still and know that I AM

Be still and KNOW

Be STILL

BE…

The stillness at the level of being allows access to inspiration and inner wisdom. Find a comfortable place, quiet your breathing, and try repeating each line 3 times, then stay in this place for whatever time you may have; if possible, 20 or more minutes. Return restored with more clarity and energy, ready to move ahead!

Our first Call To Action is to clarify: *What is my passion?*

Then:

Where and how am I holding back?

How and with whom can I share this?

Take a moment to journal these questions. See where you light up! Use this as a roadmap to action. The insights we gain toward wholeness and the talents we receive aren't meant for us alone. They're meant to be shared!

EMOS–light workers ushering in the Aquarian Age!

REFERENCES

Andres, Lisa. *Indigo Warrior* (Self-published: 2014).

Brisk, *Sasha I Am An Indigo Child – Hear My Words (Bloomington, IN: Balboa Press).*

Virtue, Doreen and Charles Virtue, *Awaken Your Indigo Power* (Hay House Inc., 2016).

Barbara E. Hanley, PhD, RN, FNP, is a retired nurse educator and healer passionate about holistic health care. Committed to promoting wellness at the community level, she obtained an MSN in Community Health at the University of Colorado, Denver. In Tucson, Arizona, she collaborated with a team committed to establishing multicultural primary family care at the University of Arizona-sponsored El Rio Neighborhood Health Center, where she obtained a Certificate as a Family Nurse Practitioner.

Legislative activity related to expanded nursing roles led to her PhD in Nursing at the University of Michigan and 17 years at the University of Maryland School of Nursing, teaching and doing research in the Nursing Health Policy program. To survive doctoral study, she started exploring energy healing and homeopathy. After leaving the university, she spent a year at Foo Yin College of Nursing, Taiwan, teaching Holism in Nursing and Health Care.

Returning to the US, her special interest in death and dying led her to work for 15 years in home hospice nursing.

Parallel to her academic and hospice work, there are two major threads in her life:

1. Continued study of healing modalities, including therapeutic massage and several forms of energy healing: Therapeutic Touch, Chakra Balancing, and the Braided Way with Arlyn Kline, MariEl (a form of Reiki), Usui Reiki Master, and Certification in Practice and Teaching of Multidimensional Healing.

2. Personal and Spiritual Development through Zoetic Workshops, founded by Liora Brunn, a gifted teacher, mentor, and friend. Membership in their leadership group provides her with a tribe of friends whose mission is to bring love and healing to the world.

Residence in a senior living community allows her a platform to continue her healing work in practice and teaching, developing her writing skills – and playing "Grandma and Auntie" with the young ones!

Connect with Barbara:

    Email: Behanley31@gmail.com

    Facebook: Barbara Hanley

    LinkedIn: Barbara Hanley

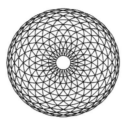

It was a million-mile journey from my head to my heart.

~ R. Scott Holmes

CHAPTER 22

EMBODIED PRESENCE

YOU DON'T NEED TO CHANGE; AWARENESS IS THE PROBLEM

R. Scott Holmes, Intuitive Energy Healer

MY STORY

My eyes snap open.

I reached out for her.

She is gone.

Emptiness fills every part of me.

Who can I be today?

Who should I be today?

What mask should I wear today?

Moira, my wife of thirty-nine years, my partner for all my adult life. Husband, protector, caregiver—my identities are all gone. A twenty-year battle against the ultimate foe, cancer, claimed her.

Moira defined home. Moira was home.

Filled with family pictures, mementos of events, and the how-tos of everyday life—everything I touched was part of her. The house was defined by her fashion sense—clutter.

Every shelf had its theme. Every corner was piled high with boxes and books, threatening to fall over. Every closet was overstuffed to the point of exploding. Children's books, Disney memorabilia, romance novels, and holiday decorations were always threatening to break out. The dining room table was stacked high with papers, making it an open-air file cabinet. The life of a teacher was how she lived every day.

Those material things brought me closer to the life that was, but I felt trapped, suffocated, and weighted down by their sheer presence.

How do I get through each day feeling so hollowed out?

The silence was ear-piercing. There was no purpose to each day. I no longer had to provide for her, care for her, or listen for her.

So, the choice: *How do I start my day? How do I start over?*

I never gave a single thought about that freedom.

Who am I now? The father? A grandfather? A friend?

All that I was and did was poured into my wife and family. My girls were grown with careers and families of their own. My friends were all married with grandchildren.

How do I break out of the shell of isolation?

And let's not even talk about being single. I hadn't been unattached since I was eighteen.

I couldn't swim in those waters. I couldn't even doggie paddle.

I had an unrestricted choice to define who I wanted to become.

What a gift! *A Pandora's box?*

All the emotions boxed in over the years and I was terrified to crack that lid even slightly. All the little-boy fears now chilled me to the bone.

As a teenager, I stumbled along oblivious, unknowing, and feeling never good enough. Later, as a young husband, I struggled to survive and provide.

Aren't I the dad who was always the rock?

Standing hard and unmovable against the uncaring world, I was the armored knight riding in to save the day, again, and again.

Where is the shelf for these parts?

I practiced yoga for ten years, on and off, occasionally more off than on. I could start my day with a cup of yoga, leaning into the spiritual, peaceful side.

Before sunrise, I rose, unfurled my mat, and sank into lotus. The marching band inside my head started to dwindle to the solo cellist playing a tune I couldn't quite remember.

Each day, I returned increasingly to my body, growing stronger and able to walk upright as the burden of loss lightened and my fear diminished. My balance was shifting, grounded, in a tree pose of possibility.

I needed guidance—help to navigate through the confusion and make sense of the unfolding lotus.

A month of digging and interviewing counselors, therapists, and psychologists led me to Dr. Stephanie. Little did I discern that this petite powerhouse would transform my life. She introduced me to EMDR, eye movement desensitization, and reprocessing.

A mouthful, to be sure.

Using an alternating light bar, she brought back traumas large and small. I became their observer, not the frightened six-year-old or thirteen-year-old, but my newly grounded self, allowing me to understand and experience the emotions boxed and shelved in my body.

Piled a mile high, as I opened each box and sensation, I understood each strongbox was a protector. I learned that emotions aren't good or bad; they're what we learned to protect ourselves.

At times, my weekly drive to her turned into such anxiety that I imagined saying I was sick, in an accident, or had fallen off a cliff. Keeping the box closed would be far easier than dealing with my inner demons.

After five years of agonizing battles, each session was a knight bracing for the fatal blow, and gradually, maddeningly, the protective armor started shedding, layer by layer. The towering castle walls that kept me safe started to crumble. Vulnerability became my new shield, and an open heart became my protection.

For years, I couldn't understand why I couldn't get close to people. They'd fade away or run. The steel and stone I surrounded myself with, acting as my security, were the obstacles that isolated me. Instead of affording me strength, these were my greatest weakness.

And then came Reiki!

Talk about getting back into your body. Self-Reiki will return you back to a deep awareness of yourself and your body. The five minutes it takes to do self-Reiki each morning changed how I negotiated the entire day.

Calm enveloped my muscles, joints, and vibrational level and allowed me to calm the gerbil running the wheel of my brain. My shoulders started up around my ears and slowly rolled down my back, freeing my neck from the constant strain of tension. The daily headaches receded.

So motivated by Reiki 1, I trained in Reiki 2 three months later. This raised my awareness and allowed me to see and feel into others' energy fields. I practiced on friends regularly, and each seemed to deeply appreciate the relief received each session. As my ego-mind diminished, I opened to experience and comprehend others' energies—where in the body it flowed, where it was blocked, and how to help them move whatever energy no longer served them.

Accepting my body and energy in this new way and understanding my life's purpose and journey poured forth as I calmly listened. I was acutely aware it was my heart (and not my mind) that was loudest, more insistent, and always guiding.

Is this what living in grace feels like?

Judgment was the next hurdle to overcome. I started working with a Yogini, learning Indian and Buddhist mantras. Using a mala, the 108-bead necklace, where the mantra is said or sung at each bead, deepened the meditations. I ended up singing in Sanskrit, slowly holding the tones and words longer and fuller. Not bad for someone who can't carry a tune in a paper bag. It was beautifully liberating to allow my heart's voice to be heard.

One of the hardest lessons was to write down each time I passed judgment on another. As a self-described "Mass-hole" (drivers in Massachusetts are notorious for their impatience and belief that everyone else is driving the wrong way), impatience and judgment bubbled forth so easily. Being aware of how these judgments drove into my awareness and having to record each held me accountable. I started to allow people to cross in front of me, slowed down to let them in traffic and I didn't need the extra thirty seconds going through a yellow light at the intersection.

This led to seeing people as they were, not what I expected them to be.

Hmm, expectations.

When expectations aren't there, life is so much simpler and less demanding, and I felt a newfound grace for myself and all others.

Was compassion and understanding developing in my everyday persona?

As my senses were awakened, deep curiosity followed. A love of reading, learning, and understanding turned my mindfulness toward travel.

The world began to open for me, and the thrill of new adventures fully opened the box of my consciousness. One of my best friends and I traveled through Central Europe in a rented car for seventeen days, never knowing where we would be sleeping the next night or which direction we would be heading. Eight countries, 2500 miles, and a sixtieth birthday to match no other. Breakfast in Germany, lunch in France, and dinner in Switzerland. It was all directed by intuition and the knowing: *We'll be where we need to be when it's meant for us to be there.*

Ireland with a lifelong friend fulfilling a bucket list wish for him. Another seventeen-day trip through Thailand, Cambodia, and Vietnam. Twelve days in Singapore and Malaysia. Twenty days in Delhi and the Himalayas. An upcoming sixteen-day trip to Peru. Not to mention the numerous weekend and week-long US trips.

What this did for my soul!

What might this do for your soul?

What if you open your boxed heart to new possibilities?

What if you put aside all judgment and let curiosity take the lead— understand every person on this Earth is looking for the same things: family, safety, abundance, and, most of all, love.

When traveling, my senses are fully aware. Sounds are louder, tastes are more spectacular, sights are more intriguing, and I'm much more open to the people around me.

How can I share my journey so that everyone may know the potential of what is boxed away, waiting in each heart?

This thought brought me to my biggest fear: writing.

I was never afraid to write as long as no one was ever going to read it. Being a published author? Terrifying. I'd lay the best parts of my journey out on the pavement to be driven over, judged, and picked apart. And from my closest friends.

This is the sixth book, with a seventh due shortly. Each chapter is a deeper dive into the darkest, murkiest parts of my life—the emotions, healing, understanding, aha moments, and elevation of awareness has been priceless.

Each chapter another thought released from my life's journey box, wherever it is headed.

What is remaining?

Hope.

I heard the word transcendence and never thought it could or would apply to anything in my life. I now see it as overcoming, elevating understanding, and knowing this life, in all its imperfections, can be lived with complete joy. The basic practice that started after my wife passed is done daily, giving me the foundation to live this life fully.

I'm so looking forward to seeing what you can accomplish once you implement getting back to knowing yourself. I hope you will contact me and let me support your journey.

THE TOOL

Rituals are the foundation. Practice is the work.

What in your life do you practice daily that leads you to a better quality of life and awareness? The push we hear from every source is that you are the master, the goddess, the king, the empress of all you survey.

I get that. It's meant to remind you of your power.

But it's in the quiet spaces of life that we find ourselves—our true nature—the one we're born with and that has been chiseled away, repainted, and sandpapered smooth so the edges of who we are don't show.

The form your practice takes may vary day to day, but the "doing" is to be done. You owe it to yourself and to everyone around you.

What allows you to listen to your body?

Walking in nature, running on a treadmill, spin class, sitting in your favorite chair stroking the cat, watching birds out the window, or five minutes of quiet in the bathroom first thing in the morning are all ways to allow your body to ground.

Have you ever asked your body what it needs? And then waited for the answer?

Maybe it's time to ask.

Your body has a knowing within it. If you're quiet enough in mind, emotion, and spirit, the answer will be given. Only when you're fully in your body is your awareness raised to see beyond yourself. Then, the real transformation happens.

Acceptance: Allowing the idea that you're not perfect but are perfection. Life has defined for you how to act, what to be, and how to feel. When you no longer judge yourself so harshly, you then accept others and their differences more readily.

Gratitude: An amazing gift to give yourself. Being thankful and saying it aloud each and everyday changes how you view life and everyone around you. Allows grace and ease back into practice.

Forgiveness: You did the best you could with what you had at your disposal at the time. Forgive yourself for the imperfections. Forgive those you love with even greater kindness. Watch how your connections transform.

Compassion: Leading with heart is not always easy. Practicing being heart-led strengthens your ability to see beyond yourself. Vulnerability is not a weakness but a strength when put into practice.

Boundaries: Create the walls, fences, or speedbumps that define how much of you will be given. When 'no' is a complete sentence, you've arrived.

Caregiving: It's not about massages or pampering. It's the ultimate love you show for yourself. Recharging, reigniting, and refueling your core, allowing you to show up fully present in this world.

Getting back into your body allows so many amazing things to happen. For example, to travel and enjoy it fully, you must be physically stable, grounded, and able to maintain your baseline health. It's not always easy, given changing circumstances.

Having consistent routines allows your body to deal with whatever comes up.

Ground into Mother Earth. Guide your energy into your heart space. Bring yourself back to you, without worries, stress, fears, shoulds, have-tos, or expectations.

Lie in the hammock of your heart and lounge with the best parts of who you really are.

Just you without pretense, without apology, without ego, knowing your best friend was always there, right beside you.

I've developed my practice to help you find the way to your Pandora's box. Let's walk your journey together to find and unlock the hope and joy of life that awareness brings.

R. Scott Holmes is an intuitive energy practitioner and transformational coach using Reiki, polarity therapy, RYSE, ThetaHealing, and Find Your Voice coaching techniques to clear, ground, and align your energetic body. His specialty is collaborating with professional men and women, allowing them to heal and maintain their true paths in life.

He began walking in the holistic healing world when his wife of 39 years died after a 20-year battle with breast cancer. After years of caregiving for his daughter and wife, the world of coaching, healing, and energy opened. His soul journey has been to help heal others through one-on-one sessions, teaching, and volunteering.

Walk with him to find the rituals and daily practices enabling you to open those locked spaces. Allow your most authentic self to shine through. Embrace the life you are living.

Contact Scott for a free thirty minute share to see if you too can unwrap the Pandora's box carried in your heart.

Website: https://www.rscottholmes.com

Contact him at rscott_holmes@yahoo.com

Facebook: https://www.facebook.com/Scott.Holmes.31105674

Instagram: https://www.instagram.com/r.scottholmes

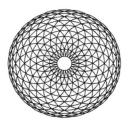

---

*Fear crept in. I placed the welcome mat outside my door
and allowed it to enter. I gave it permission to take control
of my life. I had willingly surrendered to fear with open arms.
Have you left your door open?*

~ Donna O'Toole

CHAPTER 23

LETTING GO TO CONQUER FEAR

HOW TO EMBRACE THE LIFE YOU WERE MEANT TO LIVE

Donna O'Toole,
RN, B.Ed., Reiki Master, Energy Healer, Intuitive

MY STORY

"I am so sorry you are going through this again so soon." Bill just learned he had less than six months to live, but his first thought was for me. My husband, John, died ten years before from complications of ALS. As a marriage counselor, Bill understood the grieving process. Little did we know that Bill would die a short three and a half weeks later.

But this time was so immensely different. Bill and I moved one year before to a foreign country, and I learned a new language to assimilate. We chose to buy a large farm out in a rural area, living among the people of this country. We created a property filled with exquisite landscapes and beautiful gardens. It was a serene and peaceful sanctuary that welcomed and housed many species of birds and animals. It was a natural paradise for us. We opened our gates each morning to welcome anyone in the community to visit us.

Ten days prior to Bill's death, two men on four-wheelers came onto our property and wanted to gain access to our home. "Donna, go outside and stall them so I have time to retrieve my gun."

With my heart pounding loudly in my ears, I somehow miraculously stalled them with my limited knowledge of their language. Out of the corner of my eye, I saw Bill, so I squatted down to give him a clear path to fire his revolver if necessary.

The men followed my gaze and saw Bill standing at the door with one arm tucked behind his back, disguising it as a held gun. They understood. The gardener escorted them off the property without incident and closed our gates. A knot twisted in my heart as I realized I could no longer have our open-door policy. As Bill held me in his arms, no words were necessary because I felt his concern that the peaceful world we built would no longer exist.

One hour later, Bill asked me to help him to bed. I wrapped my arm around Bill's waist as we slowly ascended the stairs for the last time. Bill never came downstairs again.

I was alone with my grief.

In the foggy mist, fear sneakily came rolling in to drip its putrid, pungent stench on me.

What am I going to do now without him in my life?

How am I going to protect myself?

What am I going to do when it takes the police at least an hour to respond to a call?

Can I live alone in a foreign country?

Who would ever move to a foreign country to live with me?

What do I know about running a farm?

How am I going to take care of this farm by myself?

I am afraid to be in this large house by myself.

I am afraid to come home after dark.

I am afraid of growing old by myself.

I am afraid I will walk alone.

I am afraid of. . .

You name it, I was afraid of it.

Did you know there's even a word for the fear of vacuum cleaners? Zuigerphobia. *Who knew? At least there was one fear I did not have.*

I lived in a constant state of fear. It became a mindset that influenced my every decision. My judgment was clouded, and I made decisions defensively or impulsively. *How would a burglar get into this house? I need bars surrounding the carport, additional security lights, holster a gun after dark.*

Life decisions based on fear will lead to a life you don't want or one you'll regret. *I wish I hadn't married again, my life's biggest mistake and regret.* I looked for immediate relief, not even considering any long-term consequences from the decisions I made.

Fear becomes a very powerful emotion, putting up roadblocks to prevent you from letting go and moving on—letting go of relationships, habits, jobs, limited or outdated beliefs, judgments, and mindsets, to name a few. Fear of the unknown or change can make even the strongest person stop dead in their tracks and resist acknowledging the fear residing in their body. The only thing constant in our life is change.

I discovered that acknowledging the fear is the first step in letting go. Looking within and analyzing the fear you're experiencing will make the emotion more manageable. Accepting that change is necessary will propel you forward in your personal growth and overall well-being.

Where did this fear come from? Probing deeper into the root causes of your fear will give insight to making the necessary changes to address the fear you are experiencing. As you explore those root causes, remember to stop that hypercritical voice within you and show yourself compassion.

How could you have been so stupid? Did you even stop to think?

Stop It! You are a kind, loving and intelligent woman. You were in a vulnerable place and sometimes people will take advantage of you. You did your best at the time.

Understand that letting go is a journey with many paths and stops along the way. Accept that fear is just a part of our human experience and, in many circumstances, can save someone's life. Remember to recognize fear doesn't necessarily dictate your actions and life decisions.

Take time to reflect on how the situation caused by the fear is impacting you. What emotions are directly tied to the fear? What is the overall status of your health and well-being? Why are you holding onto the fear or the emotions associated with it? Take the time to ponder the positive outcome for yourself if you could let go of the fear? What would your life look like? Focus on the benefits you could bring into your life!

Remember to take small steps to avoid being overwhelmed. Letting go is a process. Seek support from friends, family, or professionals as needed. The process of letting go does not need to be a solo journey. You do not have to do this process of letting go alone. Remember, each person's journey is unique to them, so be patient and loving with yourself. Practice self-compassion and self-care. Celebrate each step no matter how minor they may seem.

I wrote this poem while I was on my journey.

Letting Go

I am in a home surrounded by nature
Serenaded by the sweet lullabies of birds, insects, and animals,
Large groves of bamboo captured my attention
Swaying gently by the fresh breeze,
Rhythmically clattering and toning their unique melodious songs,
Until I became immersed within nature's symphony.

Bamboo dancing and bending majestically
Created a refuge where I could escape from the chaos
To a place of tranquility and peace and harmony.
Urging me to seek inner peace
By uncovering the hidden unconscious thoughts and beliefs
That hold me back from being my authentic self.

I continued to listen to the enchantments of the cloud forest
Bamboo shoots whistle their lofty musical notes

Harmonizing with the cadence of the insects
Lulled in the quietness of the rain
Filtering mistily to the earth
Cleansing the air and
Filling my nostrils with the smell of change.

And I was in awe as I discovered
The pure essence of knowing
I can easily draw each breath
To fill my essence with peace and love.

In this serene and calm place
Where the light and dark are in balance
I discovered a profound dark silence
Stilling the chatter in my mind.

Whispers began stirring within me
Unveiling secrets and
Opening the portal
Until
I was finally receptive to truly listen
To the shadows within me.
Winding their way around my heart.

Embracing my fears and untrue assumptions
I broke their chains
To set my soul free.

Acknowledging those shadows
I openly chose to let them go
I released them to the winds
I released them to the rainfalls
I named them all
And they all started with
Fear.

As I let go of all that
No longer served my highest good.
I discovered there is such freedom
In letting go.
The space that was created,
A sanctuary within me
That held only pure love.

There was a life-altering, precious gift
Bestowed to me
By the bamboo groves and nature sounds
Of the cloud forest.

The following guided meditation will resonate with is for anyone in the process of releasing and letting go.

I prefer to use the "I AM" statements or affirmations within guided meditations. "I AM" affirmations connect you directly to your subconscious and alert the universe with the message, that effectively says "Reflect or manifest my inner reality into my outer reality or physical world."

THE TOOL

A Guided Meditation to Release and Let Go of What No Longer Serves Your Highest Good

Get comfortable. Close your eyes if you choose to do so. Place your hand or hands over your heart and connect to this sacred space.

Take three deep breaths and fill your heart space with love.

As you breathe deeply in and out, imagine roots going down into the soil. Deep down into the Earth through every crack and fissure, winding and weaving deeper into the rock until you reach the core of the Earth. You will feel firmly grounded and connected to Mother Earth.

Begin by drawing unconditional love up into the lower chakras and the heart. This is the love of the Divine Feminine, which you may visualize as emanating from Mother Earth. You draw this love up through the soles of your feet, up through your lower three chakras, and into your heart.

As you continue to draw love into your heart on each inspiration, you will also begin to draw Creator-Light down through your crown chakra into your sacred mind and then your heart. This is the light of the Divine masculine, which you can visualize as coming from Father Sun, the heavens, the Supreme Creator, or from the angels. This divine light enters through the crown chakra of your head, which is the gateway to your higher self. From there, draw the light down into your sacred mind and then into your heart, where it merges with the unconditional love from Mother Earth.

In the merging, unconditional love and divine light become activated and empowered so they can be sent out through your expiration to the rest of your body, engulfing and infusing every cell. From there, you'll send this divine love light mixture through a thousand points of light to the rest of the world and beyond.

This loving empowerment process on each breath cycle will continue automatically without you thinking about it.

When you're ready, visualize a sacred place or place of power that holds special meaning to you. Feel its unique energy and infuse yourself with it. Breathe this unique energy into your heart space, and then let it engulf your whole being.

As you sit in this sacred place, you will automatically continue to breathe in the divine love and light. Ask for your spirit guides, animal guides, angels, guardian angels, ascended masters, or the presence of a higher spirit to come and sit with you in your sacred place.

Breathe in love, feel the love, then exhale love.

Breathe in compassion, feel the compassion, then exhale compassion.

Breathe in gratitude, feel the gratitude, then exhale gratitude.

Feel the love, compassion, and gratitude in your heart and heart space, and exhale love, compassion, and gratitude.

Breathe in peace.

Feel the peace in your heart and heart space, then exhale peace.

Feel the love, compassion, and healing taking place.

Turn your attention inward and slowly acknowledge various aspects of your life:

Relationships with parents, spouse, children, friends, co-workers.

Beliefs: Spiritual, self, roles in life, death, afterlife.

Emotions: Fear, anger, resentment.

Repetitive judgments like: *I'm not good enough, I'm such a failure, Who could love me*, or any other that just came to you.

Habits and actions.

With a compassionate heart, gently review these aspects, recognizing those that may no longer serve your highest good. Like the changes of the seasons, your life journeys through cycles, and it is natural for one to outgrow certain energies.

Notice areas in your body where you may feel tense or some type of sensation when you think of those recognized aspects that no longer serve you.

Send love to your wounds, known and unknown, for healing. See this empowered and activated divine love and light energies locating and reaching all your wounds, known and unknown.

In this serene, sacred place, you notice a nearby stream. Take those aspects you have identified, releasing the old, stagnant energies that keep you anchored to the past and place them in the nearby stream. Allow all those thoughts and energies to float away like delicate leaves carried by a gentle breeze. Your gaze follows them as they float away until you no longer see them.

Embrace this sensation of freedom that comes from letting go. You're making space for growth, expansion, and the manifestation of your truest and highest self.

The following "I AM" affirmations serve as powerful statements to assist you with the intention to release what no longer serves your highest good. As you read each "I AM" affirmation, feel the resonance of these words in your heart and mind, and then allow the power of your intentions and the "I AM" affirmations to permeate every cell in your body:

I AM connected to and guided by a higher divine power.

I AM divinely guided as I AM trusting the process of releasing what no longer serves me and I AM renewing and replenishing to continue my journey.

I AM worthy of releasing what no longer serves my highest good.

I AM a vessel of divine Love and Light, releasing all darkness that obscures my soul growth and spiritual path.

I AM recognizing and freeing myself from the bondage and chains of my limited beliefs.

I AM recognizing and releasing any emotions associated with anything that does not serve my highest good.

I AM acknowledging and releasing fear as I AM embracing the boundless possibilities of the present moment.

I AM living in the present moment.

I AM removing any habits that no longer support my personal well-being and soul growth.

I AM letting go of relationships that hinder my journey to self-discovery and impede my soul growth.

I AM forgiving myself and others, liberating my heart from the weight of anger and resentment.

I AM grounded in the present moment as I AM releasing attachments to the past and to matters of the future.

I AM letting go of attachments to outcomes.

I AM releasing all known and unknown concepts, beliefs, people, situations, and anything else from my life that no longer serves my highest good.

I AM creating space for love, joy, bliss, compassion, grace, and abundance to flow effortlessly into my life.

I AM setting and honoring healthy boundaries with myself and others.

I AM a beacon of light and positivity, attracting only what aligns with my highest good.

I AM stepping into my power, releasing the need for validation from others.

I AM welcoming and embracing change as a catalyst for personal growth and spiritual transformation.

I AM grateful for the lessons I have learned from what I AM releasing, as I AM acknowledging those lessons have shaped my steps along my sacred soul journey and path.

I AM experiencing life with heightened awareness and mindfulness.

I AM consciously creating an energetic shift to raise my vibrational patterns and welcoming positive changes within my body and mind.

I AM connecting with the realms of the divine, and I AM living in alignment with my highest and most vibrant self.

I AM ushering in life-changing soul growth.

I AM experiencing soul-awakening abundance.

I AM Living Gratitude and Loving Wisdom.

I AM enhancing and living my authentic spiritual life and path.

Give thanks and gratitude for the insight, guidance, clarity and direction to the desires and questions of your heart. Give thanks to those spirit guides who have joined you in seeking your answers.

Feel the lightness that comes with releasing what no longer serves your highest good. Recognize that the universe conspires in your favor when you align with your highest self.

Slowly bring your consciousness back to this time and space. You will bring this newfound wisdom, peace, joy, and love with you and will be able to recall these feelings anytime you need them as they dwell within your joyful and loving self.

And So It Is!

Namaste.

You can use these affirmations even without the meditation. Repeat these affirmations regularly, preferably in a quiet and focused state. The affirmations reinforce positive beliefs, and align your energy with the qualities associated with each affirmation. Bring in the energy of each word of the affirmations and hold them in your heart space.

Everything in life is a choice. You can choose to live in fear or you can choose to embrace the life you were meant to live by learning the art of letting go.

I encourage you to sweep the fear from your welcome mat and replace it with one that says, "I AM embracing the life I was meant to live."

Read my bio to take advantage of a free offer.

Are you ready to don the badge of courage and take that first step, brave warrior?

Donna O'Toole, RN, B.Ed., Massage Therapist, Druid Priestess, Intuitive, Energy Healer, Awen Awakener.

After caring for her husband of 14 years, who died from ALS, Donna knew something was missing from Western teachings. This led her to search and study across many fields. As a result, she merges the Western and Eastern philosophies to enhance and enrich how one lives their life.

Donna bridges this work with many other teachings as a Reiki Master, Karuna Reiki Master, crystal, sound, and color healer, clearing and blessing homes and spaces, intuitive, poet, actress, singer, and guided meditation leader. She is in her third decade of embracing the healing arts, energy work, sound healing, crystal healing, crystal grids, Celtic and Irish study, druidism, and meditation, to name a few of her varied interests.

Donna's expertise focuses, as she feels called, on those individuals who need help with alternative healing options, transitioning from this earth plane, and those who have had the trauma of childhood sexual abuse.

Donna started writing poetry 13 years ago and found this method of writing, as well as journal writing, has led her to further healing for herself and her readers.

She also brings healing through guided meditations using focused "I AM" statements. Through Donna's years of stage and theatre work, she has learned how to use her voice and lends those talents to her voice-guided meditations, setting the right tone for delivery.

Donna truly believes it's important to live your authentic spiritual life and to be guided to dwell where it *makes your soul sing.*

Be one of the first five people to email Donna and win a free Zoom meditation session. Just put in the subject line: Free meditation

Connect with Donna:

Email: drsharingjoys@gmail.com

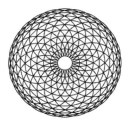

Compassion. Compassion. Compassion.

~ Arlene Nock

CHAPTER 24

PREVENTING HEALER FATIGUE

WHY EMPATHY IS NOT
ALWAYS THE BEST CHOICE

Arlene Nock, M.D.

MY STORY

In the early evening of June 22, 1969, I was driving home from my waitressing job at a summer resort in the Catskills. I stopped to pick up ice cream for my older brother, Bob, and was looking forward to getting into comfy clothes and relaxing. The quiet country road ran next to a lake, and the evening sun was creating gold streaks over the water. With pale blue skies, a few wisps of clouds, and air that was dry and cool, it was the best of upstate New York's summer days.

Suddenly, the cars in front of me slowed down and then stopped altogether. I couldn't see what was wrong because there was a curve in the road. Cars ahead of me were turning around to take alternate routes.

I wonder what happened? Shoot, I guess I'll turn around and go home the long way.

Suddenly, my heart started pounding in my chest.

Why is my heart pounding?! Why am I so scared? Am I connected to what's around that curve?

One by one, the cars turned and drove away. An ambulance sped by on my left, sirens blaring, my heart still beating fast. As each car turned, I got closer and closer until I could see around the curve.

I don't recognize either of those cars, thank goodness, because it's a terrible crash. One car was pushed into that old stone wall and knocked it down. It was weird that I was so nervous. I feel bad for the people involved though. How awful.

I turned around, relieved that my heart racing didn't mean anything, and drove home.

My younger brother Rich was home alone, and he looked surprisingly worried.

"Hi Rich, where is everybody?"

"Mom and Dad are at the hospital because Bob was in an accident."

"What do you mean he was in an accident? What happened?!"

"That's all I know. We were at the neighbor's house for a picnic and Bob left with a few people to take someone home, and a while later, the hospital called and said there was an accident, and Mom and Dad and some others left. That's all I know. I've been waiting for them to call."

Oh my God, no! That couldn't be the accident I saw. Is that why my heart was pounding?! No, no, no!

"I saw an accident on the way home, but I didn't recognize either of the cars."

"They left in the neighbor's car."

The neighbor's car! That's why I didn't recognize it. The neighbor's son was driving. But Bob hardly knew him. Why would he be in his car?

Time blurred from then on. I only remember the moments seared into my memory. I remember my mother sitting in a chair in a dark corner of the family room, eyes closed, her face distorted by the agony only a mother knows, saying over and over, "Why couldn't it have been me? Why couldn't it have been me?" I could feel her pain, and it terrified me.

I remember going to work. When I was home, I tried to help by keeping up with household chores, but all I remember was ironing. I don't remember any conversations with my parents or brother except when my dad called us into the living room to tell us that Bob was badly hurt but still alive. I didn't know how to make sense of anything I experienced.

My brother Bob, who was 24 years old, was paralyzed from the neck down in that accident.

No, please, no. That can't be! Bob? Paralyzed?! This can't be happening. Maybe if I hadn't stopped to get him that ice cream, I would have been in front of their car, and they couldn't have been driving so fast.

I visited Bob once in the hospital. He was lying in a hospital bed with a steel halo on his head, holding his broken neck in traction. I brought in a chair because I was afraid I'd faint. Seeing my discomfort, Bob smiled at me, trying to put me at ease.

What's wrong with me? Here he is; he can't move, and he's trying to make ME comfortable! What do I say? What can I do?!

I have no idea what I said or if I said anything at all. In my memory, I can see myself from outside my body, which was trying to fold in on itself and couldn't talk or move. My body didn't know what to do with all my feelings of fear and pain. I have no idea how long I stayed with Bob or when I left him there in the hospital.

I never visited him again.

***

I experienced overwhelming empathy. My 19-year-old self couldn't have known that or named it. I only knew I couldn't bear the fear and pain I felt when I was around my family, who were suffering with intense emotional pain.

My boyfriend visited that summer. We went to the Jersey Shore. I was completely disconnected from my family. I returned to college in September. I dropped out of college after my junior year and spent the next 25 years running away to Mexico, Oklahoma, New Mexico, California, North Dakota, France, and Malaysia.

Miraculously, amidst the chaos of my life, at the age of 31, I started medical school and completed my residency in psychiatry when I was 39. I married when I was 33 and had three daughters by the time I was 42. We gradually moved closer and closer to New York, and in 1995, at

45 years old, we moved into a house two doors away from my parents and Bob.

Running away was fast; walking back took a long time. I'm grateful for the five years I had with my family until my mother and Bob died within three weeks of each other in 2000.

***

I often see and hear the words *empathy* and *compassion* used interchangeably. However, the work of researchers such as Richard Davidson, Helen Weng, and Tania Singer, who were all assisted by the Dalai Lama, shows us that empathy and compassion are very different neurological processes.

In 1992, Carla Joinson used the term "compassion fatigue" to describe the burnout that emergency department nurses experience. This was unfortunate because while it's true that those of us in the healing professions can be overwhelmed by the suffering of others, it's unchecked *empathy* that causes fatigue, *not* compassion.

The neurobiology of these processes is complex, but it will benefit clinicians to appreciate the significant differences, even though simplified, between empathy and compassion. The importance of understanding these differences goes beyond just academic clarification. Knowing the differences can ensure you remain a healer without burning out because you will know how to tame your empathy and strengthen your compassion. That will enable you to provide care without fatigue.

Interestingly, although the brain's capacity for empathy has been present for millions of years, the word did not appear in the English language until around 1909. It came from the German word "einfuhlung" meaning "feeling in." There was an evolutionary advantage for early humans who had empathy because it allowed their brains to experience the emotional aspects of pain or disgust by just seeing someone in pain or listening to someone talk about their *actual* physical pain. This ability meant that only one member of your clan needed to suffer scratches from walking into a yummy berry patch. When someone came back with terrible scratches and told the others about it, the clan members felt the same pain as if they were hurt themselves. They learned to pick berries carefully without being injured.

Think about your own reaction if your friend told you about slamming their fingers in the car door. You'd probably wince as though you felt the pain, pull your hand back, and shake or hold your fingers because your brain had the same emotional reaction as your friend. Both of your brains learned to be more careful when closing the car door, but only one set of fingers suffered.

We have the strongest empathic responses to negative experiences such as pain or disgust. While we appreciate the positive feelings of joy or pleasure in another person, we don't feel them in our bodies as strongly as the negative ones. This makes sense when you think of empathy as a protective behavior. We don't need to be protected from positive experiences, only from dangerous ones.

We all know how comforting it is when someone shares our pain. However, empathy isn't primarily a prosocial behavior; it doesn't always involve a desire to relieve another's suffering. As you saw in my case when I was 19 years old, my empathy didn't propel me toward those who suffered; instead, the fear of the pain I felt propelled me to run away. Empathy evolved to improve the survival of the group, not just the individual.

Empathy involves connections among many structures in the brain, but it will help us understand how it differs from compassion if we simplify it. One part of the brain involved in empathy is the *insula*, which lies deep in the brain. Make a fist with your thumb facing you. Imagine your index finger is your frontal lobe, and your thumb is your temporal lobe. Now, unroll your index finger slightly and peek inside; you will see where the insula would be. The insula monitors our body's experience and remembers reactions the body has to interactions with the environment, including our emotional experience of pain. If you've experienced food poisoning, the reason you feel disgusted by the thought of eating that same food again is due to your insula's memory of being sick. The insula enables us to remember what a cold day feels like, so we remember to grab a jacket.

Key to understanding empathy is the fact that the insula has connections to the amygdala. The amygdala is commonly associated with fear, but it processes almost all inputs from the environment and gives each experience an emotional "tag." The insula and the amygdala share information coming into the brain from the environment. Some of that information comes from the body the brain resides in, and some comes from the empathic emotions we feel in someone else's body. Either way, if the amygdala records it as dangerous, it will send you signals to stay away.

People who have lost a child or lost someone to suicide tell me they feel so isolated. They feel isolated because their friends and family "don't know what to say," so they stop reaching out. Yet those friends are certainly feeling strong empathic responses and are likely sharing those feelings with other friends or family members. The problem isn't not knowing what to say; *the problem is not knowing how to calm their fear of it happening to them.*

There have been times when I shared a personal experience with a patient that I thought might let them know I understood something they were going through. It never helped. This puzzled me until I remembered the nature of empathy. Although my intention was to say, "I've gone through something similar, so I understand, and you're not alone," what their empathic brain heard was, "Oh, great, now I have to feel their loss in addition to my own." There is an unspoken agreement in therapy that the patient doesn't have to worry about having to experience any emotions other than their own.

We need to be vigilant about our empathic responses to be sure we neither run away from feelings that are too painful nor yield to feelings of wanting to share too much.

Unlike the word *empathy*, the word *compassion* has been around for millennia. It's contained in every religion's sacred text, such as the Quran, the Bible, the Tao Te Ching, and the Bhagavad Gita, to name just a few. Compassion is attributed to the deity as each religion understands it and is characterized as feelings of kindness, caring, and concern for the suffering of others. There is no mention of shared emotions.

This is the hallmark of compassion: it generates a heartfelt sense of kindness for others. It's a prosocial quality that allows us to be in the presence of another's suffering without being hurt by it. Unlike empathy, it's not an innate survival response of the brain to the environment. It's something we must train our brains to do. With practice, we can decrease the strength of the connection between the insula and the amygdala and strengthen the connections among the prefrontal cortex, the insula, and the nucleus accumbans. The nucleus accumbans is a part of the reward system in the brain, and when activated, it produces positive feelings of well-being. When we practice feelings of kindness toward others, we are stimulating our nucleus accumbans. This experience of compassion creates a feeling that is personally rewarding to our brain. We can be in the presence of suffering and not have to turn away because we are *with* someone's feelings without being *in* someone's feelings.

The trick is that we must practice compassion and strengthen it. At the same time, we need to monitor and tame our empathy toward clients because it involves our survival pathways. Our brain will *react* with empathy unless we take charge and intentionally create a state of compassion when we're with our clients. So, let's see how to do that!

THE TOOL

This version of the tool is short and suitable for busy workdays. This loving-kindness practice originated in India over 2,500 years ago, probably before Buddha's time, but it has been shared in the earliest Buddhist teachings. The goal of the loving-kindness practice is to strengthen the pathways in the brain that build compassion. I added a short exercise to do first so that we remember to tame our innate use of empathy.

The Busy Day Tool Part 1: Taming Empathy

First, bring your next client to mind. I find it's easier to close my eyes and picture them, but use whatever works best for you to think of them. If it's a client with a trauma history, you can bring to mind what they might be working on in this session. The goal is to feel a connection with them.

Next, notice what your body feels in relation to your client. Do you feel a heaviness in your heart? Does your stomach feel queasy? Do you feel nervous? Do you feel pain? Are you looking forward to seeing them, or do you feel drained? Notice any body reaction or emotion that arises when thinking about your client.

Finally, consciously remind yourself that you don't need to mirror these feelings or emotions. They are not yours, and you do not need to take them on yourself. In neurological terms, you want to disconnect your insula from your amygdala so that your brain is free to connect your insula to your nucleus accumbans.

The Busy Day Tool Part 2: Building up Compassion

This is an abbreviated loving-kindness practice. A more complete practice will be described in the next section.

First, offer compassion to yourself. You have compassion for other healers, and you want to show that same compassion to yourself. I like to place my hand over my heart and, if possible, say this out loud. However, you could also be walking to the waiting room saying the phrases silently:

May I be happy

May I be safe

May I be free from suffering

May I be at peace

Next, bring your client to mind and offer them compassion:

May you be happy

May you be safe

May you be free from suffering

May you be at peace

That's it! You can do this in 30 seconds if that's all you have. You can do it while you're walking down the hall to meet your client. You can take ten minutes and really give your compassion a workout. You can also change the phrases to ones that are more meaningful to you. The goal is to remove the pain of empathy and turn it into a rewarding feeling that allows you to be in the presence of suffering without needing to turn away.

A Traditional Loving-Kindness Practice

Feel free to practice this seated on the floor or pillow, eyes closed, sitting still, or while washing dishes, taking a walk, or in the shower. You can also change the phrases if something else is more suitable. Keep in mind that these are *not* affirmations. We're extending kindness to ourselves and all beings. It's not "I will be happy" as in an affirmation, but "May I be Happy" as the result of the kindness I'm offering.

To start, imagine a person, pet, or place that represents loving kindness for you, and see them sitting in front of you, and you want to offer them loving kindness. So you say:

> May you be happy
> May you be safe
> May you be free from suffering
> May you be at peace

(You can personalize these phrases, e.g. "May your heart be open" "May you be healthy" "May you be free from fear", etc.)

After a few repetitions, imagine them offering the loving kindness back to you and say:

> May I be happy
> May I be safe
> May I be free from suffering
> May I be at peace

After a few repetitions, extend the object of your loving kindness to a friend or colleague that you bring to mind:

> May you be happy
> May you be safe
> May you be free from suffering
> May you be at peace

You can then extend the same offering to a stranger, and if you want to feel challenged, offer this to a difficult person in your life. This isn't about *liking* someone, but rather practicing being with them and offering kindness. There is no judgement.

You can then extend it to everyone in your city, town, state, or country.

Finally, you will be able to extend kindness to all beings by saying:

> May all beings be happy
> May all beings be safe
> May all beings be free from suffering
> May all beings be at peace

Dr. Arlene Nock is a board-certified psychiatrist living in an 1847 brownstone on Washington Park in Troy, NY. Her neighborhood was turned into 19th-century New York City for the HBO series *The Gilded Age.* After dropping out of college in 1971, she hitchhiked around Mexico and luckily lived to tell her tales! She eventually found herself in Santa Fe, New Mexico, where she finished her bachelor's degree in 1975 and then worked for five years at the Los Alamos Scientific Laboratory. She was accepted into medical school but turned it down to save the world in Malaysia. After realizing that saving the world was harder than she thought, she applied to medical school again and started her training in 1981 at the University of New Mexico in Albuquerque. Since completing her psychiatric residency in Albany, NY, in 1989, she has worked in a variety of clinical settings. Her drive to understand the brain intensified when her middle daughter was diagnosed with autism in 1990. Her primary interest is understanding how the brain interacts with the environment starting from the moment of birth, especially in response to neglect and trauma. She has felt called to work with people with multiplicity (dissociative identity disorder) since so many found their way to her practice. Through this work, she has learned that one body can have more than one soul. She understands consciousness as fundamental and that efforts to show that the brain creates consciousness will fail because the illusion of our physical reality is created by Consciousness. Her website serves as a "handbook" for people living with multiple identities to foster the understanding and acceptance of the brilliant adaptions that the Self and the brain make when faced with overwhelming childhood experiences.

Connect with Arlene:

https://www.doctornock.com

https://www.linkedin.com/in/doctornock

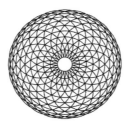

When you have a witness, there's more healing.
You can do the work of healing within (it's necessary),
but when you heal in community, more magic happens.

~ Laura Di Franco

CHAPTER 25

HEALING IS MORE THAN AN INSIDE JOB

THE POWER OF COMMUNITY TO AMPLIFY TRANSFORMATION

Laura Di Franco, MPT, Publisher

MY STORY

"What do you need, Laura?"

"I'm not sure. When I figure it out, I'll let you know."

I pace the strip of hardwood floor between the kitchen and the back sliding glass door. I feel the slight bracing in my gut and force an exhale, trying to unclench. Leo is staring at me, working a half-wag. I can tell he isn't sure what to do with me.

What do I need? I don't know. I'm not sure I ever really learned how to ask for help. I learned doing everything by myself was the path to success. Aren't I the one who should be mindful of the needs of others, first? God, I suck at this!

Learning to receive (and ask for what I need) is a work-in-progress practice for me. I imagine for many of you, too.

This book was part of a bigger vision to bring my Brave Healer community together for a retreat as we created it. That vision was shared with me (with great excitement) as an idea and business strategy to ponder in 2022. We were going to Sedona, one of my favorite healing places on the planet. "Yes, maybe we should do this!" I felt excited, already having participated in prior wildly amazing and successful similar projects.

Seems like a no-brainer: Affordable for my participants. Huge over-deliver for them. Great chance to make a profit and give back to the community.

After the trauma and trial that happened with my daughter and our win in court (read that paragraph in Chapter 1), my dad passed. I remember getting the phone call from my sister. "Dad died in his sleep last night."

Now, Dad? Really?

I was sad and mad. I was preparing to go to Mexico for my second author journey with Freedom, Folk & Soul. I was exhausted. I needed a break from the four years of clenching. I needed that trip for my own healing. I needed it so badly. I was mad at my dad's timing.

I realized at that point (and very late in the game because I forgot to look at my contract in a timely manner) that I hadn't sold enough tickets to make a go of the Sedona retreat; I called the retreat manager and surrendered.

"I'm sorry, I can't make it happen. My dad just passed. I have to let this go." I forfeited a $15,000 deposit, the biggest "mistake" of my business career.

"I'm going to Mexico," I told my sister. "We can go out to San Francisco, and I'll help you with Dad's stuff when I return, okay?" There was no rush and no plans, so I packed for Mexico.

During a sharing time in a sacred circle with my brave healer authors in Teotihuacan, I had a huge aha: *Of course, you could go now, Dad. You finished your mission. You helped prepare me my entire life to be brave enough to fight this fight. And we won, Dad! We won. Rest in peace. I love you.*

My aha felt easy, complete, and peaceful, very unlike my actual relationship with Dad.

My dad and I never got along. I spoke to him on Father's Day, his birthday, my birthday, and Christmas every year since I moved to the East

Coast from San Francisco in 1994. The obligatory love I tried to feel for my dad taught me a lot about life and myself over decades of trying to feel worthy. It's another book, y'all.

I was at the airport weeks after Mexico, waiting to fly to San Francisco to meet my sister and take care of my dad's belongings, when the retreat manager called me.

"We have a sister property in New York, and we'd like to offer to transfer your deposit to that location for next year; you can pick any dates you want."

I held back tears. I'd been given a huge gift. The Universe had my back. What I didn't know is how big that gift would actually turn out to be.

The short story? The love my community poured on and into me before, during, and since that rescheduled retreat was nothing short of transformational. The fact that I was burned out, exhausted, healing from surgery, and dealing with an iffy pap smear result as I prepared to travel to New York created a necessary action: asking for help and receiving.

I suppose the Universe has her way of transforming stubborn people.

After the trial and my dad's passing, during the year of retreat planning in the new location, she also gave me two herniated discs and unrelenting nerve pain to deal with.

You're benched, I heard the Universe say.

It makes me chuckle now. It wasn't funny then. I stared at the ceiling most of those days because 'flat on my back' was the only position I didn't hurt in. Workouts (my normal coping strategy) stopped. *Doing* stopped. I had to ask for help for my business, and I had to ask for help at home, and then, I had to ask for help to make the retreat happen.

That's a lot of help.

When my mom (my right hand for retreat planning) got sick and had to be driven home two nights after arriving in New York, I had to ask for more help.

Okay, okay. I get it. At that point, I was a little annoyed with the Universe. I may have eye-rolled the sky.

Why the Hell does it feel like it takes courage to ask for help?

That was the thought in that scene, but I'm asking you, too, dear reader.

My guess is that along the way, we learned asking for help meant you were weak, inferior, or incapable. I don't know. It feels silly as I type it.

It takes a village, right?

You *can* do it all on your own. And most likely, you'll survive. You might even thrive to some degree. However, it takes a village to realize the amount of love, support, and connection that's possible. The village takes you further than you can go on your own. It challenges you to stay on the path.

The village is what helps you figure out what else is possible (for love, healing, and life).

For some of us, asking for help is the evolution we need to make. Asking for help and gratefully receiving help is a manifesting strategy. Opening up and gratefully receiving help is a gift you give the giver because giving feels good and creates a feeling of purpose in the giver. If there were no receivers, there'd be a lot less purposeful feelings. We need to be and do both.

When I hear, "Healing is a solo act, an inside job," I feel torn. We do the work of healing, and specifically the work of connecting to our own inner wisdom, healer, and power, by building a connection and trust within. Nobody does that for you. That's a solo adventure.

Then, when we're in community with each other, we amplify the healing. Sometimes, my journal provides a witness (me). When there's a fellow human acting as a witness to your process, something even more powerful happens. The safe space a fellow journeyer creates by listening and mirroring your soul back to you is magic. Mirroring is the magic and power of all great coaching, therapy, and personal transformation.

Authentic healers understand that they're guides or facilitators of this process and that the greatest thing they ever do is lead you to your own awareness and healing power. Creating a community that does that for each other is priceless. It's not just any village, it's a safe one that we need—one that practices awareness, listening, love, and healing.

I never used to include testimonials in my books. I was afraid. This time, I want you to feel the love I felt as my community gathered around me and showered love on me. I want you to understand what happens when you show up as your authentic self, allow people to see you, ask for help, and then receive. I want you to feel the reward of being brave with a community that isn't afraid to love bigger. I want you to feel the love warrior in yourself and let her out to play.

> *"Going on retreat with Laura Di Franco is like taking a Ph.D. in writing, business, personal transformation, and soul-level connection in one action-packed weekend. Each segment built the energy to a final crescendo that sent us home inspired and burning with passion to write and serve our mission to help as many people as possible with our gifts."*
>
> ~ Laurie Morin, Writing Coach

> *"Laura Di Franco brought her badass healing energy to this retreat in one of the most magical and perfect spaces. I knew the moment I arrived I wasn't leaving unscathed. Healing requires something of us, and for me, it meant addressing some wounds that needed tending before I could fully step into my power. And step into my power I did with the help of the presenters and Laura herself. The programming had me writing every day and night. Poetry flew through me. Chapters started writing themselves, and my heart opened to connection in a way I didn't expect. I would do this again and again."*
>
> ~ Michol Mae, Poet, Performer

> *"Laura is not only teaching me to be a better writer, but she's helping me open up. She got me to see that the stories I hold deep inside are the stories I need to share. They're the stories that will heal the masses!"*
>
> ~ Carrie Dahle, CEO Thrive Mindset

"Laura Di Franco is a force of nature. That is a common phrase I seldom use. Hurricanes, floods, tornadoes—these are forces of nature. But, with Laura, just as there are good witches and bad witches, there are destructive forces of nature and positive ones. Laura will take the tornado and help you land that house back in Kansas where it belongs with the love that only you could have found for yourself."

~ Dr. Pamela J. Pine, Director, Stop the Silence

"Life changing. Write changing. Perspective changing. You've allowed me to see my vision in clear lines without the mist of confusion wrapping itself around my will to step forward. Thank you for empowering me to be a better writer, a better practitioner, and a much better, braver person."

~R. Scott Holmes

"To be in the same room with people that bring nothing but positive energy was transforming. I'm learning here with a new family—people who will help me reach my goals and dreams!"

~Tanya Stokes, Graphic Designer and artist

I'm still basking in the more than thirty messages I received the day I was brave enough to ask for them. "I'm going to make wallpaper out of them," I joked with some of the presenters, who were also basking in the messages *they* received. And then I thought of something better—*put them here, out loud, and make them real.*

Remember those two comments I received that I shared in Chapter 1? What I'm realizing is that when someone is living an authentic, soul-led life, that energy is intense. It does take stamina to roll with people like that. And I wouldn't ever give an ounce of it up. It's not a lonely road anymore. I'm loved for being me. I'm free.

Here's the secret about creating a community—it starts with one person. At first I thought it was a failure if you didn't have hundreds in your community. I quickly figured out that one person could be your community (and your witness) and create transformation.

Growing a community is a powerful life tool. I'm not talking about any community. I'm talking about people who practice showing up with awareness, taking responsibility for how they show up and the energy they show up with, and adjusting as they go. I'm talking about people who make you feel like the best you, people who lift you up and celebrate all of you, good, bad, ugly, and awesome.

Your inner circle should be able to call you out on your bullshit and help you feel loved while they do it. The community you build around you is part of your legacy. It's part of how you get up in the morning on a tough week. It's how you keep your eyes on your purpose.

Purpose has a face and a name, y'all, and it only takes one.

Your closest inner circle is your first and most powerful community. Do you know the quote about the five people you spend the most time with? Yeah, *that* community. Taking a hard look at that inner circle can be tough. It can wake you up to the life you're creating and the support you receive to fulfill your dreams.

I beg you to be brave about this. Choose wisely. It might be time to weed.

I've prepared a simple tool to help you assess your current community. This will allow you to begin crafting your most magnificent, flourishing circle—the community that shines a light on who you were meant to be and why you were born, the one that feeds your soul and supports your biggest, wildest, craziest, most world-changing dreams.

Those are your people. They love you no matter what. They always see the best in you. They believe in your dreams more than you some days. And they are always on the sidelines with the biggest pompoms—purple glitter sparkled.

The first step is assessing where we're at.

> *"You can't clean house until you first see the dirt."*
> ~ Louise Hay

Let's get to it.

THE TOOL

Your Inner Circle Assessment

These are five big questions you can ask yourself and journal about to assess the people you've surrounded yourself with and determine if they're helping you live the life you dream of.

Heads up: This is scary work. It's not always easy to see the weeds in the garden. It can feel overwhelming. In many instances, you may feel stuck in your situation with certain people and not know how to escape or change the circumstances.

Don't worry; you're not taking that action first. Today, you'll ponder, reflect, and hopefully experience some ahas about it as a first step. With awareness, you have a choice. Awareness is badass. Having more awareness is a powerful ninja move.

What you need: A quiet, sacred writing space where you won't be distracted and your notebook and pen.

Journal on the following questions paying particular attention to how you feel with each.

1. Who in my inner circle helps me feel good about myself and encourages my desires, dreams, and goals? How do they make me feel?

2. Who in my inner circle believes in me, helps me believe in myself, and is always offering a solution to problems, issues, or challenges in a positive way by helping me discover my power and inner wisdom? How do they do that?

3. Who in my inner circle listens without judgment and mirrors back to me in a way that helps me discover new things about myself and feel brave?

4. Who in my life feels great to be around and shows up with positive energy, excitement, gratitude, and love?

5. Who in my life helps me feel excited about life and brings more joy to it?

I purposefully crafted these questions positively to keep you focused. When you weed people from your life, you do that because they're the opposite of the kinds of people I've asked you about.

What we focus on grows.

This applies to people, money, resources, energy, outlook, mood, jobs, everything. I'm trying to focus and pay attention to the things I want to grow. It matters. It's how you manifest the life of your dreams. Fine-tuning this skill leads to a peak performance life. Creating your village or community to purposefully support you is how you do things in life you never dreamed you could do.

Answering the above questions will shed light on anyone not fitting in these categories, or worse, feels toxic to you in any way. This isn't rocket science. You have the awareness to feel the difference. Most times, you're just afraid to do something about it.

Taking action to change something that doesn't feel good is brave.

Taking action to change something that is just okay for something better is even more brave. It takes a warrior to decide to make a change and then go through with it.

At the beginning of this practice, it helps to start by focusing on the people bringing you the most joy. That focus is what starts the momentum and helps you be more brave about making changes. When you realize how great it feels to spend more time with badass people, and you begin to attract more of that energy into your life, you'll naturally gravitate to them more often.

Then, pay attention: some relationships may start to feel like a very heavy weight. That's a good thing. With awareness, you have a choice. I know; I've typed that last sentence several times already. But some phrases must be repeated. It's the repetition of a thought, word, or behavior that creates a good habit and a new, healthier pattern, which eventually turns into your life.

Note: When the possible consequences of your actions feel unsafe, it's time to get help. Safety is always the priority. Please read Chapter 18 by Tiffany Thomas for resources.

Brave Healers, love warriors, you're never alone, and this book is way more than just a book. It's a generous community of people who've devoted their lives to this amazing healing journey and who care about you and your goals and dreams.

The next step is to reach out to any of the authors here, ask a question, carry on the conversation, explore their world or offerings, and create an inner circle and community that will feel like someone has tapped your head with a magic wand of awesomeness.

That is how I feel every time I look around at mine. Thank you for that, Brave Healers. I love you.

Big warrior love,

Laura

You can join our Brave Badass Healers, A Community for World-Changers Facebook group and get started by hanging with people who get it here:

https://www.facebook.com/groups/YourHighVibeBusiness

Laura Di Franco is the CEO of Brave Healer Productions, an award-winning publisher for holistic health and wellness professionals and those who serve them. Read more about her in the About the Author section at the end of the book.

https://BraveHealer.com

A RAMPAGE OF GRATITUDE

To the stellar cast of co-authors who stepped up with their "Hell yes!" Thanks for walking beside me on this journey and for the love and support that keeps me burning in my purpose every day. Thank you for getting my collaborative spirit and for being here with yours. Thanks for having the stamina to roll with me!

To our book launch team: You're badasses! Thank you so much for reading this book and for the love and support you're pouring into this community. We love your Amazon reviews, y'all. They keep us authors going on a bad day. Thank you so much for the time, energy, and effort you have put into helping us.

To Kelly Kaschula, our Brave Healer Productions publishing manager. Without you, growing this business into the empire it is today wouldn't have happened. Thank you so much for who you are and what you do in the world, and especially for your patience with this alien soul.

Jenny Hawkyard: Your cover art is magic. I'm honored it's a part of what we're sharing with the world. *The Lightbearer* brings a level of vibration to this book I couldn't have dreamed of. Thank you.

Dino Marino: Thank you for working with me to create this brilliant book. When your designs are a part of our books, I have the benefit of knowing they will shine among all the rest in the world. You're talented beyond words. And working with you is a dream.

Maggie McLaughlin: Your Amazon and book expertise and care help our systems and processes run smoothly, but you bring a level of personal service to this that I'm so grateful for. Thank you for being a part of this vision and our team.

To the authors, presenters, and master teachers who said yes to my invitation to join us at The Brave Healer Writer's Retreat: Thank you so much for surrounding me with your love. You've shown me what's possible when we collaborate for something bigger in a way I hadn't experienced before. That was a huge gift and will set a bar forever more.

ABOUT THE AUTHOR

Laura Di Franco, MPT, is the CEO of Brave Healer Productions, an award-winning publisher specializing in business strategy for healers and those who serve them. The publishing house includes Brave Kids Books and Brave Business Books and specializes in expert book collaborations. They offer programs that serve author-entrepreneurs well past their book launch.

Laura spent 30 years in holistic physical therapy (12 in private practice) before making the pivot to publishing. With 14 years of training in the martial arts, 13 of her own books, and a community of over 2000 authors (including over 80 Amazon bestsellers and counting), she knows how to help you share your brave words in a way that builds your business and your dream life.

Her daily mission is to help fellow holistic wellness professionals by paying forward everything she's learned in business and healing. She shares her authentic passion, wisdom, and expertise with refreshing transparency and straightforward badassery. Hold on to your seat because riding alongside her means you'll be pushed beyond your comfort zone and have way more fun with your purpose-driven fears on a regular basis.

When Laura chills out, you'll find her at a poetry event with friends, walking in the woods, driving her Mustang, bouncing to the beat at a rave, or on a beach in Mexico with something made of dark chocolate in her mouth. Joy is her compass and her business strategy.

Connect with Laura:

Website: https://BraveHealer.com

YouTube:
https://www.youtube.com/@bravehealerproductions2444

Free Facebook Group:
https://www.facebook.com/groups/YourHighVibeBusiness

Instagram: https://www.Instagram.com/BraveHealerProductions
https://www.instagram.com/bravekidsbooks/

LinkedIn: https://www.linkedin.com/in/laura-di-franco-mpt-1b037a5/

Good Morning Joy Episode:
https://youtu.be/vvYyMJGpP_U?si=Cbs5rTsbGRLsxfZS

Get access to The Brave Healer Resources Vault with thousands in training/master classes/workshops for author-entrepreneurs:
https://lauradifranco.com/resources-vault/

BECOME A BESTSELLING AUTHOR

Your words change the world when you're brave enough to share them. It's time to be brave.

Are you ready to become an author in one of our bestselling books? Or lead your own book project? Brave Healer Productions, Brave Kids Books, and Brave Business Books are waiting for you!

Reach out to speak to the Brave Healer Productions publishing team by emailing: support@LauraDiFranco.com

THE BRAVE HEALER TRANSFORMATION SCHOOL

Ready to teach your business or health and wellness course online? We make that easy. Start earning passive income with your digital course!

BraveHealerTransformationSchool.com

THE BRAVE HEALER WRITER'S CIRCLE

Want a safe space to write in community and stay accountable to your goals? The Writer's Circle meets up to five times each month and provides the support, teaching, and accountability you're looking for. Check our schedule, including the guest writing experts coming to share their wisdom. Topics include business writing, writing to heal, creative fiction and non-fiction writing, and more!

https://lauradifranco.com/writers-circle/

If you want to take your life to another level of bliss, at some point, you'll need to get over your purpose-driven fears, invest in yourself, your vision, and your purpose, and take the action your soul is yearning for you to take.

You're not alone. Your life, message, and work matter.
You're worthy.

That fear of not-good-enough is boring.

This isn't about you anymore.
It's about the life you'll save when you share your brave words.
It's time to be brave.

With warrior love,

Laura

BraveHealer.com

Made in the USA
Columbia, SC
25 October 2024

44636927R10176